MW01223594

Critical Pedagogical Strategies
to Transcend Hegemonic Masculinity

RADICAL ANIMAL STUDIES
AND TOTAL LIBERATION

Anthony J. Nocella II
Series Editor

Vol. 7

The Radical Animal Studies and Total Liberation series
is part of the Peter Lang Education list.
Every volume is peer reviewed and meets
the highest quality standards for content and production.

PETER LANG
New York • Bern • Berlin
Brussels • Vienna • Oxford • Warsaw

Critical Pedagogical Strategies to Transcend Hegemonic Masculinity

Edited by
Amber E. George
and Russell W. Waltz

PETER LANG
New York • Bern • Berlin
Brussels • Vienna • Oxford • Warsaw

Library of Congress Cataloging-in-Publication Data

Names: George, Amber E., editor. | Waltz, Russell W., editor.
Title: Critical pedagogical strategies to transcend hegemonic masculinity /
edited by Amber E. George and Russell W. Waltz.
Description: New York: Peter Lang, 2021.
Series: Radical animal studies and total liberation; vol. 7
ISSN 2469-3065 (print) | ISSN 2469-3081 (online)
Includes bibliographical references and index.
Identifiers: LCCN 2020033411 (print) | LCCN 2020033412 (ebook)
ISBN 978-1-4331-8337-9 (paperback) | ISBN 978-1-4331-8338-6 (ebook pdf)
ISBN 978-1-4331-8339-3 (epub) | ISBN 978-1-4331-8340-9 (mobi)
Subjects: LCSH: Critical pedagogy—United States. | College
teaching—United States. | College teaching—Methodology. |
Masculinity—United States. | Male domination (Social structure)—United
States. | Men—Education—United States. | Sex differences in
education—United States.
Classification: LCC LC196.5.U6 C748 2021 (print) | LCC LC196.5.U6 (ebook) |
DDC 370.11/5—dc23
LC record available at https://lccn.loc.gov/2020033411
LC ebook record available at https://lccn.loc.gov/2020033412
DOI 10.3726/b17486

Bibliographic information published by **Die Deutsche Nationalbibliothek**.
Die Deutsche Nationalbibliothek lists this publication in the "Deutsche
Nationalbibliografie"; detailed bibliographic data are available
on the Internet at http://dnb.d-nb.de/.

© 2021 Peter Lang Publishing, Inc., New York
80 Broad Street, 5th floor, New York, NY 10004
www.peterlang.com

Table of Contents

Introduction: Why Critical Pedagogy?: Illustrating the Importance of Critical Pedagogical Strategies in the Classroom

AMBER E. GEORGE AND RUSSELL W. WALTZ

Critical Pedagogical Strategies to Transcend Hegemonic Masculinity goes beyond what many other critical pedagogy collections have contributed to the field of women's, gender, and sexuality studies since it brings together an entire collection of essays on practical critical pedagogical strategies for use in the classroom. An in-depth analysis of hegemonic masculinity is crucial to understanding how heterosexism and masculinity surfaces in the expanding interdisciplinary field of critical pedagogy studies. This collection is meant to make gender and sexuality visible so that educators can disrupt the hegemonic nature of masculinity; hegemonic masculinity is the normative ideal of manhood. As the Italian Marxist, Antonio Gramsci (1992) once stated, hegemony saturates what we think of as common sense as it becomes part of our lived system of meanings and values. We take as our foundation that gender is performative: gender is what you do, not as much who you are (Butler, 2004). Thus, the "successful" genders are learned by copying normative or hegemonic examples that are emulated generation after generation. We end up reprocessing familiar stereotypes of what it means to be feminine and masculine in the traditional sense while omitting what it means to be queer and nonbinary in gendered performances. This collection is intended to be a corrective to generate inclusive pedagogical approaches that avoid reinforcing gender inequities.

Sexism, heterosexism, and homophobia must be explored together as overlapping systems of oppression to demolish gender inequity. Sexism perpetuates rigid gendered stereotypes that keep men locked in patterns of masculinity that are toxic to not only women but also LGBTQIA+ members. Heterosexism denigrates and stigmatizes any non-heterosexual form of behavior, identity, or community, which also uses sexism to keep shallow gender roles firmly in place. Furthermore, homophobia or the irrational fear and hatred of LGBTQIA+ identity, people, or perceived LGBTQIA+ behavior further contributes to this destructive pattern. Masculinity describes the complexity of the male social position, identity, and experience as men differ according to their other social identities, including race, socioeconomic background, disability status, and sexual orientation. Men must adhere to masculinity at all costs, often at the expense of women, queer individuals, people of color, people with disabilities, and others whom they abuse in their efforts to measure up as "real men." Men often get locked into a guide of tokenizing women to repel emasculation and accusations of being queer because the fear of appearing gay (homophobia) keeps men exaggerating their masculinity. To ensure that no one gets the wrong idea about them, men often resort to sexist and heterosexist behavior that harms, limits, and destroys the lives of all those in its path.

Ignoring masculinity in academia and beyond perpetuates the power that keeps masculinity invisible, normative, and privileged. Making masculinity visible through reflective praxis and critical pedagogy will provide the tools needed to dismantle the most destructive aspects of inequity. Thus, we felt there is no better time to challenge hegemonically toxic masculinity for the harms it inflicts not only on vulnerable populations but also on the men themselves. Disrupting the stronghold of hegemonic masculinity invigorates gender and queer equity efforts and allows men to live unencumbered by antiquated notions of manhood. Unlocking the secrets behind hegemonic masculinity means that students and educators alike are offered the possibility of leading more vibrant lives with families and friends.

Critical Pedagogical Strategies to Transcend Hegemonic Masculinity interweaves theories of discourse, identity politics, feminism, critical race studies, queer studies, linguistics, religion, art, and film as a means of providing concrete strategies that educators can use to create inclusive engagement within the classroom.

Definitional Foundation

The current social climate in the United States and elsewhere has been one of social conflict and strife. A glance at the news or social media reveals that some citizens are active in promoting social justice issues, while others affirm structures of inequity. These same actions are enacted as microcosms within classrooms in the U.S. and abroad. Educators involved with critical pedagogy studies, and scholarship within research on hegemonic masculinity in higher education, can uniquely contribute to scholarship that fosters social change as well as influence others to join in the struggle against inequity. Within the walls of academia, students come to the classroom seeking knowledge, awareness, and often, inspiration to challenge assumptions that disadvantage LGBTQIA+ persons because of their sexual orientation or gender identity. Some of the most ardent supporters of fostering inclusivity and diversity are students seeking to improve their lives and the lives of others.

Critical pedagogy is defined as the practice of deconstructing scholarly works, media, and popular culture to search for deep (rather than superficial) meaning to uncover the social context and consequences of speech acts, propositional attitudes, implicit attitudes, societal customs, value judgments, norms, mores, and other socially entrenched means of expression (Friere, 1970; Shor, 1992; Giroux, 2011). The author of the label "critical pedagogy," Max Horkheimer, sought to shift away from traditional pedagogy because he recognized the need to raise class consciousness, continuing in the traditions of Georg Wilhelm Friedrich Hegel and Karl Marx (Horkheimer, 1937). Hegemonic masculinity and heterosexism have been ingrained within modern Western society through the sort of traditional pedagogy that Horkheimer rejected. It is only within environments that feature the application of a critical lens that individuals can be shown the causes, symptoms, and effects of hegemonic masculinity and heterosexism. Educators must raise the consciousness of their students like critical theorists of the past in the hope that educators succeed in awakening their students to promote equity.

What this book offers gender and sexuality studies is "illustrated" critical pedagogy. While plenty of high caliber scholarship has created a theoretical foundation for critical pedagogy in the classroom, educators still need a means for transforming their classrooms into spaces of inclusion where hegemonic masculinity and heteronormativity can be eliminated. We hope that by challenging hegemonic masculinity and heteronormativity in their classrooms, educators will be able to offer students a more equitable environment in which to share ideas, cooperate with their peers, and grow both academically and personally. The desire is to provide educators with a tangible guide that could prove invaluable during attempts to create an equitable learning environment for all students, and especially those students who identify as women and members of the LGBTQIA+ community.

This book is invaluable to educators who wish to create inclusive engagement in the classroom. Far too often, students self-segregate and create both mental and physical divisions in the classroom. Some of the concrete strategies and activities in this book can be used by educators to work through the mire created by hegemonic masculinity and form collaborative bonds with one another in the classroom. Establishing cooperative relationships fosters an environment of listening and reflecting upon the experiences of others, rather than traditional pedagogy that often pits students against one another during clashes of intellectual combat fueled by unchecked drives toward competition.

Part One: Feminist Approaches to Disrupting Hegemonic Masculinity and Sexism

We have organized this book into two main parts to highlight how educators might disrupt hegemonic masculinity and sexism in their classrooms, according to Feminist and anti-heterosexist approaches. The chapters in Part One of this book investigate the grip that hegemonic masculinity, misogyny, and sexism has in the classroom. By examining traditional pedagogical practices and curricula, as well as providing strategies, activities, and conceptual models, educators will learn how to transform their classrooms into inclusive incubators for student learning.

In Chapter One, "She Really Got You: Transcending Hegemonic Masculinity at a College for Men," Crystal Benedicks and Adriel M. Trott feature practical critical pedagogical engagement stemming from their experiences teaching at a small liberal arts college in the Midwest whose student body is comprised entirely of men. As a result of the unique student body at Trott's and Benedicks's institution, they are well-poised to explore the ways that hegemonic masculinity affects, and often limits, men students' learning. In their chapter, Trott and Benedicks articulate pedagogical strategies that they have developed to help erode toxic masculinity and offer more nuanced and constructive possibilities for men to be and, thus, to learn. They approach this project at three different institutional levels. At the classroom level, they developed strategic pedagogies to circumvent the obstacles that toxic masculinity poses to student learning. These include careful attention to how competition manifests in the classroom, strategies to emphasize listening, ways of building trust in the classroom, and ways of fostering productive "failure." At the faculty level, they developed a yearlong series of workshops beginning with a half-day all-faculty forum to articulate the problem of toxic masculinity in the classroom and to pool resources across disciplines and from various positionalities. At the programmatic level, they developed a gender studies minor (one of the only in the country populated entirely by men students) to help students think critically about masculinity. This chapter addresses the goals of this anthology, to "transform traditional discussions of gender to highlight how employing different pedagogical strategies, styles, and curriculum can change the oppressive and harmful impact of toxic masculinity."

In Chapter Two, "We Are How We Teach: Black Feminist Pedagogy as a Move Towards the Legibility and Liberation of All," Jenn M. Jackson and Hilary N. Tackie argue that it is not only masculinity that sits at the foundation of the academy, but masculinity defined as white, cis, able-bodied, middle-class, and heterosexual. Thus, as Black queer womyn, they consistently oppose the normative form of Western intellectual tradition. The methods and texts of traditional classrooms do not include Black queer womyn as they were never expected to possess them. The adherence to a queer Black Feminist pedagogy often does not come from training alone. Instead, it comes from academic experiences of exclusion, silencing, and intellectual and emotional violence. When bringing such an approach into the university classroom, Tackie and Jackson anticipate productive discomfort for many, but especially for white men, as Black queer womyn push for practices that actualize their legibility, recognition, and liberation. Tackie and Jackson discuss the development and realities of (queer) Black Feminist pedagogical practice through a synthesis of Black Feminist philosophers such as Audre Lorde, bell hooks, Kimberlé Crenshaw, and Patricia Hill Collins, in conversation with their own experiences, as well as Black radical tradition, and movement logics. Fundamentally, these logics and praxes allow for new forms of hegemonic resistance for students and educators while decentering exclusive masculinist traditions of academic knowledge production.

In Chapter Three, "I'll Huff, and I'll Puff: Becoming Masculine in Fables," Jessica Ruth Austin discusses *Fables*, which was a comic book series featuring modern-day versions of fable and fairy-tale characters. Austin's analysis suggests that the representation of masculinity in *Fables* is pro-Feminist, which is essential since the comic book genre and fandom has often been accused of producing hegemonic and toxic masculine characters. By using scholarly work from the fan studies discipline, Austin addresses violence in the narrative and how these stories can be framed as fighting against toxic masculinity. This chapter provides a Feminist pedagogy based on the "unruly woman" framework created by Kathleen Rowe (1995) to argue that there is also an "unruly man" in popular culture. Like the "unruly woman," who uses mimesis to become overly feminine and thus subvert and twist patriarchal views of femininity to reclaim characters as Feminist, the "unruly man" described in this chapter does too. This chapter examines the masculinity portrayed in Fables, which shows that a male does not have to follow violent masculinity "to be a man" but also that violent actions taken are not always due to hegemonic masculinity but can be a product of mimesis. Readers will come to understand how *Fables* can be read as a Feminist text since it uses traditionally described as "subordinate" masculinities to characterize important male characters. This chapter provides a theoretical framework to provide academics and students a way to discuss popular culture texts and subvert the meanings of hegemonic masculinity that may appear in them. This pedagogical strategy can be used in academia to allow scholars to reclaim previously proclaimed hegemonically masculine characters and disrupt these narratives. Educators can adapt this framework to enact social commentary within comic books to empower female and queer perspectives within the genre.

In Chapter Four, "Feminist Mythmaking: Reclaiming the Myth," Purnur Ozbirinci argues that myths are the narrative patterns that provide individuals with the necessary experience, language, words, or stories that shape their lives and identities, and unite a group of people. Thus, mythmakers have the power to adjust, manipulate, and change societies. However, for centuries some people were withheld from creating their myths and truths. More powerful groups, who could access the "word," imposed their myths upon these "others." One of these "othered" groups consists of women. For centuries, their identities, and the social roles required of them have been established by experts of the "word." Today, women have discovered that their existence depends on their power to use the word. They will exist when their experiences find a name; when their myths are retold and accepted to link them to the contemporary social order. Paulo Freire (2005) proposes the oppressed take steps to achieve liberation. The first step for those who have been deprived of their power is to accept and to reveal their oppression, and then to commit to changing this oppressive system. The second stage requires the "expulsion of the myths created and developed in the old order" (Freire, 2005, p. 37). Following this pedagogy, women must continuously unveil the sexism in myths while creating and retelling their myths to progress into the future. Revisionist drama serves as a primary tool for producing and transmitting women's "word," their myth, their experiences, and voices. Ozbirinci uses drama/theatre to uncover the journey of the women playwright, turning into a mythmaker, in the pursuit of reclaiming the power to use the "word." This chapter's analysis provides examples from the rewritten versions of the myth of Oedipus, Antigone, Medea, and Philomela and Procne. The comparative analysis of such retellings coming from the perspectives of the historically suppressed figures decentralizes the power retained from the privilege to use the "word." Therefore, exploring revisionism, rewriting, and mythmaking in the college classroom offers educators and students tools to challenge the status quo through praxis. The goal of such pedagogy in the academy must be to achieve cultural plurality in the classroom, to urge the students to "self-actualize" (hooks, 1994, p. 15), and to realize their power and responsibility in ending dehumanization to liberate the oppressed as well as the oppressor.

In Chapter Five, "Implicit Attitudes and Explicit Harms: Combating Biases that Hinder Inclusivity," Russell W. Waltz concludes Part One by arguing that implicit attitudes work in tandem with hegemonic masculinity to pose a serious challenge to educators in the higher education classroom. When such biases are present, creating and maintaining an inclusive learning environment is difficult. Students who exhibit implicit biases, such as confirmation bias, disconfirmation bias, or outgroup homogeneity bias, while also harboring heteronormative views, struggle to participate in an inclusive classroom. The traditional pedagogical approach to counteracting these biases typically involves presenting students with critical thinking instruction grounded in informal logic. When this traditional approach to identifying and eradicating implicit biases fails, it is because such biases are affective rather than rational prejudices. Waltz explores pedagogical strategies that could enable students to reflect on implicit attitudes and hegemonic masculinity. Waltz hopes that when educators adopt an affective, rather than a rational approach to teaching course content, students will overcome their implicit attitudes that often thwarts educators' efforts to create an inclusive classroom.

Part Two: Anti-heterosexist Approaches to Disrupting Hegemonic Masculinity and Sexism

The chapters in Part Two of this book investigate the negative influence of homophobia and transphobia on the student learning environment to present educators with strategies, activities, and conceptual anti-heterosexist models that can promote inclusive engagement among students. The first chapter in this part, "Sex≠Gender: Reframing Cultural and Linguistic Assumptions in Undergraduate Courses," by Mária Cipriani, chronicles five years of teaching an undergraduate course called Women & Media. The course challenges media studies students to become aware of the cultural, linguistic, and personal gendered assumptions that they make day by day, minute by minute, encouraging them to begin to see the world differently. Cipriani's stated learning objective is for students to leave the course looking at, thinking about, and understanding the world differently, especially regarding how they interact with, and "consume" media. Cipriani uses case studies to describe specific course content, key discomfiting questions, and challenges encountered by participants, both faculty and students, as they grapple with their lifelong assumptions, presumptions, and "malfunctions." Anecdotal descriptions include considerations of inclusivity as pedagogical praxis and methods for maintaining professionalism while simultaneously modeling the concept that the political is personal. Additional key features of this pedagogy include addressing chauvinism, homophobia, sexism, transphobia, and misogyny in media and the classroom that offer opportunities to cultivate unique "teaching moments" like a discussion about the distinction between a passionate professor and not just another angry Feminist.

In Chapter Seven, "Grammatical Gender Trouble: Counteracting the Discriminatory Nature of Grammatically Gendered Languages," Zuzanna Jusińska analyzes how grammatically gendered languages render intersex, non-binary, and genderqueer people invisible, and is thus, discriminatory against them. Additionally, grammatically gendered languages reinforce the belief that a person's gender is relevant in every situation. Grammatical gender is a noun class system that divides nouns into two or three classes (i.e., feminine, masculine, and neutral). Still, it is also manifested in other parts of speech such as pronouns, adjectives, and verbs whose forms have to agree with the gender of the noun to which they refer. The grammatical gendering of nouns designating people and nonhuman animals usually corresponds to the sex/gender of the referent. By using grammatical gendering, they often are forced to gender themselves and others, even if the information about someone's gender is not what they want to communicate, the language they use requires that they do so. The main two consequences of grammatical gender in the social and political area are one, the ubiquity of information about people's gender, and two, the imposition of a gender binary. In this chapter, using J.L. Austin's (1962) speech act theory and H.P. Grice's (1975) conversational maxims, Jusińska analyzes how these effects bear out on members of society. Examining how using expressions with grammatical gender contribute to cisnormative, heteronormative, and binary way of thinking fuels hegemonic masculinity is a necessary step towards overcoming such hegemony. Providing a normative account of language helps explain how linguistic practices constitute norms dictating what can and cannot be said and thus what can and cannot exist. Understanding this is especially important when teaching languages with grammatical gender, whether as a foreign or first language. Jusińska concludes by offering practical alternative linguistic practices within languages with grammatical gender that could promote pro- Feminist, pro-LGBTQIA+, inclusive outcomes. To do this, Jusińska provides strategies for language-teaching that incorporate these practices and that facilitate critical thinking about language, providing a means for understanding how language can be oppressive not only regarding content but also through form and grammar.

In Chapter Eight, "Putting the T and Q into First-Year Composition: Using Queer Theory to Make Courses Trans-inclusive," Emily Donovan argues that English rhetoric and composition and its instructors have failed to tap into the full potential of queer theory. Scholars Jonathan Alexander and David Wallace (2009) find that English rhetoric and composition's limited application of queer theory has catered almost exclusively to cisgender gays and lesbians. Meanwhile, first-year trans and gender-nonconforming college students demonstrate a dire need for support in academia, as high rates of harassment and assault lead most to report attending school was the most traumatic aspect of growing up. Trans activists, as discussed by trans historian Susan Stryker (2017), have a long history of using powerful rhetorical approaches to draw attention to how queer movements have failed to be inclusive. As such, Alexander and Wallace find, queer theory has not made a significant impact on composition theory or pedagogy. Meanwhile, queer theory as envisioned by Feminist theorist Judith Butler (2004) and transwomen professor of law Amy D. Ronner (2013) has centered trans and gender-nonconforming individuals, leading queer feminism's vision of queer theory to critique the validity of the gender binary and thereby equipping its scholars to deconstruct categorical binaries at large. Many issues trans and gender-nonconforming students face are complex and institutional. Still, best practices that instructors could take to make their classrooms more inclusive, and thereby broaden their students' conception of gender, are simple and easy to adopt. Donovan outlines how educators can apply a more radical queer theory to first-year composition pedagogy. Educators learn how these practices in the classroom could intervene at a critical time to create a generation of scholars, trans, gender-nonconforming, and cisgender alike, who understand just how deeply political and socially constructed the personal can be.

In Chapter Nine, "Disrupting Hegemonic Masculinity: An Argument for Restructuring the Literature Classroom," Camille Alexander makes the case that despite the belief that colleges and universities are centers of liberalism, the nature of the academy is relatively conservative, reflecting the hegemonic masculinity permeating both public and private educational institutions. Sexism, which remains a troubling issue in academia, is the direct result of a social culture of hegemonic masculinity and leads to other forms of bias, such as racism, xenophobia, and homophobia. While many academics profess to have a liberal agenda, meaning that they oppose all forms of bias, the approaches taken in the classroom indicate that they remain influenced by a culture of hegemonic masculinity. Alexander proposes a shift in pedagogical approaches in the English/Literature classroom to strategies that challenge the hegemonic masculinity pervading the academy, the "liberal" arts, and literary studies. The goal of Alexander's research is to propose pedagogical methods that can disrupt the sexist narratives that have become enmeshed in literary studies and academia. First, Alexander recommends a shift in the reading material typically assigned. Working with prior research on this subject (Schaub, 2003; Alexander, 2011), Alexander examines incorporating texts by women, writers of color, non-Christian, non-Western(ized), and LGBTQIA+ writers into every literature course in conjunction with canonical pieces. Second, Alexander advises that beginning in the first- and second-year courses, literary theories that challenge hegemonic masculinity, such as gender studies, queer theory, postcolonial studies, Marxism, and ethnic studies, be incorporated into literature courses. Finally, Alexander suggests that instructors place more emphasis on classroom discussions that, using the reading material and literary theories, allow students to carefully examine their notions about bias through more active engagement with the text and challenge hegemonic masculinity in their verbal and written responses.

In Chapter Ten, "Queer Pedagogy and Engaging Cinema in LGBTQIA+ Discourse in Africa," Stephen Ogheneruro Okpadah explains that poststructuralism, postcolonialism, postmodernism, and posthumanism ignited a rapid growth in counter-discourses and oppositional cultures in the late twentieth and early twenty-first centuries. Among these oppositions are feminism, separatist nationalist movements, animal rights movements, and queer culture. The oppositional forces are a marginalized minority whose aim is to create space(s) for themselves in society. Silenced by the power, discourse, and knowledge of dominant cultures, countercultures strive to speak for themselves and resist all forms of subjugation and marginalization. In the West, oppositional cultures have been able to create a queer cinema of resistance. While queer cinema continues to thrive in developed nations, African cinemas have been slow in exploring the queer genre. African queer cinematic engagement came late with Mohammed Camara's 1997 film-*Dakan*, which is believed to be the first film focused primarily on LGBTQIA+ themes from West Africa. Ever since the above Guinean-French film pushed the queer sexual orientation into the center of discourse in Africa, film industries such as Nollywood in Nigeria, Ghollywood in Ghana, the South African film enterprise, among others, have followed suit. It is against this backdrop that Okpadah examines African queer cinema as a struggle against heteronormative and oppressive tendencies. Employing Michel Foucault's (2016) perspective on knowledge and power and discourse as theory, Okpadah uses content analysis to interrogate selected African queer cinematic narratives. Among other findings, Okpadah argues that African queer cinema resists heteronormativity and other sexually oppressive categories and that this enterprise is geared towards creating a voice for the LGBTQIA+ community across the African continent.

In Chapter Eleven, "Becoming an Ally in the College Classroom: One Front in the Battle against Homophobia," Omar Swartz establishes that while anti-queer bias is anachronistic, homophobia, transphobia, and heteronormativity persist in our society, requiring us to think more deeply about what it means to live in the twenty-first century as a multicultural community. Following philosopher Richard Rorty (1989, 2007), Swartz argues that progress in moral and intellectual matters occurs by offering reasons for why outdated attitudes should give way to contemporary inclusive ideas, and, along with those modern attitudes, inclusive practices. In so doing, Swartz operationalizes three important terms (homophobia, heteronormativity, and ally) to help educators consider the ways they can encourage inclusivity within the higher education classroom. Swartz uses himself as an example of an ally inside and outside of the college classroom and offers a discussion of best practices for creating an LGBTQIA+-inclusive classroom. These include tips for enacting one's identity as an ally and modeling for students' ways of interacting with others that are worthy of respect and acceptance. Doing so involves acknowledging what one does not know and being open to learning from the experiences of our students. Also discussed is how to be respectful to religious people who oppose gay and transgender rights. Overall, these best practices are situated in mindfulness. When engaged in social justice education, teaching a vast array of students with diverse needs and experiences, it is essential to be mindful that each student is an individual and, no matter their views, deserves a voice in the classroom. It is the multiplicity of voices that contribute best to a robust and rigorous learning environment.

The critical pedagogy contained within this book poses a direct challenge to traditional classroom pedagogical practices to empower educators and lessening the hold of toxic masculinity in the classroom, and in course material itself. Gendered scholarship often limits the ability of students to gain a broad-context perspective of concepts and ideas necessary for attaining a rich appreciation for social issues, problems, and individuals situated in those events. We hope that this book will inspire educators to transform their teaching practices and classrooms into inclusive spaces where gender and sexual diversity are modeled and valued. We believe this book is a valuable bridge-builder for understanding the intersections of oppression among disciplines and alliance politics. We hope that the ideas in this book are readily consumable for those who are interested in rejecting toxic masculinity and desirous to make their professional and personal lives more inclusive spaces.

References

Alexander, C. (2011). Teaching against the tide: Transgressing norms in the American college composition classroom. *Akademisk Kvarter*, *3*, 66–80.

Alexander, J., & Wallace, D. (2009). The queer turn in composition studies: Reviewing and assessing an emerging scholarship. *College Composition and Communication*, *61*, 300–320.

Austin, J. L. (1962). *How to do things with words*. U.K.: Clarendon Press.

Butler, J. (2004). *Undoing gender*. New York, NY: Routledge.

Foucault, M. (2016). *Social theory-rewired*. UK: Routledge Taylor and Francis Group.

Freire, P. (2005). *The pedagogy of the oppressed* (M. B. Ramos, Trans.). New York, NY: Continuum (Original work published 1970).

Giroux, H. A. (2011). *On critical pedagogy*. New York: Continuum.

Gramsci, A., Buttigieg, J. A., & Callari, A. (1992). *Prison notebooks*. NY: Columbia University Press.

Grice, H. P. (1975). Logic and conversation. In P. Cole, & J. L. Morgan (Eds.), *Syntax and semantics, Vol. 3, speech acts,* (pp. 41–58). New York: Academic Press.

hooks, b. (1994). *Teaching to transgress: Education as the price of freedom*. New York: Routledge.

Horkheimer, M. (1937). *Critical theory: Selected essays*. London: Continuum Publishing Corporation.

Ronner, A. D. (2013). Let's get the 'trans' and 'sex' out of it and free us all. *The Journal of Gender, Race and Justice*, *16*, 859–916.

Rorty, R. (1989). *Contingency, irony, and solidarity*. New York: Cambridge University Press.

Rorty, R. (2007). *Philosophy as cultural politics*. New York: Cambridge University Press.

Rowe, K. (1995). *The unruly woman: Gender and the genres of laughter*. USA: University of Texas Press.

Schaub, M. (2003). Beyond these shores: An argument for internationalizing composition. *Pedagogy: Critical Approaches to Teaching Literature, Language, Composition, and Culture*, *3*(1), 85–98.

Shor, I. (1992). *Empowering education: Critical teaching for social change*. Chicago, IL: The University of Chicago Press.

Stryker, S. (2017). *Transgender history: The roots of today's revolution* (Second edition). New York: Seal Press.

PART ONE

FEMINIST APPROACHES TO DISRUPTING HEGEMONIC MASCULINITY AND SEXISM

CHAPTER ONE

"She Really Got You": Transcending Hegemonic Masculinity at a College for Men

CRYSTAL BENEDICKS AND ADRIEL M. TROTT

Introduction

In *The Man They Wanted Me to Be: Toxic Masculinity and a Crisis of Our Own Making,* journalist Jared Yates Sexton (2019) recounts growing up in rural, working-class Indiana, where his father and other men in his family enforced a brand of traditional masculinity based on aggression, dominance, and emotional repression. The first in his family to go to college, he recalls arriving eagerly on campus only to be instantly "overcome with a panic that made it hard to breathe or walk" (Sexton, 2019, p. 144). To cope with the fear, he put on a persona that would have pleased his father: "I strolled into class and pretended I didn't care about anything. I practiced the nonchalant air the men around me projected, I stifled my natural inclination to talk and express myself" (p. 145). Most teachers are familiar with men students like Sexton, hiding behind a seemingly impenetrable mask. For Sexton and many other young men, the challenge posed by attending college amounts to a kind of existential threat. His performance of gendered norms helped ward off that threat, while also dampening the classroom environment and damaging his ability to learn. Here Sexton speaks from his position as an able-bodied, heterosexual, white man on an upward economic trajectory, raising the perhaps unanswerable but haunting question of how much more severe the emotional and mental costs of entering academia may be for men who are none of those things, men who are racially underrepresented, economically disadvantaged, disabled, queer, or a combination thereof. Sexton's experience, and that of countless other men who have faced similar challenges, demonstrates the need for pedagogical strategies that reach men and illuminate ways of navigating hegemonic masculinity that foster learning and a healthy classroom environment for everyone involved.

As a philosophy professor and an English professor at one of the only three remaining colleges for men in the United States, we are uniquely situated to analyze the relationships among the lived experiences of young men and the expectations of hegemonic masculinity and how these dynamics inform our pedagogical and curricular choices. The homosocial space of a college for men is a useful environment for thinking through the relationships among gender, learning, and identity (Smyth, 2010).

While most approaches to emancipatory pedagogy originate in feminist scholarship and focus on how hegemonic masculinity affects women, we argue that an important complement to this approach is focusing on how hegemonic masculinity affects men's learning. As women and girls' learning has been supported by feminism, which paved the way for greater educational and workplace access and greater attention to the way stereotypes about femininity can interfere with girls' learning, masculinity studies scholars like Jason A. Laker suggest that men would benefit from a parallel consideration. He writes, "we can effectively improve the engagement and success of boys and men … by considering gender socialization's influences of boy's and men's notions of education, men's motivation to participate in and complete educational programs, and how faculty and staff can use these analyses to positively design effective interventions and educational processes" (2011, p. 63).

In the book, *Gender and Power: Society, the Person and Sexual Politics*, that introduces the now-canonical term "hegemonic masculinity," R.W. Connell claims that there are a range of ways of being a man or a woman, but that these ways, particularly in regards to men, are muted and subordinated to dominant ideals. The defining structural feature of these forms in a patriarchal society is "the global dominance of men over women" (1987, p. 183). Connell proceeds to show that hegemonic masculinity rests not only on power over women, but also on power over other, alternative performances of masculinity. In Connell's formulation, hegemonic masculinity is defined as "aggressive, physically dominant masculinity" that emphasizes "power, authority," heterosexuality, and emotional flatness. Masculinities that fall outside of this model are suppressed to the point that it is sometimes difficult to imagine what they would be like: "indeed, achieving hegemonic masculinity may consist precisely in preventing alternatives gaining cultural definition and recognition as alternatives, confining them to ghettos, to privacy, to unconsciousness" (1987, p. 186).

Yet, while hegemonic masculinity is the premiere socially-sanctioned form of masculinity, no individual man can fully embody it, even as patriarchy is sustained when that avatar is protected and projected. There is an interesting slippage here: hegemonic masculinity is an always receding, never realistic ideal, but other options for masculine behavior are actively suppressed even when adherence to hegemonic masculinity strategies are harmful. For example, conformity to masculine norms has been correlated to male depression associated with suicide for which men rarely seek help (Wide et al., 2011), which is further compounded by race (Powell et al., 2016). While higher incomes lead to better help-seeking for mental health issues among white men, they are negatively associated with help-seeking among Black men (Parent et al., 2018). This study suggests that the cost for seeking help is greater for Black men than it is for white men, which suggests further that masculinity pressures and privileges accrue to white men so that challenges to the expectations are permitted for white men and not for Black men.

In the classroom, this paradox becomes an obstacle to student learning when young men encounter intellectual challenges. Showing vulnerability, admitting to not knowing, listening carefully to others, grappling with open-ended questions that cannot be easily solved or conquered: all of these are strategies of good learners and critical thinkers, but are discouraged by hegemonic masculinity. No other models of masculinity are "legal." One of the goals of a social-justice-oriented educator of young men, then, must be to help them excavate, however piecemeal, alternate ways of inhabiting their masculine identities that are more compatible with learning. Our hope is that if men grapple critically with both the restrictive and empowering aspects of performing masculinity in a patriarchal society, we will move towards a more inclusive society.

The strategies we present in this chapter, while honed at a college for men, are relevant to all educators who share these goals. These strategies include classroom level, faculty level, and programmatic level interventions. At the classroom level, we developed strategic pedagogies to circumvent the obstacles that hegemonic masculinity poses to student learning. These include careful attention to the ways competition manifests in the classroom, strategies to emphasize listening, ways of building trust in the classroom, and ways of fostering productive "failure." At the faculty level, we developed a yearlong series of workshops beginning with a half-day all-faculty forum to articulate the effects of hegemonic masculinity in the classroom and to pool resources across disciplines and from various positionalities including staff and coaches. At the programmatic level, we developed a gender studies minor (one of the only in the country populated entirely by students who are men) to help students think critically about masculinity.

Classroom Pedagogical Strategies

One of us (Trott) is a historian of philosophy who often tells her students, if you are not aware that your thinking is influenced by the tradition you inherit, then you are subjected to it and not able to consider whether you really want to accept it or think otherwise. Men growing up today find themselves in this situation. Certain social forces pressure men to perform in ways that they do not really choose and yet those ways of showing up can be sources of oppression for others. Finding ways to recognize these social forces and pressures, understand how those forces work, and consider possibilities for resisting those forces is part of how we can help students be freed from these expectations.

Researchers have noted how traits associated with hegemonic masculinity discourage success in the classroom. As a recent article in *American Journal for Men's Health* notes, "[d]efined as the dominant set of norms and behaviors that allow men to maintain power and privilege" (Green et al., 2018), masculine norms broadly include dominance, violence, anti-femininity, emotional control, and self-reliance. Adherence to these norms has been associated with many forms of negative emotionality, including depression (Addis, 2008; Good & Wood, 1995), aggression and hostility (Cohn & Zeichner, 2006), and poorer overall psychological well-being (Alfred et al., 2014). Researchers and clinicians have argued that additional aspects of masculine gender socialization may predispose some men to engage in suicidal and self-damaging behaviors, including the desire for emotional control and self-reliance (Green & Jakupcak, 2015; Green et al., 2018). Since masculinity seems to foreclose experiencing or expressing negative emotions in ways that often lead to further harm, men are not generally habituated to deal with their frustration and failure even in mediated learning contexts.

One such example of this phenomenon took place when Trott was teaching an upper division course on the work of Hannah Arendt. She spent considerable time in class talking to students about the connection between more fruitful thinking and discussion. After one class, a student she knew well came to her office and told her that some students in the class approach discussion as a matter of winning. With some probing, she learned that some students plan for discussion by coming to class with one point they want to say and then once they have said it consider their work done. When they are corrected in class, they feel defeated, and often say to one another outside of class, "She really got you."

Not all students approach discussion in this competitive way, but it is useful for educators to know how ingrained competition is to students' perceptions of what being a good student means. An unofficial school motto at Wabash College is "Wabash Always Fights," or WAF. Many students use "WAF" in their email signatures (in the place where "sincerely" or "thank you" might otherwise go). It is used by faculty, staff, and students alike as a rallying cry or an inspirational message when the going gets tough. While "WAF" is particular to Wabash culture, it is also a distillation of hegemonic masculinity attitudes at large and can illuminate the ways in which young men conceive of their student identities. As a mantra, it may motivate students to persevere in their academic work, but it also promotes aggression and suggests that the answer to any difficulty lies in "fighting it harder," which is an exhausting and Sisyphean prospect that shuts down a range of other reactions to scholastic challenges by focusing on an individualistic and romanticized battle for victory. Under the dictates of this mantra, it makes sense that students would approach class discussion as a competition to win, a battle for intellectual supremacy. This tendency is only compounded by academic practices like class rankings and the competitiveness implicit in assigning grades. As WAF makes clear, competition is the preferred, the most sanctioned, form of male interaction; men must "always" and "only" be fighting. This mentality prevents some men students from using discussion as an opportunity to flesh out a problem or follow an idea without a clear predetermined course for where it will go. Instead, they think that success in the classroom requires defeating one another. With this awareness, we can address students' gendered assumptions about discussion expectations which will ultimately help in our efforts to keep students engaging even when they sense their contributions are wrong. As teachers, we can recognize and be responsive to a certain anxiety that is in play when they feel like winning is the goal and they are not winning. It is worth noting that women are permitted to fail and keep going in ways that our expectations on what it means to be a man makes it much harder and riskier for them to persevere when they are not immediately successful at the projects to which they put their hand (Rich, 2018). These observations are consistent with Communication scholars' work on gendered communication, where boys' communication styles are found to emphasize individuality and competition that perceives communication as a means toward another goal and not for the sake of itself. Boys' communication also tends to focus on action, where listening instead of speaking, a key element of successful discussion, might be perceived as being passive. By contrast, girls develop communication styles through forms of play that encourage cooperation (Wood, 2009, pp. 127–128).

If competition and the need to win restricts men's learning in one regard, men's hesitancy to ask for help is another obstacle to their learning. Addis and Mahalik (2003) use social constructivist and feminist analyses of masculinity to highlight this obstacle. They maintain that gender is actively reinforced by men's continued engagement in stereotypically masculine behavior. Addis and Mahalik follow feminist theorists who note that men's aversion to dependence and their insistence on self-reliance help men maintain structural power. If men perceive an action as potentially threatening to that power then they avoid it (2003, p. 11). Addis and Mahalik argue that men can use masculine scripts, which are interpersonal ways of acting and speaking that shape social identity (Nagel et al., 2015) to avoid seeking help as well as to seek help when no other options work. If men can construe seeking help according to a masculine script, like taking control, or if they can envision themselves reciprocating the help, they are more likely to ask for it (2015, pp. 10–11). Therefore, masculine scripts can be used to encourage men to pursue learning strategies typically associated with femininity. This notion will be explored in more depth at the end of this section.

One of the obstacles to teaching young men is the dearth of cultural imagination about masculinity, as Connell (1987) points out. The prescribed behaviors of hegemonic masculinity require a repudiation of all that is not "manly;" in other words, being "a man" means aggressively not being a woman. As Sarah Rich (2018) states in a recent article in The Atlantic, "To embrace anything feminine, if you're not biologically female, causes discomfort and confusion, because throughout most of history and in most parts of the world, being a woman has been a disadvantage. Why would a boy, born into all the power of maleness, reach outside his privileged domain? It doesn't compute." Rich points out that girls and young women are encouraged to take on stereotypical male characteristics like courage, strength, competitiveness, ambition, but boys and young men are rarely encouraged to take on stereotypically feminine characteristics. Girls and young women have more leeway to adopt stereotypical masculine characteristics like athleticism, courage, and ambition. Of course, girls and women face potential risks when they violate gender expectations, but a man who acts "like a woman" is often considered shameful or self-demeaning.

If it is hard for us as a society to imagine what men could be if not stereotypically manly, it is that much harder for individual young men sitting in college classrooms who are dealing with the common college problems of homesickness, self-doubt in the face of a more rigorous curriculum, interpersonal relationship issues, and so on. An effective educator of young men has to explore the barriers to men's full participation in their emotional lives and question what this might look like as a pedagogical strategy. One way to delve into these issues is by talking explicitly with men students about their struggles. Educators can pair a conversation about inner struggles with readings on contemporary masculinity and mental health. Examples of such texts include Jared Sexton Yates' memoir *The Man They Wanted Me To Be* (2019) with which we began this chapter; Wil Hylton's "My Cousin Was My Hero. Until The Day He Tried To Kill Me" (2019), a *New York Times Magazine* feature article about a man coming to terms with his attraction to violent and unhealthy men role models; or Sarah Rich's "Today's Masculinity is Stifling" (2018), an *Atlantic* article from the perspective of a mother worrying about the social and emotional costs of her son's gender non-conforming behavior. Another technique might be to simply ask open-ended questions about their coping strategies. One colleague asks students to spend the first five minutes of class in pairs, asking their partner how they are doing and what is on their mind. For this exercise, no "it's all good" or "living the dream"-type answers are permitted. Of course, it is not easy to get young men to give honest answers to these questions, as they are conditioned to project confidence at best and indifference at worst. One Wabash professor notes, "I employ the "three question" rule. "How's it going?" "Fine," is the inevitable first response. "How it going?" I ask again. "Hey, I really can't complain." "Oh, really, why not? How is it really going?" And here, after making a nuisance of myself, I fairly often get an authentic response, and some specifics, and can move on from there, providing a sympathetic ear, offering some advice, or making a referral to the counseling or academic support office." (Rosenberg, 2018). Building the trust required to allow men to lower the "mask of masculinity" is critical to the success of this approach (Rosenberg, 2018). Both of us, and many of our colleagues, meet regularly with students one-on-one or in small groups to establish a more personal connection.

Jason A. Laker (2011) advises that we "Invoke, Invite, and Inspire Utilizing Masculine Script Narratives" in our classrooms. To this end, Wabash professor of English emeritus and masculinity studies scholar Warren Rosenberg (2018) describes assigning first-year students Paul Monette's *Becoming a Man: Half a Life Story* (2014), a memoir by a gay man who struggles with coming to terms with his sexuality in the 50s and 60s. Rosenberg's reading is met with resistance from young men students steeped in the homophobia of bro culture. He draws on a kind of "man-up masculinity script" to encourage them to push through the reading even if it makes them uncomfortable. Finally, he notes, his students begin to root for the memoir writer, even wishing he would just hurry up and come out and have the courage to be himself. Here Rosenberg capitalizes on the energy of common male scripts (hard work, courage, standing up for oneself), but turns them against themselves at the point where those scripts become harmful or hateful (Rosenberg, 2018). In a way, this brings us back to Trott's example earlier in this section. In the classroom, the male script of competitiveness and winning can overwrite the larger goal of generative scholarly discussion. One of the biggest challenges is to keep what is powerful about this masculine script of competitiveness, such as its motivational qualities and its demand for courage to do the right thing, but steer students away from naive allegiance to it by illuminating a range of strategies that men students can employ.

Trott teaches a course on the uses of the concept of nature in arguments about what gender is and how and whether it should organize our social world. In one class, students read Todd Reeser's *Masculinities in Theory* (2010), which led to a discussion about how gendered expectations often restrict their reactions despite not wanting to accept a hegemonic conception of masculinity. Students discussed how the costs associated with acting outside hegemonic masculinity's expectations of toughness and lack of emotion resulted in being called feminine or gay, which were taken to perceived as lower on the social scale. One student shared that despite not buying into hegemonic notions of masculinity, he hesitates to resist those gendered expectations because he fears losing heteronormative privilege attached to hegemonic masculinity. Thus, it follows that even men who wish to resist hegemonic masculinity, still accept its leading claim that being associated with what is feminine or gay is insulting and could result in a loss of hetero-masculine power.

This dynamic wherein men students recognize the dangers of gendered expectations while finding themselves unable to reject them appears to play out in the classroom. In the *Introduction to Gender Studies* course, for example, men students can recognize and articulate in writing the ways that gendered expectations are applied to women through cultural artifacts like Valentine's Day cards, after a reading of Sandra Lee Bartky's (1997) "Foucault, Feminism, and the Modernization of Patriarchy." However, despite this knowledge, men students still hesitate to address the constructed, and therefore, unstable nature of gendered expectations under hegemonic masculinity. In light of this dynamic, we have students work in small groups where they discuss among themselves the contradictions and harms associated with hegemonic masculinity. This small group setting helps relieve some of the anxiety attached to investigating their masculinity in front of a group of thirty other men students. Furthermore, independent writing assignments allow them to communicate their hesitancy and resistance to hegemonic masculinity without feeling like they are going to lose something in relation to their peers. A third strategy is helping students understand the shared insights that can be gleaned from their writing assignments. This way, they can come to see one another as allies against the demands of hegemonic masculinity instead of nodes in the disciplinary matrix of enforcing hegemonic masculinity's demands and punishments. An example of this strategy is used by Benedicks when she asks students to write a brief, informal, anonymous essay in which they describe one instance of meeting society's expectations of them as men, and one way in which they defy those expectations. Responses are then shared anonymously among the group to demonstrate the range of "normal deviations."

In sum, we find that the strict expectations of masculinity limit the range of possibilities allotted to men both by themselves and by one another as they each become nodes in the web of disciplinary power through which gender roles are learned and perpetuated (Foucault, 1977; Bartky, 1997). Excavating these expectations as they influence men's students' understanding of what learning for men should and should not look like allows us to understand the roadblocks that prevent these men from learning and improving in their coursework. Not every intervention of this kind explicitly addresses gendered expectations, even though gender expectations are influencing what they think they should be doing in the classroom. Trott did not lecture her students on how gender expectations were informing their discussion, rather, she identified how discussion often requires engagement that is often considered more feminine, such as listening, recognizing one's own limitations, pursuing collaboration over competition. As a result, students began to understand that discussion goes beyond a planned set of statements aimed at "overcoming" or "defeating" the statements of others. Rather their statements should be aimed at eliciting genuine interaction that moves participants to a place of understanding beyond where they started. While some elements of competition may remain, the goal is no longer personal victory, but growing knowledge as a group. This shift also involves seeing success in the classroom not as the result of innate intellectual capacity but in terms of the ability to grow interpersonally.

Faculty Development Strategies

Just as we encourage students to understand how hegemonic gender paradigms inflect their behavior and belief structures, educators must also be mindful of these trappings in their own thinking and learning. Rosenberg notes, "I believe it is critical to examine our own gendered attitudes towards our students. In what ways do our perhaps not fully conscious attitudes and stereotypes about men and women (identity and sexuality) affect our teaching? (2018, para. 6)." Here, Rosenberg highlights that educators do not exist outside of the gendered expectations that effect students. Like students, we also navigate the pressures of hegemonic gender standards—and, like students, we can best counter these pressures when we are aware of how we produce and reproduce them in our own thinking. Rosenberg provides an example of this type of self-analysis when he frankly describes his sometimes negative view of some young men's behavior: they "walk silently, their faces stern and unsmiling," they seem cocky (Rosenberg, 2018, para. 7).

His weary disdain crumbles, however, when he gets into a long conversation with a student who has spent the summer mulling over the problematics of race in Melville's *Moby-Dick*. Moved by the student's thoughtfulness, Rosenberg notes, "[b]ehind the 'masks of masculinity,' as I well knew, our male students are fully and complicatedly human, a fact those masks are designed to make us forget" (Rosenberg, 2018). Similarly, Laker (2011) points out the prevalence of what he calls "Bad Dog" responses to men students' behaviors, that is, when faculty fall into the easy assumption that boys are naturally rowdy or inappropriate and need reigning in. This assumption, argues Laker, leads teachers and administrators to shame men when they say or do something problematic, such as say something intentionally or unintentionally sexist or homophobic in class. The shaming approach, argues Laker, may not be as effective as one that is rooted in a less essentialist or dismissive understanding of men students. In other words, teachers improve their craft when they reflect seriously on the often-obscured ways in which gendered assumptions color their pedagogical choices.

To prompt a conversation about how gendered expectations (on the part of faculty, teaching staff, and students) impact student learning and to share best practices for teaching men, we focused Wabash College's 2018 faculty and teaching staff development efforts on the theme of "teaching men." We both serve on the Teaching & Learning Committee: Trott as chair and Benedicks *ex officio*. This chapter is focused on many of the observations and insights we gleaned from facilitating these workshops (Trott, 2018). The program was comprised of a half-day faculty and teaching staff retreat before the start of the fall semester and a series of lunch talks and workshops throughout the year. Our aim for this programming was to inspire faculty development efforts as a way to combat hegemonic masculinity's negative effects in the classroom, including the ways in which it limits men's ability to learn. We began from the conviction that bearing witness to men students' learning and classroom behaviors, as well as excavating our own unconscious assumptions about men, is a necessary strategy for becoming better teachers of them. While we did not expect to achieve the difficult, shifting, and context-bound task of finding solutions to all the issues we raised, we believe that articulating those barriers to men's learning is itself a crucial faculty-development strategy, an end (if not *the* end) in itself.

One of the first outcomes of planning and preparing this program revolving around the "Teaching Men" theme was the pushback we received. Some faculty members were vocal in their belief that this discussion of masculinity would automatically be prescriptive and punitive. Although our workshops were explicitly aimed at surfacing best practices for teaching men, it was assumed that the program would have a politicized agenda of punishing or shaming our men students for their masculine identities and privilege. We tell this story not to cast blame or inscribe ourselves as victims, but to draw attention to the ways in which it remains difficult for anyone to open a public discourse about masculinity in academia without invoking a range of political and social assumptions about one's goals that range from suspicion of complicity with male privilege on the one hand to charges of a caricature-ish radical feminist agenda of symbolic castration on the other. These reactions are rooted in cultural debates, but they are also keenly emotional and embodied responses that speak to the cognitive dissonance reverberating around the idea of masculinity in contemporary society. Scholars have long argued that hegemonic masculinity is a tenuous mask or performance that must always be protected, affirmed or defended because of how nebulous it actually is (Connell, 1987; Laker & Davis, 2011; Kimmel, 2008, 2011; Sexton, 2019; Rosenberg, 2018). Public discourse about masculinity, then, is also fraught: what are we talking about and why are we doing it? These questions are steeped in fear, defensiveness, and suspicion. Nevertheless, we maintain that teaching men to think critically (and especially teaching them to notice, name, and transcend the trap of hegemonic masculinity) cannot be effective unless educators directly address the question of gender, in general, and masculinity, in particular. Our faculty and teaching staff development retreat was an attempt to put this conviction into action.

The event was well-attended by a large majority of the college's faculty members, and critically, members of the coaching and counseling staff, whose experiences with students in teaching situations outside of class illuminated the ways hegemonic masculinity and its effects follow students everywhere they go on campus and off and whose expertise in less traditional teaching situations shed light on faculty's pedagogical efforts. Over the course of the day, we asked several key questions:

- How do we understand the expectations of masculinity generally? How do the men who are Wabash students fit or not fit into those expectations?
- What are the different pressures men and women face as agents in the world? How can keeping these pressures in mind inflect our teaching?
- Thinking about and studying gender has traditionally been thought about as work by and for women. What does it mean to do this work in the context of a college for men?
- What are the challenges and opportunities of teaching men?

Faculty and staff addressed these questions individually in short sessions of informal writing and collectively in small group conversations. Our emphasis was less on arriving at conclusions or "solving" the "problem" of classroom gender dynamics, and more on collectively unearthing our attitudes and observations about men students. This act of bearing witness to masculinity is important because of the tendency to think about gender in terms of women students. Similarly, learning is traditionally assumed to be a habit of mind, disconnected from the embodied business of going through life as a man or woman. Drawing attention to these ingrained ways of thinking in order to develop new habits of engaging men students can be hard work. In what follows, we describe several themes that emerged from this effort:

Men Students Tend to Be Guarded

Several faculty and staff members noted that a challenge of teaching men is what one of them referred to as men students' "low affect." Indeed, most college teachers have encountered expressionless young men who remain unreadable and disengaged throughout entire classes. As one respondent put it, men students "don't laugh at my jokes." Several respondents spoke to the difficulty of helping men "overcom[e] guardedness and reluctance to be vulnerable in front of peers," linking low affect to fear of perceived failure.

Men Students Are Often More Eager to Compete Than to Collaborate

We referred to this issue in the section above, but it is worth noting that many faculty and staff identify male competitiveness as both an opportunity and a challenge. The fact that these responses came up so often demonstrates to us the need to create opportunities for faculty to meet together and discuss this issue. Some faculty noted that the competition could be harnessed to encourage them to collaborate with team members against those with whom they are competing in a way that allows them to hold on to their sense that winning is the goal even as the real work of learning is happening in the collaborative process with teammates.

In a Homosocial Environment, Men Take on Roles That Are Usually Assigned to Women

Many faculty and staff members deplored the lack of gender diversity in a college for men. One person wrote that one of the challenges of teaching only men is the "burden on female faculty to be the sole female perspective in the classroom and to challenge ideas that female students might otherwise challenge if they were present." However, the corresponding opportunity to the dearth of gender diversity is that men take on a greater diversity of roles. Here are some representative faculty and staff responses to the prompt that asked them about the opportunities afforded by teaching only men:

- "Male students take on roles traditionally ascribed to women."
- There is a "diversification of ways of being a man in an all-male student body."
- "Men fill traditionally female-gendered roles" by doing "emotional labor."
- "All roles need to be filled, so men explore those roles."
- "Students may develop closer and more intimate friendships with other men."

In other words, men provide each other with more emotional support than they might in heterosocial environments. Here, men are actively resisting the dictates of hegemonic masculinity by rejecting relationships built on dominance in favor of those built on cooperation and mutual vulnerability. This phenomenon is particularly visible in male homosocial environments, but teachers and staff at coeducational colleges can also encourage men to explore roles outside of hegemonic masculinity by normalizing empathy, male friendships, and men in caretaker roles. One interesting aspect of the all-men student body is that men do have to find different ways of engaging one another when the social triangulation of women is no longer available to them (Sedgwick, 1985).

One critical piece of Wabash's faculty development efforts around teaching men has to do with the active participation of the coaching staff and counseling staff. The coaching staff in particular has been instrumental in inviting students to take questions of masculinity seriously, especially as they relate to sexual violence. This past fall, almost all of the athletes at Wabash under the direction of the coaching staff participated in sexual violence prevention workshops led by experts in masculinity and sexual violence Don McPherson and Jacqueline Schuman. During that visit, Jacqueline Schuman (Colby College) met with all women staff on campus to surface their various experiences as women faculty, administrators and staff and discuss the ways that the college could improve the environment for women. The faculty who are affiliated with the Gender Studies minor met with McPherson to discuss challenges and opportunities for teaching men. The football coach, who serves on the Gender Issues Committee, a committee on campus whose "general objectives are to enrich the curriculum and the quality of life at Wabash College by encouraging perspectives that recognize and actively address issues of gender," helped spearhead this effort, which helped athletes who like the coach and trust their team members engage earnestly in the workshop.

A highlight of the workshop was a panel on teaching men composed of a counselor, the writing center director, and the track and field coach. The track and field coach spoke of encouraging his runners to learn when to compete and when not to compete, how to judge the different work required for practice and the meet, and how to control one's energy throughout. This advice from the coaching staff has been referenced regularly throughout the year. What was particularly helpful was having a track coach describe his efforts to teach his runners the difference between the time to compete and the time to train. We found that this distinction could help men students reframe the classroom as a space for training.

Overall, our recommendations for faculty development aimed at transcending hegemonic masculinity revolve around interrogating how our own implicit assumptions about our students' gender a/effect our pedagogy, creating ample opportunities for unpacking teaching experiences related to gender, and building partnerships with other college stakeholders, particularly coaching and counseling staff who are trusted by students.

Programmatic and Curricular Strategies

In our introduction to the teaching workshop, we invited faculty to think about "what would our teaching, our faculty development, and our curriculum look like if it considered specifically the kinds of issues that men face in living up to a certain image of masculinity that demands that they not be like women, that they be tough, that they always be winning." We looked at ways that our teaching and faculty development focused on critical masculinity pedagogy, and we would now like to think about curriculum and programming.

We have developed a gender studies minor at Wabash College to facilitate the discussion of masculinity and foster an understanding of the experiences of other genders. The minor includes an introductory course and a senior capstone and then three courses cross-listed from other departments. Such courses include but are not limited to feminist philosophy from the philosophy department, human sexuality and a course on fatherhood from the psychology department, a course on masculinity and sport and a course on the history of gender and sexuality from the history department, a course on gender, family and politics from the political science department and courses on fascism and gender, queer theory, Latina women writers, and disability studies from the English department.

Of teaching men, Laker writes: "Girls' and woman's advances have actually taught us that gendered analysis and interventions can be highly effective, and we should therefore learn what we have learned about supporting girls and women to the current situation of boys and men" (2011, p. 63). Laker uses the useful term "gender-informed pedagogies" and calls attention to the need to articulate the script and provide counter-models. The fatherhood course is a good example of a course that gives students new possibilities for thinking masculinity. The professor invites men faculty from other departments to speak to the class about their experiences that are often at odds with hegemonic masculinity's expectations, including discussions of male infertility and men taking on the main caregiver role for children. Another example is Benedicks' queer theory course, in which the first assignment is for students to write about (nonsexual) ways that they "queer" heteronormative assumptions about themselves as men.

In 2016, Wabash offered its first GEN 101: Introduction to Gender Studies course, the only course in the country populated entirely by men. Seventeen men enrolled. Two students reported in faculty discussions with seniors about their experience at the college that the introduction to gender studies course was one of the courses they took at the college that they found to be most relevant to their lived experience. Another student commented at the close of the course that the course should be required by all students on campus. We take these responses as evidence that men benefit not only by becoming more thoughtful about how to relate to others, but by learning about the ways that masculinity restricts their own being in the world and considering avenues of resistance. The last two years have seen thirty students enroll in the course each year.

It is worth noting the high number of athletes who enroll in the introductory course. We think part of the reason for the involvement of athletes, who are commonly considered at the top of the hegemonic masculinity hierarchy, is the vocal support and involvement of many members of the coaching staff. We recognize that this collaboration between faculty and staff might be more easily developed and sustained at a small liberal arts college, but we find the involvement of coaches critical to getting students to buy into the value of studying and discussing gender. This is an example of using the demands of masculinity where athletics is perceived as a sphere for expressing masculinity to encourage students to imagine other ways of being men, ways that are not tied to the rejection of what are often considered feminine traits.

In addition to these efforts, our required freshmen seminar course includes a module on gender. The assigned text has shifted over the years from an article on masculinity by Michael Kimmel (1997) to Ursula K. Le Guin's short story,

"The Matter of Seggri" (1994). Faculty across the college teach this course and compose the syllabus and share the understanding that men students need to be thinking about gender. Faculty members have the choice to supplement the common readings with choices of their own: Nate Marshall, a former English professor at Wabash, teaches the podcast Scene on the Radio's Season Three: MEN series (Biewen & Headlee, 2018), which discusses the history of patriarchy, sexual harassment in the workplace, Kate Manne's concept of "himpathy" (Manne, 2017), gender in the military and more. As Marshall said in explaining his choice, if we aren't talking about masculinity in [this] course, then what are we doing here (Biewen & Headlee, 2018)?

The gender studies minor and the freshman seminar module on gender are both relatively recent additions to our curriculum that speak to a growing desire on the part of students, faculty, and staff to talk rigorously about masculinity. We believe that addressing the issues that face young men directly is a necessary step in deflating hegemonic masculinity's power; as we described above, the resistance with which these conversations are sometimes met is also an index of their destabilizing potential. Our college's efforts to have these conversations have been highlighted in the national press: journalist Eleanor Clift, one of the first women journalists on a syndicated political talk show, visited the campus in 2018, sitting in on a Gender Studies 101 class and participating in a campus-wide forum about the #MeToo movement, and specifically men's responsibilities within that movement. Clift's article (2018) is titled "#MeToo is Doing Well—At An All-Male College in Indiana," with the tag-line "Wabash College is a small, all-male school in a small town smack in the middle of Trump country. You'd never know any of that after talking to these young men" (Clift, 2018). The headline and the accompanying story draw attention to the juxtaposition of a perceived conservative institution ("all-male," "Trump country") with potentially liberal values ("Where else would you find a gender studies class that is all male?" [Clift, 2018]). The intersection of these forces can be a fruitfully disruptive and generative site for thinking about and enacting alternatives for young men to the expectations of hegemonic masculinity.

Conclusion

We do not intend to suggest that hegemonic masculinity is not harmful to women in the classroom or that it does not mute other voices. We suggest that, in addition to being harmful to women, hegemonic masculinity produces pressures and expectations for men that limit their options for how to act and appear to one another that become obstacles to their learning. This recognition of male privilege and pressures makes the various issues that men face and that we face in the classroom teaching men different than in both women student bodies and co-educational environments. Here, we hope to export some of the practices and questions that have worked for us as teachers of men. We proceed from the belief that hegemonic masculinity keeps men from learning effectively, and thus keeps us from teaching effectively. We hold that hegemonic masculinity needs to be addressed directly with students, in on-going conversation with faculty, and the shape of the curriculum. If we as educators fail to do this, we risk underwriting men students' unhealthy and unproductive habits of hegemonic masculinity, and moreover, we also risk perpetuating those habits ourselves when we implicitly accept and encourage them, or fail to interrogate them in our pedagogical choices. One of the affordances of approaching hegemonic masculinity as a specifically pedagogical issue is that it invites men to reflect on the ways that it is an obstacle to their own learning, thus investing them in the process of resisting a social, economic, and political structure (patriarchy in general and hegemonic masculinity in particular) that many young men are not encouraged or inclined to question. Instead of challenging the ethics and politics of hegemonic masculinity as a larger structure, we are appealing to students to question the workings of hegemonic masculinity to make them better learners and to make us better teachers. Investing men students in this project works through investing them in their learning and seeing the ways that hegemonic masculinity is an obstacle to it.

References

Addis, M. E. (2008). Gender and depression in men. *Clinical Psychology: Science and Practice, 15*, 153–168.

Addis, M. E., & Mahalik, J. R. (2003). Men, masculinity, and the contexts of help seeking. *American Psychology, 58*(1), 5–14.

Alfred, G. C., Hammer, J. H., & Good, G. E. (2014). Male student veterans: Hardiness, psychological well-being, and masculine norms. *Psychology of Men & Masculinity, 15*, 95–99.

Bartky, S. E. (1997). Foucault, femininity, and the modernization of patriarchy. In K. Conboy, N. Medina, & S. Stanbury (Eds.), *Writing on the body: Female embodiment and feminist theory* (pp. 129–154). New York: Columbia University Press.

Biewen, J., & Headlee, C. (2018). MEN Series, Scene on the Radio. Podcast: http://www.sceneonradio.org/men/

Clift, E. (2018). #MeToo is doing well—at an all-male college in Indiana. *Daily Beast*. Retrieved from https://www.thedailybeast.com/metoo-is-doing-wellat-an-all-male-college-in-indiana.

Cohn, A., & Zeichner A. (2006). Effects of masculine identity and gender role stress on aggression in men. *Psychology of Men & Masculinity*, 7, 179–190.

Connell, R. W. (1987). *Gender and power: Society, the person and sexual politics.* Stanford, CA: Stanford UP.

Connell, R. W., & Messerschmidt, J. W. (2005). Hegemonic masculinity: Rethinking the concept. *Gender & Society*, 19, 829–859.

Foucault, M. (1977). *Discipline and power: The birth of the prison.* Trans. by Alan Sheridan. New York: Vintage Books.

Good, G. E., & Wood, P. K. (1995). Male gender role conflict, depression, and help seeking: Do college men face double jeopardy? *Journal of Counseling & Development*, 74, 70–75.

Green, J., & Jakupcak, M. (2016). Masculinity and men's self-harm behaviors: Implications for non-suicidal self-injury disorder. *Psychology of Men & Masculinity*, 17(2), 147–155.

Green, J. D., Kearns, J. C., Ledoux, A. M., Addis, M. E., & Marx, B. P. (2018). The association between masculinity and nonsuicidal self-injury. *American Journal of Men's Health*, 12(1), 30–40.

Hylton, W. S. (2019). My cousin was my hero. Until the day he tried to kill me. *The New York Times Magazine.* Retrieved from https://www.nytimes.com/2019/05/08/magazine/cousin-kill-me-male-violence.html

Kimmel, M. (1997). Masculinity as homophobia: Fear, shame and silence in the construction of gender identity. In M. M. Gergen & S. N. Davis (Eds.), *Toward a new psychology of gender* (pp. 223–242). Florence, KY, US: Taylor & Frances/Routledge.

Kimmel, M. (2008). *Guyland: The perilous world where boys become men.* NY: Harper Collins.

Kimmel, M. (2011). Mapping guyland in college. In J. A. Laker & T. Davis (Eds.), *Masculinities in higher education: Theoretical and practical considerations* (pp. 3–15). New York: Routledge.

Laker, J. A. (2011). Inviting and inspiring men: Gendered pedagogical considerations for undergraduate teaching and learning environments. In J. A. Laker & T. Davis (Eds.), *Masculinities in higher education: Theoretical and practical considerations* (pp. 63–78). New York: Routledge.

Laker, J. A., & Davis, T. (2011). *Masculinities in higher education: Theoretical and practical considerations.* New York: Routledge.

Mahalik, J. R., Good, G. E., & Englar-Carlson, M. (2003). Masculinity scripts, presenting concerns, and help seeking: Implications for practice and training. *Professional Psychology: Research and Practice*, 34, 123–131.

Manne, K. (2017). *Down girl: The logic of misogyny.* Oxford: Oxford University Press.

Nagel, E., Kalish, R., & Kimmel, M. (2015). Scripts of masculinity. *International Encyclopedia of the Social & Behavioral Sciences*, 14, 685–689.

Parent, M. C., Hammer, J. H., Bradstreet, T. C., Schwartz, E. N., & Jobe, T. (2018). Men's mental health help-seeking behaviors: An intersectional analysis. *American Journal of Men's Health*, 12(1), 64–73. doi:10.1177/1557988315625776.

Powell, W., Adams, L. B., Cole-Lewis, Y., Agyemang, A., & Upton, R. D. (2016). Masculinity and race-related factors as barriers to health help-seeking among African American men. *Behavioral Medicine, 42*(3), 150–63. doi:10.1080/08964289.2016.1165174.

Reeser, T. (2010). *Masculinities in theory: An introduction.* Malden, MA: Wiley-Blackwell.

Rich, S. (2018). Today's masculinity is stifling. *The Atlantic Monthly.* Retrieved from https://www.theatlantic.com/family/archive/2018/06/imagining-a-better-boyhood/562232/

Rosenberg, W. (2018). Teaching men: What difference does it make? What difference can it make? GLCA / GLAA Consortium for Teaching and Learning blog. Retrieved from https://glcateachlearn.org/teaching-men-what-difference-does-it-make-what-difference-can-it-make/

Sedgwick, E. K. (1985). *Between men: English literature and male homosocial desire.* New York City: Columbia University Press.

Sexton, J. Y. (2019). *The man they wanted me to be: Toxic masculinity and a crisis of our own making.* Berkeley, CA: Counterpoint.

Smyth, E. (2010). Single-sex education: What does research tell us. *Revue française de pedagogie, 171,* 47–55.

Trott, A. M. (2018). Teaching men. *Wabash College Teaching and Learning blog.* Retrieved from https://blog.wabash.edu/teachingandlearning/2018/09/27/teaching-men/#more-225.

Wide, J., Mok, H., McKenna, M., & Ogrodniczuk, J. S. (2011). Effect of gender socialization on the presentation of depression among men: A pilot study. *Canadian Family Physician, 57,* e74–e78.

Wood, J. (2009). *Gendered lives: Communication, gender, and culture.* Boston: Wadsworth.

CHAPTER TWO

We Are How We Teach: Black Feminist Pedagogy as a Move Towards the Legibility and Liberation of All

JENN M. JACKSON AND HILARY N. TACKIE

Education in the United States is still fraught with tensions. College campuses have become increasingly neoliberal. Public secondary education in the United States is too often tethered to the financial whims of racially segregated communities. Despite claims of post-racialism and "colorblindness," the long histories of colonialism, genocide, racial discrimination, and gender-based violence in the United States and across the Americas continue to structure the institutions and systems regulating social norms and order. Though time has passed since groundbreaking decisions like *Brown v. Board of Education* (1954), which formally desegregated American classrooms, many traditional classroom conditions prevail. From pre-kindergarten through postsecondary, Black students, and other students of color, rarely see authentic representations of their experiences reflected in their courses or the pedagogical methods employed in their classrooms. Moreover, multiply marginalized learners, at the intersections of race, class, gender, sexuality, embodiment, and disability, often endure the multiple and interlocking burdens of struggling against stereotypes, biases, and structural exclusions while trying to be fully present learners. Thus, since the classroom is still a political site—in which how material is taught, which material is taught, and who it is taught by have significance for learning and development—teaching is a political act.

In this chapter, we focus on the political import of the classroom, insisting on a Black Feminist mode of teaching based on Black women's experiences and ideas. This Black Feminist pedagogical approach, "aims to develop a mindset that stands in contradiction to the Western intellectual tradition of exclusivity and chauvinism" (Omolade, 1987, p. 32). It is through Black Feminist pedagogy, that the potential radicalism of the classroom is made clearer. Through processes of unlearning the socialization of white supremacist hegemony, learners and educators engage in a transformative process of knowledge creation and consciousness-building that is foundational to seeding liberatory politics and behaviors.

In specific reference to the objective of this collection, introducing a Black Feminist pedagogy asks all to be critical of the normative assumptions of the classroom which cast non-white, non-cismen participants as others to be accommodated. As bell hooks explains, "there has to be some deconstruction of the traditional notion that only the professor is responsible for classroom dynamics. That responsibility is relative to status" (hooks, 1994, p. 8). This process requires the dismantling of artificial hierarchies and boundaries between the academy and the "real-world." Most importantly, this process requires mindful and deliberate interrogation of how we have been taught, what we have learned, and how we teach others.

Several guiding questions emerge from this analysis. First, what does the persistence of white, cisgender, heterosexual, masculinity in educational spaces make legible or illegible for students and educators? Second, what can be learned from both the experiential and theoretical precepts of Black Feminist pedagogy and critique? Third, how does a commitment to Black Feminist pedagogical practice contribute to the possibility of liberation for all people? We argue that the specific experiences with exclusion, silencing, intellectual, and emotional violence that Black womyn, femmes, and other non-men experience in their daily lives are fundamental in shaping a Black Feminist pedagogical approach. Moreover, these experiences and knowledge banks supply critical rubrics for decentering white masculinity and instead centering multiply marginalized learners.

In what follows, we discuss the roles of learning and legibility in the classroom in upholding gendered and racialized normativity. Further, we parse out the process of "productive discomfort," a pedagogical tool meant to challenge learners to work through the discomfort of unlearning existing racial, gender, and class paradigms that are often reinforced in traditional classroom environments. Penultimately, we supply a framework for using the classroom as a site of social and political transformation. Lastly, we address identity, feminist scholarship, and the critical roles of prior knowledge and experience at play in shaping the learning experiences of educators and students.

Learning and Legibility

The learning process is dynamic. But many traditional pedagogical methods have not fully accounted for the full potential of the teaching environment. According to Paulo Freire (1972), these highly structured and rigid teaching methods fall under the "banking" concept of education. In this form, teaching is primarily the act of depositing information into the minds of students to be taken in without critique and preserved. In this traditional pedagogical approach, learning, then, boils down to processes of memorization, regurgitation, and content mastery rather than active and rigorous engagement, careful and deliberate analysis, or the production of new forms of knowledge. However, the true aim of a Black Feminist classroom must first rest on dismantling these pedagogical methods. To produce knowledge that challenges existing hegemonic systems of heteropatriarchy, white supremacy, and gendered exclusion, learners must first have agency and autonomy in the class environment. Freire explains that "knowledge emerges only through invention and re-invention, through the restless, impatient, continuing, hopeful inquiry human beings pursue in the world, with the world, and with each other" (1972, p. 72). By challenging the long-standing "banking" concept of education, through deliberate inclusion, purposeful inquiry, and diligent introspection, educators can make formative contributions to the ideas and behaviors of learners. This is just the first step in fostering a learning environment that is compatible with a Black Feminist pedagogical approach.

For classrooms to offer adequate points of entry to all participants they must be legible to all. The mechanics, often unwritten and unspoken rules, standards, and pedagogical aims must be transparent. "Legibility," in its most basic form, means clarity, and refers to the process by which a phenomenon or issue is made clear enough to understand. Frequently, legibility in the classroom environment is reduced to the use of "proper" terminology. However, the deployment of terminology alone, or the practice of naming bodies, experiences, and phenomena, does not sufficiently tap into the full possibility of the classroom. In their critical essay examining terminology and the pedagogical tenants of a transgender studies course, Toby Beauchamp illustrates how the focus on terminology, especially in courses focused on learning transgender studies, fails to fully account for how students and learners in these courses often arrive in class with corollary expectations, needs, and objectives. Beauchamp is one of the few, and perhaps the only, faculty member on their campus who focuses on transgender studies. In Beauchamp's experience, students frequently share private information about their medical needs, transition status, and other non-academic issues because they need support which exceeds traditional in-class pedagogical models. Beauchamp says, "each time students engage me in these ways, I am struck by the unfulfilled needs implied by such conversations; they suggest to me a persistent desire for recognition and legibility that, for many of my students, is otherwise absent on campus" (2018, p. 26). Beauchamp makes it clear that the inclusive and knowledge-driven classroom carries the possibility of supplying experiential connectedness and real-world navigational techniques which rest outside of traditional hegemonic norms. While students and learners often come to these courses seeking mutually recognizable language to articulate their experiences, to make their prior knowledge legible both to themselves and to others, they, too, are frequently still struggling against systemic and structural barriers which delimit their ability to fully access the knowledge bases, resources, and repositories needed to assist them in that endeavor. Thus, the traditional classroom and the banking method of education make these student needs and aims illegible. To be clear, the traditional classroom and the banking method of education rely so heavily on hierarchical relationships between students and educators that they undermine efforts to draw material connections between course content and real-world experiences. Instead, in Beauchamp's classroom, the collapsing of the traditional classroom hierarchy enables students to be vulnerable.

Because the learning process is vastly improved upon when educators commit to cooperative knowledge production, active forms of student inquiry, and fastidious care for student inclusion, the learning environment also has the potential to affect how learners situate themselves with respect to the content and others in the classroom. Elizabeth Higginbotham explains that "learning to identify myth and misinformation about people of color is a critical task in course and curriculum revision" (1995, p. 478). Myth and misinformation do not only prevail where it concerns people of color, however. There are mythical gender biases and stereotypes, class-based norms, and beliefs, ableist course structures, and antagonisms rooted in fears of non-heterosexual coupling and intimacy. These enduring notions, rooted in the white cis-heteropatriarchal nature of the status quo, must be uprooted to effectively and with purpose reorient student learning outcomes. Educators with the intention to disrupt myth will "be better prepared to interrupt and challenge racist, sexist, class-bias, and homophobic remarks made in the classroom" (Higginbotham, 1995, p. 478). Learning and legibility intermingle to create a crucible wherein students and educators may (a) prepare themselves for both learning and unlearning; (b) critically engage with the existing narratives, frameworks, and systems that negatively shape the classroom environment; and (c) open up the educational space for the possibility of both knowing *and* doing otherwise in the classroom and in the "real-world."

(Un)Learning in the Classroom

There is a pervasive myth that classrooms are nurturing safe spaces. This myth often clouds the ability to see the variety of violence and discomforts that can occur in classrooms. Violence in the classroom is often policed on the student-to-student interactional level through discipline policies and efforts to teach young people proper decorum. However, this does not account for a large swath of the harms that occur in the classroom. The presumed safety of the classroom leads us to see the information that has been considered by dominant society as worth knowing as relatively safe. While learning may tax students intellectually, it is not expected to challenge them on a personal level nor to affect their identity formation and meaning making processes. If we expand our definition of violence and harm, we can see that classroom harm comes in the form of cultural denial, silencing, and erasure, ignorance, tokenization, and shaming among many other manifestations. Students of marginalized identities most often experience these types of harms. Whether in a primary, secondary, or postsecondary setting, the traditional classroom still holds onto the fundamental practices and values that initially shaped it centuries ago. However, since that time, the overwhelming demographics of the student and learner population has transformed to include a variety of embodiments that historically would not have been granted entrance. Given that the education system no longer exclusively serves white cisgender men, it is unfortunate that the format and content of the classroom has not adequately changed in response.

We ask students of color and learners of other marginalized identities to leave their identities at the door as they read texts that were never intended for their consumption. The white men who wrote these texts likely did not ever consider that such individuals would be reading their work. The list of required texts for most courses has remained vastly the same over time since texts by white European men still dominate reading lists. The effects on students of color reading about their so-called primitive and barbaric ancestors, when there is opportunity to read about them at all, is given little to no thought. This is not to say that texts written by white European men should not be read, or that they have no value, but that we need to adjust our approach as to how we teach them. Traditional works need to be taught in context, and especially through a critical lens. Annette Henry claims that, "all topics can be studied in respect to women and girls or from feminist frameworks" (2005, p. 96). Applying a critical lens, students are encouraged to question what they know and how they have previously learned to perceive the world. Without this framing, the absence of differing perspectives in curricula can be harmful to all students. As Henry claims, students "lose the opportunity for growth and change if they cannot clearly examine and understand the historical dimensions of current societal dilemmas and oppressions of the ways in which they may help dismantle them. This lack of analysis misleads students to believe and accept that existing societal problems and educational inequities are in reality "natural," "inevitable," or due to the inherent characteristics of certain classes and cultures" (Henry, 2005, p. 96). The lack of added analysis also allows students to continue without questioning the assumptions upon which the content they learn is based. Presently, a traditional classroom can easily function to alienate marginalized students and perpetuate reductive forms of thought.

Pushing students to question what they know, although ultimately productive, can make them feel vulnerable and uncomfortable. However, this is not the same as the discomfort that marginalized students may feel in the traditional classroom which has little function but to spawn inferiority complexes, distance personal from academic identity, and trigger disengagement—a precursor to dropout. This latter type of discomfort is distinctly harmful and unproductive. However, if educators are to encourage students to question their worlds as they know them and critique the systems and structures that shape their lives, it is impossible to conduct a classroom that allows all students to always be comfortable that also results in any meaningful learning. Instead, a Black feminist pedagogy, as a transformative pedagogy, encourages students through productive discomfort. In this way, we can refer to Black feminist pedagogy as a pedagogy of discomfort (Zembylas, 2015) as it forces students to reconsider their own lines of thought and ways of knowing. Pedagogies of discomfort have been discussed most commonly in reference to the teaching of emotional, controversial, or violent topics that can challenge the assumption of classroom safety. We argue that for some students, a reframing and evaluation of content from a social position other than their own, a process that requires compassion and sympathy, can have comparable results.

In an effort towards social transformation, supporting students through discomfort eases unlearning necessary to destabilize current hegemonic and disenfranchising systems and patterns of thought. We put forth that there are at least five aspects of unlearning integral to our Black feminist pedagogical project: (1) unlearning what authority looks like; (2) unlearning a traditional conception of knowledge; (3) unlearning the banking educational format; (4) unlearning the classroom as an unemotional space; and (5) unlearning the traditional purpose of education.

Unlearning Authority

On a representational level, by simply being present in places of authority or leadership, educators of marginalized identities can disrupt traditional ways of thinking. Their presence as authority often requires that students reflect on their assumptions about who holds diverse types of expertise. As the body at the front of the classroom, such educators can dislodge a multiplicity of conflicting associations students have with the presented identities allowing "the complex interplay between the personal, intellectual, and political to flourish" (Lewis, 2011, p. 54). Unfortunately, much of this process begins before they are even able to communicate, and so the concept of legibility can also be applied to the role of the educator. Mel Michelle Lewis (2011) discusses her own "body as text" in describing the interactions she has with the students in her classes. Simply her presence as a Black queer body is a disruption in the normative university classroom that serves to question implicitly and explicitly what her students know about who has authority over knowledge. This makes some students uncomfortable as they are forced to consider how their words land on someone whose identity politics can never be invisible. Her body is part of her pedagogy bringing to mind hooks's assertion that "to call attention to the body is to betray the legacy of repression and denial that has been handed down to us by our professional elders, who have been usually white and male" (1994, p. 191). Acknowledging the body in the classroom allows both educator and student to bring their entire self into the discussion.

However, it does not necessitate a Black or oppressed body to have the effect Lewis has on her students. As Beauboeuf-Lafontant (2002) states, with reference to womanist educators, as a political position, the uptake of a Black feminist ethic is a choice that an individual of any social position can make, just as anyone can subscribe to maintaining the status quo As we all have bodies that hold social and political significance, it is a pedagogical shift that is required. The move towards an inclusive classroom that recognizes the whole self and brings multiply marginalized individuals towards the center may challenge white cisgender students who are not used to having their perspectives questioned or feeling othered. But decentering is not equivalent to delegitimizing.

Rather than simply dethroning the traditional academic gaze, such a shift aims to bring all students into a place of authority by acknowledging them as experts of their own experiences. A traditional classroom relies on the educator to be the ultimate authority in the classroom. The educator directs how the classroom will run as well as what will be learned. A Black feminist classroom would push for a more collaborative process, one where students are empowered to have some control over their own educational experiences. This distribution of power encourages greater engagement and inclusion. In this way, the educator becomes less of an authoritarian and more of a facilitator.

Unlearning Traditional Conceptions of Knowledge

A classroom centered around a Black feminist ethic, in recognizing those who are commonly left out of academic discourse, also recognizes the variety of knowledges held by marginalized individuals that is commonly relegated to non- or anti-academic spaces. Moll et al., define an individual's 'fund of knowledge' as "historically accumulated and culturally developed bodies of knowledge essential for household or individual functioning and well-being" (1992, p. 133). The lessons that make up one's fund of knowledge are often taught by people who know the person on multiple levels; therefore, these educators can see the whole multidimensional person rather than a mere student. These historical, cultural, or communal educators can then acknowledge an individual's past experiences, interests, and prior knowledge, building upon them to relate new lessons on a deeper level.

Without intentional attempts at affirming difference, it is possible that the values held by youth, learned through past experiences, may conflict with those put forth by the education system. Consistent conflict and denial of students' prior ways of knowing can be demoralizing. How a student processes in-class content is affected by what they already know and therefore using this fund of knowledge can improve engagement, relevance, and connectedness. Simultaneously, when educators encourage students to bring their whole selves into the classroom and value the knowledge or expertise students already have, they are also affirming students and concretizing their place in an educational environment. Valuing individual experience aids in the effort to move students from banks to critics and producers of knowledge.

Unlearning the Banking Educational Model

As earlier discussed, the traditional classroom relies on what Paulo Freire (1972) referred to as the "banking" model. Adjusting how one thinks of the role of the educator and expanding what content we value as meaningful knowledge shifts from a system that simply asks students to regurgitate facts. Instead, the classroom can become a place of dialogic exchange between educator and student as well as between students. In Freire's terms, the educator becomes an educator-student, which acknowledges that the educator is not omniscient. In this framework, students become student-educators, recognizing that students enter classrooms with information that can be valuable to their peers (Freire, 1972, p. 80). Educators can and should take part in learning as well, making themselves vulnerable enough to express when they do not know something and to receive student-driven knowledge.

Moving away from the banking model also asks students to engage more deeply with course material. Students must process rather than absorb content.

This latter approach requires the teaching, learning, and rehearsal of analytical skills so that they can be used in future educational, social, and political situations. The information, therefore, becomes more real and applicable as students are asked to think about what they are learning within the context of their own lives and listen to their fellow students reflect similarly.

Unlearning the Classroom as an Unemotional Space

The depiction of the classroom as a place where educators give information, and students receive it, allows for a passionless understanding of education. The emphasis on assessment, grading, and the accumulation of facts perpetuates an impersonal classroom where not even the educator is expected to have an affective stake in course content. Despite this expectation, media romanticizes the passionate classroom. As hooks states: "[e]ven though many viewers may applaud a movie like *The Dead Poets Society*, possibly identifying with the passion of the professor and his students, rarely is such passion institutionally affirmed" (1994, p. 198). However, if education can be alienating and education can be confirming, then education must be an emotional process. To acknowledge that students feel uncomfortable in class is to acknowledge that students are emotional beings. Learning meaningfully should be an emotional experience as engaging in such a process will influence how an individual relates to the world and how they see themselves. Since meaningful education affects identity and personal development, it is inherently emotional.

Moving students through discomfort requires what has been referred to as pedagogical care (Zembylas, 2015). By building a relationship with their students, being responsive to their needs, and showing concern for their progress, educators can create a transformative environment. Through exercising pedagogical care, educators can create spaces that, although not without discomfort, allow students to experience a different kind of safety. In this classroom, while students are supported and respected by their educators, they also support and respect each other. These layers of support reduce the fear of being challenged. Developing a classroom in this way expands what is allowed regarding emotional displays. Learning can be emotional. Learning can be maddening just as it can be enjoyable. In conversation with bell hooks, Ron Scapp states that "pleasure in the classroom is feared … because the idea of reciprocity, of respect, is never assumed" (1994, p. 145). Recognizing the classroom as an emotional environment allows us to reinforce it as a transformational and political space by allowing the entrance and analysis of sufficiently complex and intersectional beings.

Unlearning the Purpose of Education

A Black Feminist pedagogy stresses that learning is not simply about accumulating facts. In moving away from a "banking" model, we must re-evaluate the purpose of education. The "banking" model falls in line with a capitalist or imperialist ethos that sees education as both a means to an economic end and as a form of social control. Black feminist pedagogy seeks for all to be free. It asks its subjects to recognize themselves as agents of change. The sole objective of education is no longer for workplace preparation nor proving intelligence through scored performance on a standardized test, but to help individuals understand and push against their place in the existing social order, engage with their world, and work towards various forms of social justice.

Classrooms as Sites of Social and Political Transformation

Since college campuses are microcosms of non-academic settings, classrooms often reproduce negative gender, race or other identity-related messages, narratives, and practices that originate in students' personal and experiential worlds. This fact may obfuscate the radical potential of the classroom setting. Sites of transformation are physical locations in which new ways of being, thinking, and becoming are explored and become possible. However, these sites are not immune from mainstream expectations encouraging alignment to dominant norms. For this reason, potential sites of transformation must be actively supported in both intentional and explicit ways. Eder and McCluskey claim that, even though students may resist classroom changes which challenge their ideological commitments and biases, "[t]eaching/communicating across barriers of race, class, and gender interrupts business-as-usual in the academy, and offers an arena for knowledge-production by marginalized and excluded groups" (1996, pp. 46–47).

It is through the deliberate act of status quo interruption that both educators and student learners begin to use the radical potential of the classroom environment. Moreover, these challenges to the normative, traditional models of teaching and learning transgress the artificial boundaries which implicitly loom between race, gender, sexuality, class, and ability difference in the learning environment.

However, while sites of transformation hold radical potential, they do not develop on their own. Many of these sites of transformation emerge from community-based movement organizations, moments of political protest, and through the relationships forged despite systems of oppression and colonization that dominate our daily lives (Bassichis et al., 2011). "Sometimes these spaces for transformation are easier to spot than others—but you can find them everywhere, from church halls to lecture halls, from the lessons of our grandmothers to the lessons we learn surviving in the world" (Bassichis et al., 2011, p. 34). That means that educators, along with students and learners, have the power to draw together the myriad lessons, both formal and informal, that help them navigate the social world. It also means that educators are positioned to turn the lens of the learning environment back onto themselves and students. In his discussion of the Student Non-Violent Coordinating Committee and organizing Freedom Schools in the Deep South in the 1960s, Charles E. Cobb explains that the schools emerged out of organizing and of a desire to "encourage people to challenge their ideas and habits" (2008, p. 71). In these learning environments, educators must tap into opportunities to confront existing forms of knowledge and learning. These opportunities might emerge via lessons on diversity and inclusion, acknowledgments of descriptive differences across students and teaching staff, and incorporating real-world examples into the classroom via course design and lecture adjustments. Navigating classrooms as sites of transformation also requires that educators normalize the teaching and learning process as one of nonhierarchical co-accountability and mutual respect. By doing so, educators empower and embolden students to take control of their own learning processes rather than function as passive receivers of information. Taking control of the learning process includes interrogating the socialization, beliefs, biases, practices, and ideas that both educators and students bring into the classroom. According to Omolade, "If students transform the learning process until it becomes the study of themselves by others like themselves, they can transform their institution and overturn those who have imposed a 'foreign' understanding of the world upon them" (1987, p. 38). This process of transformation could follow a three-step form. As a first step, students and educators embark on a process of self-reflection and acknowledgment of innate difference. Secondarily, they transform their self-reflection and introspection into motivation toward self-determination and re-imagining the possible ways of being both inside the classroom and out. Finally, as a concluding step, students, and educators use their self-determination to disrupt existing social norms and instantiate new modes of existing. Thus, the classroom has transformative potential, and that potential is activated only when these lessons and experiences are combined with formal instruction and pedagogy.

As an empirical case, in *Teaching to Transgress* (1994), bell hooks details the progression of her educational experiences from segregated "all-Black" grade schools to the desegregated, white schools in Kentucky. Recalling her early experiences being taught by almost all Black women at Booker T. Washington

Elementary School, hooks writes that she and her classmates "learned early that [their] devotion to learning, to a life of the mind, was a counter-hegemonic act, a fundamental way to resist every strategy of white racial colonization … a revolutionary pedagogy of resistance that was profoundly revolutionary" (hooks, 1994, p. 2). When educators teach through the lens of Black Feminist pedagogy, they encourage students and learners, especially those at the intersections of race, gender, class, sexuality, and ability, to oppose the very systems which delimit their full humanity. The Black Feminist pedagogical approach, then, is a tool wherein educators may treat marginalized student experiences, their prior knowledgebases, as expert wisdom to help contribute to the radical possibility of the classroom.

There are three fundamental steps that educators may take to fully access the transformative potential of the classroom. First, educators must acknowledge their own orientations toward power and how their social position informs their prior knowledge, experiences, socialization, and shapes the classroom dynamic. In many instances, Black women educators, especially those who are queer, poor, have a disability or some combination of these marginalized identities, are unfairly burdened with spearheading social and political transformation within campus departments all while white male colleagues often undermine those efforts (Omolade, 1987). Moreover, they are often persecuted for their status and identities. Audre Lorde explains that "[t]hose of us who stand outside the circle of this society's definition of acceptable women; those of us who have been forged in the crucibles of difference—those of us who are poor, who are lesbians, who are Black, who are older—know that survival is not an academic skill" (1984, p. 112). It is learning how to stand alone, unpopular and sometimes reviled, and how to make common cause with those others identified as outside the structures in order to define and seek a world in which we can all flourish (2007, p. 112). In so defining outsider status as a potential site of knowledge and solidarity, Lorde helps to articulate why social position along marginalized identities is an asset in teaching and developing Black Feminist Pedagogy.

Second, tapping into the transformative nature of the classroom requires an enduring commitment to the praxis (e.g., theory and practice) of Black Feminist ideals rather than simply performance. As hooks explains, "commitment to feminist politics and black liberation struggle means that I must be able to confront issues of race and gender in a black context, providing meaningful answers to problematic questions as well as appropriate accessible ways to communicate them" (1994, p. 112). Third, educators and students must sense that the classroom is a safe yet contested space for learning, metabolizing, and reformulating the knowledge they create together. Safe spaces alone may perpetuate the notion that students with privileged identities should hold fast to their biases, stereotypes, or animus toward marginalized groups. According to Ludlow, "students who identify with privileged groups often perceive a threat to privilege and suspension of safety in the very construction of feminist/diversity classes" (2004, p. 41). Instead, a safe yet contested space ensures that all those present in the learning environment are open and available to being challenged and pressured in ways that they may not have been before the start of the course. These steps promote transformation because they promote forms of knowledge production that require thinking and doing anew.

Conclusion

The uptake of a Black feminist pedagogical practice requires several concrete steps including hiring teaching staff that represents marginalized identities, a pedagogical shift from a banking to a dialogic model and encouraging students to share their personal experiences in the classroom. It also pushes for several ideological shifts in how we understand knowledge, how we perceive authority, and overall how we imagine the function and form of the classroom. If we are committed to working towards liberation for all, from the multiply oppressed to the most privileged, we must adjust our tactics. Relying on the traditional classroom as a source of transformation will leave us wanting as it continues to invalidate the experiences of marginalized learners at the intersections of race, class, gender, ability, and sexuality.

Making space for students to bring their whole selves into the classroom is not a simple task but will ultimately allow for the establishment of a collaborative and humanizing educational experience centered on dialogic exchange (San Pedro & Kinloch, 2017, p. 390S). We acknowledge that the process of inviting students to be their whole selves is neither effortless nor without risk. For both educators and students, assimilation, respectability, and "normalcy" are reliable crutches upon which to lean as they often reduce hypervisibility, surveillance, and other forms of unwanted scrutiny. However, in this social and political moment, we argue that it is the responsibility of educators to allow space for a fuller student experience. As such, the classroom operates in a multi-modal fashion, as a place of imagination, possibility, potential, and change.

As we have described above, the move towards the explicit recognition of the classroom as a site of political transformation requires humility, vulnerability, and a willingness to sit with discomfort. While traditional forms of knowledge production and accumulation encourage students and educators to claim expertise over the objective facts of their content, a Black Feminist Pedagogical approach is rooted in the process of discovery, the process of not knowing, and embarking upon new intellectual ways of being through mutual experiential contact. M. Jacqui Alexander explains, "There is something quite profound about not knowing, claiming not to know, or not gaining access to knowledge that enables us to know that we are not the sole (re)producers of our lives" (2005, p. 109). Black Feminism, as both a theoretical tool and philosophical practice, is rooted in both self-determination and self-discovery, as Alexander elucidates with this pedagogical framework. By embracing the notion that "the personal is political," we also embrace the fact that our learning environments and practices are co-constructed through repeated instances of pressure, reflection, contestation, and confrontation. As we take up a Black Feminist Pedagogical approach to teaching, we may meet unforeseen obstacles and unfortunate drawbacks as we look to dismantle existing modes of knowledge production. But what is more important, is that we persist in our course toward justice and liberation through accountable, deliberate, and inclusive pedagogy. While we may not yet know for sure where this pedagogical approach will take us, we can be certain that it will not take us back to where we started.

References

Alexander, M. J. (2005). *Pedagogies of crossing: Meditations on feminism, sexual politics, memory, and the sacred.* Durham, NC: Duke University Press.

Bassichis, M., Lee, A., & Spade, D. (2011). Building an abolitionist trans and queer movement with everything we've got. In E. A. Stanley, & N. Stanley (Eds.), *Captive genders: Trans embodiment and the prison industrial complex* (2nd ed., pp. 21–46). Oakland, CA: AK Press.

Beauboeuf-Lafontant, T. (2002). A womanist experience of caring: Understanding the pedagogy of exemplary black women teachers. *The Urban Review, 34*(1), 71–85.

Beauchamp, T. (2018). Clutching on: Teaching identity and terminology in transgender studies. *Feminist Formations, 30*(3), 25–33.

Cobb, C. E. (2008). Organizing freedom schools. In C. M. Payne & C. S. Strickland (Ed.), *Teach freedom: Education for liberation in the African-American tradition* (pp. 69–74). New York, NY: Teachers College Press.

Eder, D., & McCluskey, A. (1996). Teaching across the barriers: The classroom as a site of Transformation. *Transformations: The Journal of Inclusive Scholarship and Pedagogy, 7*(1), 37–54.

Freire, P. (1972). *Pedagogy of the oppressed.* New York, NY: Herder and Herder.

Henry, A. (2005). Black Feminist pedagogy: Critiques and contributions. In W. Watkins (Ed.), *Counterpoints: Black Protest Thought and Education,* (pp. 89–105). New York, NY: Peter Lang.

Higginbotham, E. (1995). Designing an inclusive curriculum: Bringing all women into the core. In B. Guy-Sheftall (Ed.), *Words of fire: An anthology of African-American feminist thought* (pp. 474–486). New York, NY: New Press.

hooks, b. (1994). *Teaching to transgress: Education as the practice of freedom.* New York, NY: Routledge.

Lewis, M. M. (2011). Body of knowledge: Black queer feminist pedagogy, praxis, and embodied text. *Journal of Lesbian Studies, 15,* 49–57.

Lorde, A. (1984). The master's tools will never dismantle the master's house. In *Sister outsider: Essays and speeches* (pp. 110–114). Berkeley, CA: Crossing Press.

Ludlow, J. (2004). From safe space to contested space in the feminist classroom. *Transformations: The Journal of Inclusive Scholarship and Pedagogy, 15*(1), 40–56.

Moll, L., Amanti, C., Neff, D., & Gonzalez, N. (1992). Funds of knowledge for teaching: Using a qualitative approach to connect homes and classrooms. *Theory Into Practice, 31*(2), 132–141. Retrieved November 24, 2020, from http://www.jstor.org/stable/1476399

Omolade, B. (1987). A Black Feminist pedagogy. *Women's Studies Quarterly, 15*(3/4), 32–39.

San Pedro, T., & Kinloch, V. (2017). Toward projects in humanization: Research on co-creating and sustaining dialogic relationships. *American Educational Research Journal, 54*(1S), 373S–394S.

Zembylas, M. (2015). 'Pedagogy of discomfort' and its ethical implications: The tensions of ethical violence in social justice education. *Ethics and Education, 10*(2), 163–174.

CHAPTER THREE

"I'll Huff and I'll Puff": Becoming Masculine in *Fables*

JESSICA RUTH AUSTIN

The comic book genre has invited critical analysis from many fields of scholarship and in recent years has been used in classroom pedagogy as a way to teach history (Ravelo, 2013). This chapter develops further ways in which we can incorporate comics into the classroom using them as a cultural product to investigate masculinity in an academic setting. This framework shows educators in four easy-to-follow stages how the comic book series *Fables* (2002–2015) can be used to avoid perpetuating hegemonic masculinity. This is becoming increasingly important in a university classroom setting as recent pedagogy suggests that hegemonic masculinities can negatively affect learning in students who demonstrate different masculinities across racial lines in universities in the USA (Chou et al., 2012).

Hegemony entails a presumption of social dominance of one group over another, and masculinity refers to the behavior of men. These terms together suggest that there is a "culturally normative" idea of "what a man should act like," and men who do not adhere to this idea become subordinate masculinities (Connell, 1995). Scholarly literature has often featured arguments that comic book representations of masculinity have negative overtones by privileging whiteness and "macho" hegemonic masculinities over more realistic representations. There has also been a pernicious preoccupation with linking violence and masculine comic book characters together. Subsequently, the portrayal of hegemonic masculinity in the comic book world, especially that of superheroes, has become an important field of inquiry, making *Fables* an appropriate text to analyze. The framework suggested in this chapter is a tool which focuses on the use of violence as a marker of Western hegemonic masculinity, a gendered violence against any identity which does not conform to hegemony, and how critique can break this down.

The series *Fables* was created by Bill Willingham and ran from 2002 until 2015. It won 14 Eisner awards making it a critical and commercial success, leading to nine spin-off mini-series as well as a video game. At first glance, this series may appear to promote a hegemonic version of masculinity which has been noted to be problematic by scholars. One of the most prominent characters to appear across the series is Bigby Wolf, who is often portrayed as rude, dismissive, and violent. Bigby is also the main character is *The Wolf Among Us* video game (Telltale Games, 2013), which also perpetuates a "sexist" trope of a woman character enduring violence as a plot device (Simone, 1999). Despite this, *Fables* is based off fairytale stories that many students will be aware of from their childhood. This creates an interesting scenario where students can use a critical lens on stories from which they are familiar; from where many learnt traditional gender roles such as the helpless princess needing saving from a handsome prince.

It should be noted that no cultural product is perfect or offers every angle for analysis to battle the harms of hegemonic masculinity and *Fables* falters in two aspects: racial diversity and heterocentrism. Although a fictional version of Baghdad and Arabian fables are introduced in 2005, racial undertones appear in the treatment of the "passing as human." The basis of the comic being that these fictional characters now live alongside us in the "real" world. Therefore, any character in the comic who cannot "pass" (they may be a talking animal, based on common Disney characters) are banned from living in cities where a regular human may spot them. Sara Silah argues that "race-thinking is a form of speciesism that is highly invested in notions of the animal and the human" (2007, p. 96). She notes that particular animals are associated with "certain kinds of humans" and often these kinds of animal association are extremely harmful and racist. For example, Black individuals have often been described and associated with mere apes rather than humans (Silah, 2007, p. 98). This is not just a problem with *Fables* however, the majority of the superheroes who have been chosen for a reincarnation on the big screen in Marvel's Cinematic Universe (MCU) have been white men. The only MCU film which has not been led by masculine, white men was *Black Panther* (Coogler, 2017) which explains why it has been culturally significant for both scholars and viewers alike (LaRue, 2018).

Moreover, *Fables* has an overbearing focus on heterocentrism and lacks any discernible LGBTQIA characters. All of the relationships present in the series are heterosexual in nature, leaving any other identities omitted. This privileging of heterosexual identities supports hegemonic masculinity that is particularly harmful to women and LGBTQIA individuals. Since *Fables* uses as its source material older tales and folklore, they arguably would not have used LGBTQIA identified characters. Despite this omission, the storylines of *Fables* are an effective conduit for students to explore masculinity from these stories and why they are harmful in the present day. Furthermore, it was beyond the scope of this book chapter to investigate the omission of LGBTQIA perspectives but is an important site for future research.

Jeffrey Brown (2000) explores how Black superheroes are marginalized in the comic book genre due to their "undesirable" masculinity which is characterized as deviant in society. According to Brown, compared to the larger comic book producers (such as DC and Marvel), Milestone comics was one of the few to successfully produce empowering Black comic book characters (Brown, 2000, p. 180). Further, another character suffering from racial and gendered misappropriation is that of Glenn Rhee, who represents an unbalanced "model-minority" character from *The Walking Dead* (Kirkman, 2003-2020) comic character and later television program. Scholarly work on comic book characters has become increasingly important, especially when considering that these characters have moved into mainstream culture. Gone are the days where comic books were reserved for the "nerdy fanboy" evident by the billions in revenue Disney and Marvel now make in the international box office. Comic book characters are more likely to be known by those in a classroom setting and the general populous, and therefore, are more enjoyable and appropriate to use for teaching theory.

Comic studies have already noted the way that the body is used as a site of hyper-masculinity. Hyper-masculinity is where great emphasis is placed on physical strength, aggression, and (heterosexual) sexuality and if these are what is valued culturally then it forms part of hegemonic masculinity. Hegemonic masculinity is not always related to hyper-masculine traits but in the Western world these two are deeply entwined. Thus, analyzing body types and behaviors to find hegemonic displays of masculinity in comic books can be made relevant to students who read them. A framework that subverts hyper-masculinity can tackle the more harmful aspects of hegemonic masculinity that emanate from these texts. This has been especially important in discussing the super body that, "fills a particular place in the construction of fantasies that go beyond gender stereotypes: often they take a stereotype and push it into the absurd or even the surreal" (Salter & Blodgett, 2017, p. 110). Thus, super bodies pose a serious problem as findings indicate that societal values projected through media, such as the consumption of traditionally muscular superheroes, harms body image of those who consume them (Ferguson, 2018; Teo & Collinson, 2018; Mabe et al., 2014).

The Culture of Fandom

Educators should also consider studying the culture of fandom when exploring specific texts in the classroom because comic book fans may engage in sexist practices that are exclusionary of women aiding hegemonic masculinity claims. Suzanne Scott suggests that comic book fans sometimes engage in toxic "masculine" practices that, "cult movie fandom['s] or other man-dominated subcultures, may welcome women if they 'opt to be one of the boys'" (Scott, 2013). However, she suggests that this cultural tide is improving as more consideration is given to women's "places and perception within comic book culture" (Scott, 2013). This may be due to increased visibility via social media, blogs, and crowdfunding; however, the "fanboy" discourse persists in other negative ways (Scott, 2013). Fanboys are men who can become angry and aggressive towards anyone deemed an "unsuitable" follower of the fandom. Fanboys are often quick to disallow members or prospective members who have a differing opinion on fandom works or media texts. In one such case, fanboys were said to be responsible for publicly protesting against women from attending the San Diego Comic-Con. The fanboys stated that girls are not proper fans because comic books are meant for boys, hence their desire to bar women from attending (Scott, 2011, p. 59). Thus, educators should consider discussing with their students what comic book culture and fandom is in relation to perpetuating hegemonic masculinity.

It is unsurprising that these fanboys assume comic books are for boys when considering the different reading practices of school age girls and boys. After analyzing the literacy habits of Australians and those in the U.K., Wayne Martino found that "dominant versions of masculinity impact on boys' literacy practices" (2001, p. 61). Martino suggests that reading is considered "passive and feminized" compared to more "sex-appropriate" activities for boys such as sport (Martino, 2001, p. 65), and thus, boys were less likely to engage in it. Most importantly, for those boys who did read, they read what was considered genres for men, and thus, acquired "particular competencies for reading and understanding masculinity according to the rules of action/adventure/science fiction genres" (Martino, 2001, p. 69). In terms of pedagogy in the classroom, it can be difficult to encourage boys to pursue other less masculine genres. As suggested by Bronwyn Davies: "in entering the realm of boys and literacy we should not underestimate the desirability and joyful sense of power that boys can gain from being positioned within dominant forms of discourse which hand them ascendancy over others" (1997, p. 15). Therefore, educators must employ pedagogical strategies that empower students to learn. As Martino notes that young boys have competency when reading genres related to comic books, this may be a good site to get university aged men to engage with texts. This is because they are comfortable with the material itself and therefore may be easier to critique and engage with than genres of which they have less competency.

From Unruly Women to Unruly Men

One pedagogical strategy educators can use to deconstruct hegemonic masculinity in textual sources is the "unruly woman" theory, as first suggested by Kathleen Rowe (1995). Rowe examines the way that comedic women characters such as Miss Piggy and Roseanne Barr subvert traditional feminine characterization. Not only do these kinds of characters "lay claim to their own desire" (Rowe, 1995, p. 31) but do not limit educators to follow a gender binary for analysis. As Rowe notes, women characters are sometimes analyzed in opposition to men characters rather than as characters within their own right.

The unruly woman framework demonstrates how women characters create disorder "by defying norms of femininity intended to keep a woman in her place" (Rowe, 1995, p. 10). This theoretical framework can work in reverse for men characters. One must ask, if the unruly woman creates disorder by dominating men and refusing to confine herself to her proper place (Rowe, 2011, p. 10), how can a man character challenge patriarchal power and hegemonic masculinity to become an "unruly man?" Taking a cue from Peter Freebody (1992), educators can teach students how to critically evaluate texts by creating classroom activities that encourage critical thinking about dominance and power. Freebody suggests having students respond to the following questions: "Who is in power? What are the socio-cultural factors associated with the composition of the text? What is being portrayed as natural? What emotions are being attached to the participants? Who or what is left out of the text? Do all participants play an active role? From whose perspective is this being written?" (Webb & Singh, 1998, p. 138). Once these questions are answered, then the educator should incorporate additional gendered questions as suggested by Mimi Schippers in her paper *Recovering the Feminine Other: Masculinity, Femininity, and Gender Hegemony* (2007). Schippers put forth a framework on how to identify multiple genders in texts by asking the following questions: "What characteristics or practices are understood as manly in the setting? What characteristics or practices are womanly? Of those practices and characteristics, which situate femininity as complementary and inferior to masculinity?" (Schippers, 2007, p. 100). This framework can be co-opted for the pedagogic examination of hegemonic masculinities in most genres including comic book texts. This chapter uses the following questions as a framework to identify the subversions of hegemonic masculinity in texts:

1. What characteristics or practices are understood as hegemonically masculine in the setting?
2. What characteristics or practices are understood to be subordinate masculinity in the setting?
3. Do characteristics or practices share both hegemonic and subordinate masculinities in the setting?
4. Is hegemonic masculinity being represented negatively?

When considering what characteristics or practices are hegemonically masculine in *Fables*, it is useful to utilize Nick Trujillo's (1991) "five features" of hegemonic masculinity which is power through (1) force and control; (2) occupational achievement; (3) patriarchy; (4) frontiersman/outdoorsman persona; (5) heterosexual hierarchy. Since Trujillo's conception of hegemonic masculinity is grounded within U.S. media culture and *Fables* was written primarily for Western consumers, it makes sense to use this lens for analysis, especially as all five features appear in the comic.

The first of the five features states that hegemonic masculinity is present "when power is defined in terms of physical force and control" (Trujillo, 1991, p. 291). The idea that violence is directly related to representations of hegemonic masculinity has been extensively researched with scholars linking hegemonic masculinity to a variety of violent crimes (Messerschmidt, 1993; Newburn & Stanko, 1994). Violence is a pervasive entity in comic book narratives and *Fables* is no exception. However, how one interprets this violence can make all the difference in whether one assumes hegemonic masculinity is supported or is presented negatively within the text. Rowe argues that the presence of violence does not necessarily mean it is being encouraged, or that it be viewed negatively. In later work (2011) she argues that positive representations of women characterization sometimes lose their power due to audiences focusing on the violent content. Rowe argued that popular characters such as Buffy from *Buffy the Vampire Slayer* (1997–2003) challenged "familiar representations of femininity by affirming female friendship, agency and physical power" but that audiences were often "troubled" by her argument (2011, p. 6).

Rowe's decision to emphasize the context of violence rather than simply the violent act itself goes beyond previous comic book analyses that classified any violent as indicative of hegemonic masculinity. For example, Kirsh and Olczak's study suggests that men are significantly more interested in violent comic books than women and also find them funny (2001, p. 835). However, they failed to elaborate on what men found "funny" about these violent representations and instead theorized only that these men were probably more likely to be less restrained in "subsequent aggression" (2001, p. 836). However, if we proclaim anything that has violence to be hegemonic then we may miss texts where violence is presented negatively way. The unruly man framework proposes that representations of violence may not be automatically hegemonic, offering a different point of analysis and offering more types of masculinity to be considered.

Character Analyses of *Fables* Characters

Bluebeard

Our analysis here begins with Bluebeard as he embodies all five of Trujillo's hegemonic masculine traits (1) force and control; (2) occupational achievement; (3) patriarchy; (4) frontiersman/outdoorsman persona; (5) heterosexual hierarchy. Bluebeard is an antagonist based on a character created by Charles Perrault (1697). In Perrault's story, Bluebeard is a wealthy nobleman who murders his multiple wives, usually for an inheritance. His ruthless character as a spousal murderer and unethical opportunist is re-enacted in the *Fables* storyline showing a preoccupation for Trujillo's trait of heterosexual hierarchy and patriarchy in his treatment of his wives. Bluebeard is also known for being an opportunist by making characters pay large sums of money for any help they need and uses force when characters will not acquiesce to him, demonstrating Trujillo's first trait (force and control). His opportunism also provides him with a large fortune which he uses to exert a massive amount of influence over other characters. Bluebeard's power, wealth, and aggressive nature represents the second hegemonic feature from Trujillo's five features of masculinity due to his "occupational achievement in a capitalistic society" (1991, p. 291). At first glance, Bluebeard optimizes popular media representations of hegemonic masculinity which offer "an endless stream of violent male icons" (Kareithi, 2013, p. 27). Figures such as Bluebeard are often represented as something to aspire too, being a talented swordsman (relating to the frontiersman Trujillo trait), thus giving credence to the type of masculinity that encourages violence and aggressiveness.

However, educators should stress that Bluebeard's enactment of hegemonic masculinity is portrayed negatively in the text (considering question 4 of this framework) and thus not an encouraging one for students to adopt. Interestingly, Bluebeard dies twice at the hands of characters he perceives as performing subordinate masculinities. The first time Bluebeard is killed is where readers learn that Bluebeard had plotted to kill two other characters which is found out by Prince Charming (based on the princes from tales such as Cinderella and Sleeping Beauty) who challenges him to a duel and kills him. He is later brought back to life only to succumb to another death by Shere Khan, a tiger from *The Jungle*

Book (Kipling, 1894), who mauls and eats him. The context of both deaths must be thoroughly investigated by students so that they come to understand the nature of the characters that he considered subordinate in terms of masculinity. And, how his assertion that others were subordinate, led to his downfall (considering our second framework question).

In Bluebeard's first death, he failed to recognize the power of Prince Charming's fighting skills because he perceived him as not being a "manly" man. Prince Charming is not effeminate but, he wears fashionable clothes (unironically) and uses his charm to gain what he wants, rather than Bluebeard's straightforward and violent tactics. Prince Charming does not care for money, unlike Trujillo's capitalistic masculinity trait, which is why Bluebeard was not able to assert his control over him. However, Prince Charming has not always embodied the role of the unruly man in the *Fables* series. In early issues, he is portrayed as a rogue and a womanizer, displaying a more hegemonic masculinity. But he ends up redeeming himself and treating those around him better and becoming a hero. Applying the concept of "mimesis," a term utilized by scholar Luce Irigaray, "as a means of taking control of one's representation within discourse" (Rowe, 1995, p. 223), in the progression of his character arch, Prince Charming became an example of the "unruly man" or "mimesis" of hegemonic masculinity. This mimesis comes from the fact that he takes on the Trujillo trait of the "frontiersman" but uses that as a force for good. He ends up challenging patriarchal power by caring about others and ultimately sacrificing himself. Demonstrating to students how characters can change their portrayal of masculinity can "disrupt usual assumptions about power and the illusions and fictions that hold it in place" (Davies, 1997, p. 15).

Bluebeard's second death occurs because he wrongly assumes that Shere Khan was happy to be his second in command; "Of course you've no skills in administering a kingdom. So, I will assume the crown by necessity, once the bloodletting is done. But don't worry, Shere Khan. There'll always be a place for you in my regime" (issue 66, 2007). Here Bluebeard is perpetuating Trujillo's masculinity again because he defines his sense of manhood according to ruling a kingdom (occupational achievement). Also, by denying that Shere Khan is equal in terms of Trujillo's familial patriarchy. Before Shere Khan kills Bluebeard he says, "you've shown yourself to be nothing but a paper tiger, while I'm a real one—of the man-eating variety" (issue 66, 2007). Calling Bluebeard a "paper tiger" is especially telling because this phrase is used to describe someone (or something) that appears threatening but is superficial and thus ineffectual. Interestingly, this scene is symbolic of how masculinity should be studied according to context; something may seem hegemonic until deconstruction occurs, much like how Bluebeard seems powerful until he is killed almost instantly.

Bigby Wolf

Another character that students will be surprised to learn can be deconstructed in *Fables* is Bigby Wolf who is an amalgamation of "Big Bad Wolf" fairytale tropes. At the start of the comic series, Bigby is presented to the reader as having abandoned his pig-eating ways and is now acting as a law-abiding sheriff (but is still feared by many characters due to his past violent tendencies). When considering question one of this chapter's framework, "What characteristics or practices are understood as hegemonically masculine in the setting?", *Fables* offers many characteristics and practices that are understood as hegemonically masculine through the character of Bigby. He is well noted for using military tactics similar to Trujillo's frontiersman and force and control trait. It may also seem like his appointment as a protector fulfills a hegemonically masculine practice of Trujillo's patriarchy; men in his position are typically presented "as strong protectors and leaders who deserve to be in positions of authority over women and marginalized men" (Wolshyn et al., 2012, p. 151). Karethi (2013) suggests that hegemonic masculinity is perpetuated by men validating each other's identity through harmful practices and Bigby enacts this by making Bluebeard cry thus invalidating (for a short time) the hegemonic masculinity that Bluebeard was portraying (men don't cry). In the beginning, Bigby seems to adhere to not only hegemonic masculinity but also hypermasculine traits as wolves often symbolize masculine power but as argued in this framework, violence in a male character does not always indicate a hegemonic masculinity.

Rowe argues that the exaggerated femininity of characters such as Miss Piggy is an example of how traditional "feminized" characters can subvert these stereotypes by performing a "mimesis." Miss Piggy's hyper-sexualization simultaneously provides social commentary about how society "regulates" women's representations and reclaims this portrayal by being exaggerated stereotypes. For Rowe, "we might examine models of *returning* the male gaze, exposing and making a spectacle of the gazer, claiming the pleasure and power of making spectacles of ourselves, and beginning to negate our own visibility in the public sphere." [original italics] (Rowe, 1995, p. 12). Bigby's persona engages this kind of "mimesis" in that his violence is exaggerated, but it is not evidence of hegemony or hyper-masculinity. To explain, Hilary Neroni notes that violence in narrative has "primarily been a masculine activity," but also that "if a writer discusses violence … without at one point expressing some degree of disapproval toward violence itself, it appears as though she advocates violence" (2005, p. ix). Typically, the practice of violence would be considered hegemonically masculine and being a peaceful character understood as subordinate. With Bluebeard, using violence in a stereotypical way (violence against women or for personal gain) is represented negatively. For Bigby, mimesis occurs as Bigby takes control of the representation of violence as justifiable and necessary. Bigby's fierceness is not summoned for shock value (it is often employed to protect those less able to protect themselves) which is noteworthy as hegemonic characterizations of masculine traits are often associated with "wanton violence" (Kupers, 2005, p. 714).

In storylines where Bigby's violent behavior is unjustified and at risk of becoming hegemonic, he is chastised by other characters classified as "subordinate" characters. The hegemonic "manly man" that Bigby supposedly represents is subverted due to his willingness to engage and often rely on other characters. The relationship between Bigby and Snow White is a prime example. In volume 13 (2010), Bigby and Beast (of Disney fame) get so angry with each other that they transform into their respective beastly visages and try to tear each other apart. Snow White physically intervenes between the two and chastises his unjustified violent behavior telling him to shut up, which he does. In this way, we can assess that Bigby enacts (supposed) subordinate masculinities, in accordance with our third question, by listening to women rather than displaying Trujillo's patriarchy trait.

It seems that when Bigby's violence becomes too hegemonic, Bill Willingham uses traditionally subordinate characters to demonstrate that hegemonic violence is wrong. For students studying social commentary and ways of flipping the script, Bigby's complex character development is particularly noteworthy. Connell (1987) notes there is a hierarchical notion as to which men are hegemonically masculine and which ones are subordinate. Bigby often blurs these notions, however, as he simultaneously represents hegemonic masculinity (in that he is willing to use violence) yet also presents subordinate masculinity as he is willing to listen to feminine or other "subordinate" characters. Further, Bigby often fails to encompass the third aspect of Trujillo's five defining features of hegemonic masculinity that of "familial patriarch" (Trujillo, 1991, p. 291). His relationship with Snow White is a partnership, whereby Snow White sometimes emulates as the patriarch instead. Therefore, by adopting traits of subordinate masculinity, Bigby encompasses the "unruly man" rather than hegemonic masculinity.

Flycatcher

Another instance of Bigby's character being an unruly man, non-hegemonic character is his relationship with the character Flycatcher. Flycatcher is introduced in the first issue as a friendly, good-natured character who is always "in trouble" and thus having to endure community service constantly. His body is the opposite of a hyper-masculine comic book character, being a tall and thin character as opposed to muscular. Over the first few issues, students might be surprised to notice that Bigby is (seemingly) being unfair to Flycatcher, making him work as a janitor. Students might lament this; perhaps even suggest he is bullying a subordinate masculine character type. However, Bigby keeps Flycatcher "in constant servitude" for a noble reason that explains why their friendship is positive and not indicative of hegemonic masculinity.

Flycatcher's character, based on the story of *The Frog Prince* (Grimm, 1889), turns into a frog whenever he is startled, but a kiss from his wife will turn him back into a man. It is revealed before *Fables* began, that he is actually a king who lived in a kingdom with his family who were brutally murdered in-front of him when he was startled into becoming a frog. Suffering from the trauma of watching his family be murdered, he blocked out the memory of the event, and not knowing any better, wandered the world looking for them. Therefore, to keep him from pain and torment of searching for a family everyone knew was dead, the other fables allowed Bigby to "punish" Flycatcher by being his perpetual worker (and thus unable to leave). Although Bigby used seemingly hegemonically masculine methods to stop Flycatcher, he did so out of compassion.

It is later revealed that Flycatcher also has extensive magical powers and is incredibly powerful compared to all the other main characters. However, he does not like to use this power and prefers to use discussions over fighting, exile over execution; he uses violence as a last resort. Flycatcher's character produces an amalgamation of hegemonic and subordinate traits by the end of his story arc; he is a King with power beyond anyone's wildest dreams but, he is also a just and kind one. Flycatcher's subordinate masculine traits make him one of the more balanced characters. Flycatcher can be read as an "unruly man" because he ultimately acquires many traits associated with hegemonic masculinity (money, power, fame, a heterosexual relationship) as noted in Trujillo's five traits, but he does so as a "subordinate" masculinity and any hegemonic traits are presented positively in relation to supporting other characters.

By teaching students how to deconstruct characters like Flycatcher through the "unruly man" framework, they learn that a more developed comic character can have less violent traits while still having characteristics that may appeal to men who read these comics. At one point, Flycatcher is tempted to use his power and to gain the hegemonic masculinity traits by Trujillo, force and control; "Over the years I can depopulate entire towns, or countries, or worlds, I will become a destroyer of those foul things that destroyed me so long ago" (Vol. 10, 2007). Ultimately, Flycatcher realises that using violence for personal means is not the right thing to do, even though he is more than capable of enacting that violence.

Students and educators reading this series will notice that Flycatcher achieves a much happier ending than the toxic men characters due to his "subordinate" personality and his refusal to enact violence for his personal gain. He settles happily ever after in a new kingdom with his new wife, Red Riding Hood, and has four children.

A general comment can be made as to why *Fables* can be considered to subvert the traditional "hegemonic masculinity" of the comic book genre in general is the way it ends. The final issue released in 2015 was entitled "Farewell" (Issue 150). The final narrative arc is centered on a magical curse between the sisters Rose Red and Snow White which was compelling them to kill each other and to raise armies in which to do so. The last few issues seemingly promoting the idea that there would be one major final battle, which would consequently end with massive loss of life. Although this is in keeping with what would be expected in a traditional comic book, Bill Willingham ends the narrative with a twist. Instead of having a bloody battle, the two sisters decide not to fight and to make sure the curse which compels them to kill each other is never acted upon, they vow to never to live on the same world and never see each other again. It is important to note that at the end of *Fables* run, it was shown how violence does not have to be in the answer, and that it should not be unusual in the comic book genre for it not to be.

Fables has proved a useful case study for exploring ways that hegemony can be subverted using the framework that is suggested here especially in terms of comic book violence that appears in *Fables*. By using Rowe's framework to examine the context of violent representations, students may discern situations in which violence is positive, or even, righteous. This runs contrary to previous scholarship that suggests consuming violent material will make one violent, even though this theory has been abandoned in other cultural studies disciplines. This chapter has suggested four questions that can be used in a classroom setting for students to not only be able to identify hegemonic and "subordinate" masculinities and also suggest positive representations. This framework can be applied to further comic books in a classroom setting.

References

Brown, J. A. (2000). *Black superheroes, milestone comics, and their fans.* USA: University Press of Mississippi.

Chou, R. S., Lee, K., & Ho, S. (2012). The White Habitus and hegemonic masculinity at the Elite Southern University: Asian Americans and the need for intersectional analysis. *Sociation Today, 10*(2), np.

Connell, R. W. (1987). *Gender and power: Society, the person and sexual politics*. UK: Polity.

Connell, R. W. (1995). *Masculinities*. USA: University of California Press.

Davies, B. (1997). Constructing and deconstructing masculinities through critical literacy. *Gender and Education*, *9*(1), 9–30.

Feige, K. (Producer), & Coogler, R. (Director). (2018) *Black Panther*, [motion picture], USA: Walt Disney Studios Motion Pictures.

Ferguson, C. J. (2018). The devil wears stata: Thin-ideal media's minimal contribution to our understanding of body dissatisfaction and eating disorders. *American Psychological Association: Archives of Scientific Psychology*, *6*(1), 70–80.

Freebody, P. (1992). A socio-cultural approach: Resourcing four roles as a literacy learner. In A. Watson, & A. Badenhop (Eds.), *Prevention of reading failure*, (pp. 48–60). UK: Ashton Scholastic.

Ho, H. K. (2016). The model minority in the zombie apocalypse: Asian-American manhood on AMC's *The Walking Dead*. *The Journal of Popular Culture*, *49*(1), 57–76.

Kareithi, P. J. (2013). Hegemonic masculinity in media contents. *United Nations Educational, Scientific and Cultural Organization*. Retrieved from http://www.unesco.org/new/fileadmin/MULTIMEDIA/HQ/CI/CI/pdf/publications/gamag_research_agenda_kareithi.pdf

Kipling, R. (1894). *The jungle book*. UK: Macmillan.

Kirkman, R. (2003–2019). *The walking dead*. USA: Image Comics.

Kirsh, S. J., & Olczak, P. V. (2001). Rating comic book violence: Contributions of gender and trait hostility. *Social Behavior and Personality*, *29*(8), 833–836.

Kupers, T. A. (2005). Toxic masculinity as a barrier to mental health treatment in prison. *Journal of Clinical Psychology*, *61*(6), 713–724.

LaRue, R. (2018). 'I remember you was conflicted': Reflections on Black Panther, the African American/African divide, and scholarly positionings. *The Journal of Pan African Studies*, *11*(9), 48–52.

Mabe, A. G., Forney, K. J., & Keel, P. K. (2014). Do you 'like' my photo? Facebook use maintains eating disorder risk. *International Journal of Eating Disorders*, *47*(5), 516–524.

Martino, W. (2001). Boys and reading: Investigating the impact of masculinities on boys' reading preferences and involvement in literacy. *Australian Journal of Language and Literacy*, *5*(1), 61–74.

Messerschmidt, J. W. (1993). *Masculinities and crime: Critique and reconceptualization of theory*. UK: Rowman and Littlefield Publishers.

Neroni, H. (2005). *The violent woman: Femininity, narrative, and violence in contemporary American cinema*. USA: University of New York Press.

Newburn, T., & Stanko, E. A. (1994). *Just boys doing business? Men, masculinities and crime*. UK: Routledge.

Perrault, C. (1697). *Histoires ou contes du temps passé*. Publisher Unknown.

Ravelo, L. C. (2013). The use of comic strips as a means of teaching history in the EFL class: Proposal of activities based on two historical comic strips adhering to the principles of CLIL/EL. *Latin American Journal of Content and Language Learning*, *6*(1), 1–19.

Rowe, K. (1995). *The unruly woman: Gender and the genres of laughter.* USA: University of Texas Press.

Rowe, K. (2011). *Unruly girls, unrepentant mothers: Redefining Feminism on screen.* USA: University of Texas Press.

Salter, A., & Blodgett, B. (2017). *Toxic Geek masculinity in media: Sexism, trolling and identity politics.* UK: Palgrave MacMillan.

Schippers, M. (2007). Recovering the feminine other: Masculinity, femininity, and gender hegemony. *Theory and Society, 36*(1), 85–102.

Scott, S. (2011). *Revenge of the Fanboy: Convergence culture and the politics of incorporation,* [PhD thesis]. University of California.

Scott, S. (2013). Fangirls in refrigerators: The politics of (in)visibility in comic book culture in appropriating, interpreting, and transforming comic books. *Transformative Works and Cultures, 13.*

Silah, S. (2007). Filling up the space between mankind and ape: Racism, speciesism and the androphilic ape. *ARIEL: A Review of International English Literature, 38*(1), 95–111.

Simone, G. (1999). Women in refrigerators, *WIR.* Retrieved from http://www.lby3.com/wir/

TellTale Games. (2013). *The wolf among us.* [Computer Software]. USA.

Teo, N. S. Y., & Collinson, S. L. (2018). Instagram and risk of rumination and eating disorders: An Asian perspective. *Psychology of Popular Media Culture, 8*(4), 491–508.

The Brothers Grimm. (1889). *The frog prince.* Publisher Unknown.

Trujillo, N. (1991). Hegemonic masculinity on the mound: Media representations of nolan ryan and American sports culture. *Critical Studies in Mass Communication, 8,* 290–308.

Webb, G., & Singh, M. (1998). '… and what about the boys?' Re-reading signs of masculinities. *Australian Journal of Language and Literacy, 21*(2), 135–144.

Whedon, J., Greenwall, D., Noxon, M., Kuzui, F. R., & Kuzui, K. (Producers), (1997–2001). *Buffy the Vampire Slayer,* [television series], 20th Century Fox.

Willingham, B. (2002–2015). *Fables.* New York City: Vertigo.

Wolshyn, V., Taber, N., &Lane, L. (2012). Discourses of masculinity and femininity in *The Hunger Games:* "Scarred," "Bloody," and "Stunning." *International Journal of Social Science Studies, 1*(1), 150–160.

CHAPTER FOUR

Feminist Mythmaking: Reclaiming the Myth

PURNUR OZBIRINCI

Introduction

The need to control motivates the need to use the "word." For too long, men have had the privilege to use the word and, thus, to control reality. Through their perspectives, men have had the power to define, identify, and record the human experience. Because of this, the experiences of "the minoritized" have been voiced only through the experiences of those in power. The minoritized or, using Paulo Freire's (2005) phrase, "the oppressed" attains ontological status when minoritized experiences find a name, when their myths are retold and accepted to link them to the contemporary social order. Freire proposes that the first step to liberation is for the oppressed to "unveil the world of oppression and through the praxis commit themselves to its transformation" (2005, p. 54). However, the oppressed cannot transform the world alone. Having revealed the reality of oppression, the next step requires that the pedagogy now belongs to all people who will work together "in the process of permanent liberation" (Freire, 2005, p. 54).

For individuals deprived of power, they must first acknowledge their oppression and then commit to changing the system that maintains oppression. As Freire claims, the second stage requires the "expulsion of the myths created and developed in the old order" (2005, p. 55). Today, especially, minoritized women have discovered that their existence depends on their power to eradicate these "myths created and developed in the old order" (Freire, 2005, p. 55) and to remove the "mythic masks male artists have fastened over her human face" (Gilbert & Gubar, 1979, p. 17). Following Freire's liberation pedagogy and feminist mythmaking, this chapter focuses on creating a critical revisionist pedagogy that unveils the inequity in myths while reclaiming one's own myths to create an impartial future. Educators who wish to resist the perpetuation of hegemonic masculinity in their classrooms could adopt the modern reinterpretations of popular ancient myths presented in this chapter. By bringing critical revisionist mythmaking perspectives into the classroom, students can investigate the bias in canonical texts, allowing them to become conscious of oppressive discourses that perpetuate the patriarchal status quo.

The adoption of this revisionist mythmaking pedagogy can critically transform any classroom context that features critical thinking, literature, and writing. Critical pedagogy in the classroom demands that educators observe course material, their teaching practice, and the student learning experience through a critical lens. Moreover, critical pedagogy can produce a collective transformation of the learning environment since students enter the classroom with prior knowledge, beliefs, and perspectives. If these ideas are uniform and the curriculum does not seek to challenge established norms, education will only preserve and protect the status quo. Unfortunately, preserving and protecting the status quo will hinder the long-term development of students' critical thinking ability. Without citizens able to think critically, even equitable democracies living in prosperity will eventually reach stagnation. However, advancement and progress require change, and change requires individuals who are able to think critically. For this reason, the purpose of education must be to empower, inspire, and liberate individuals to seek collective transformation from oppression. Education must aim to achieve this freedom by developing empathy, flexibility, and consciousness of equity and democracy.

This chapter focuses on illuminating the oppressive norms in canonical texts so that contemporary feminist writers can revise these outdated myths. Students can learn the tools necessary to critically examine the rewritten texts of Oedipus, Antigone, Medea, and Philomela and Procne to demonstrate how women playwrights rewrite patriarchal myths in order to "unveil the world of oppression" (Freire, 2005, p. 54) and make these myths their own. Combining the approaches of Freire's critical pedagogy with revisionist mythmaking is used to trace the journey of several women playwrights, turned mythmakers, in the pursuit of reclaiming the power to use the word. The analysis presented in this chapter explores Liz Lochhead's *Thebans*, Franca Rame and Dario Fo's *A Woman Alone*, and Timberlake Wertenbaker's *Love of the Nightingale* for how they might inspire social change towards a more equitable society.

What Is a Myth?

Certain needs, beliefs, and shared memories are the aspects that bring people together to establish societies. There are norms, traditions, and therefore, truths, that social groups protect and pass onto future generations. These truths are coded in the cultural and social practices of peoples and represent the keys to survival. Regardless of whether the truths shared by a group possess any validity, they still supply the group with a sense of identity and belonging. William McNeill argues that "without such social cement no group can long preserve itself" (1986, p. 7). This is because sharing the consciousness of a common past "is a powerful supplement to other ways of defining who 'we' are" (McNeill, 1986, p. 7). These cultural practices, exercised primarily by authors who have been predominantly men, carry the codes of identity that exist in all myths. Here, "myth" is used to define all forms of recorded cultural practices, such as legends, novels, poems, dramas, even art, which use the "word" and the "gaze" to control an object.

The word myth is thought to be derived from the Greek word *mythos*, which means word, utterance, or story. Therefore, *mythos* does not merely mean fictional or an improbable story, it could also mean "word" and "utterance." If myth has a connection with word or utterance, this presents myth as having a connection with all means of communication established through the use of words or utterances. Myron Lustig and Jolene Koester define communication as a "symbolic process in which people create shared meanings" (1999, p. 25). Then, whoever uses the word, creates meanings. Roland Barthes defines the meaning of myth, as "a system of communication, … a message" (1973, p. 109). Consequently, whoever handles the *mythos*, either the word, the utterance, or the story, has the power to control the message, which creates meaning to construct truths. Accordingly, in Western culture, the truths of ancient civilizations have been recorded by myth-makers such as Homer, Ovid, Aeschylus, Sophocles, and Euripides who happen to be men.

Mythmaking

Today, women have discovered that their existence depends on their power to use the word. They exist when their experiences find a name; when their myths are retold and accepted to link them to the contemporary social order. As Alicia Ostriker suggests, "Whenever a poet employs a figure or story previously accepted and defined by a culture, the poet is using myth, and the potential is always present that the use will be revisionist" (1985, p. 317). Ostriker adds that this revisionist appropriation where "the old vessel [is] filled with new wine" ultimately makes "cultural change possible" (1985, p. 317). Therefore, women must continue creating and retelling their own myths to progress into the future. Drama serves as a primary tool for producing and transmitting their word, their myth, their experiences, and voices. As Jane de Gay and Lizbeth Goodman declare, "Theatre is a place and space in which we can dream such large dreams and attempt to realize them" (2003, p. 1).

Educators should use versions of both the old and the new myths to demonstrate the oppressive nature of ancient, patriarchal texts. As each new text is introduced to the class, students will develop a critical consciousness that helps them understand the power that literature has of not only perpetuating oppression but also shattering it through revisionist versions. As Freire states, reflection is the initial step in developing a critical consciousness that will lead to social transformation; however, without the power to create myths, we cannot expect any societal change. For this reason, the analysis of women's revisionary texts must accompany the search for the new myths that are created through the perspectives of these women. Exploring the opposing myths will empower students with the tools to create new, empowering myths for collective transformation.

Rewriting as Mythbreaking/Mythmaking

The act of unveiling the existing myths, as Freire (2005) suggests, requires a commitment to the deconstruction of prevailing stories. This act of deconstruction, namely, "mythbreaking," is not the goal if one is to invest in transforming the existing status quo. For this reason, the act of appropriating and rewriting these existing stories, in other words, mythmaking, must be the goal in the process of liberation. Nancy A. Walker declares that "the practice of appropriating existing stories in one's own work—borrowing, revising, recontextualizing—has a long and distinguished history that includes such unquestionably major works as Milton's *Paradise Lost* and the plays of Shakespeare" (1995, p. 1). When humans adapt to their environment, they tend to alter "the inherited stories of a cultural tradition" (Walker, 1995, p. 2) according to their own needs. Men, however, have been the primary ones to record oral literature and myth and also determine what was recorded in history. Thus, men shaped their culture, appropriated acceptable behavior patterns, and established the social norms through their own perspectives. Women were kept at a far distance from the control over the authority of the word. As Walker states, "because of the way in which Western literary traditions have been formulated, however, most male writers who have appropriated and revised previous texts have worked within a tradition that included them and their experience" (1995, p. 3). When women rewrite these patriarchal texts, they must break the encoded biases and messages found in them (Walker, 1995, p. 3). This is why Walker calls the writer who practices revisionist writing "the disobedient writer," as suggested in the title of her book. As Walker claims, "revisionary, 'disobedient' narratives, expose or upset the paradigms of authority inherent in the texts they appropriate" (1995, p. 7). Reconstructing these stories requires that women not only subvert the authoritative structure of the previous text, but also claim their own voice as existent within the reconstructed text. As two versions of a story are established through the rewriting process, neither story can assume sole authority. The disobedient woman writer, while breaking the "inherent tradition" (Walker, 1995, p. 4) the previous writer aimed to enhance, becomes a maker of her own myths. This is the goal of bringing critical revisionism into the classroom: encouraging students to assume their own power in creating myths.

If women succeed in deconstructing the patriarchal myths, then they can "radically alter the picture" (Sellers, 2001, p. 29) of women constructed through the phallocentric perspective. Consequently, the woman writer, making use of rewriting in her speculation of mythology, will not only provide her reader with the interrogative power of analysis of the known myth but also with a new perspective with which the reader can evaluate this myth. For this reason, Sellers argues that "Feminist rewriting can thus be thought of in two categories: as an act of demolition, exposing and detonating the stories that have hampered women, and as a task of construction—or bringing into being enabling alternatives" (2001, p. 30). I suggest using the term "mythbreaking" to refer to the process of the women writers' breaching the authority of overused masculine myths about women by the subversive use of these myths in women's works. As Jane de Gay (2003) believes, classical mythology can be perceived as an attack on powerful women in ancient cultures: "classical mythology celebrates the submission of matriarchal power to patriarchal" (2003, p. 14). Therefore, any attempt at teaching the classical mythology texts as recorded by men such as Homer, Ovid, Sophocles, Aeschylus, Euripides, and many more, should be revealed for their patriarchal tone toward powerful women. Moreover, Jane de Gay argues that classical mythology "rehearses and substantiates a fear of women: in other words, it is a set of narratives in which women are often villains or, if they are victims, their weakness also provokes fear" (2003, p. 14). Students should turn a critical eye toward depictions of the most well-known women in Greek myths: Medusa, Medea, Philomela, Procne, Antigone, Jocasta, Circe, Hera, Echo, Daphne, Helen, Sirens, Niobe, Arachne, and Pandora. Thus, characters should be analyzed according to the stereotypically harmful depictions of femininity and masculinity to help students understand the long-standing historical legacy of oppression and the ways repressive systems operate by silencing the minoritized.

One of the best ways to achieve praxis (reflection into action) is by having students critically reflect on their challenges and then share their own stories. This process encourages the development of empathy which is a moral motivator. It also enables students and educators to work together in determining the problems and their solutions. This is what Freire calls the "problem-posing method" which is an alternative to the banking system of education he explains in the second chapter of the *Pedagogy of the Oppressed*. Rather than depositing our knowledge into the empty vessels called students (the banking method), the problem-posing method encourages students to determine the societal problems that disrupt their well-being. Asking students to think critically about the cause and the effect of patriarchal oppression, for example, through literature should inspire them to assume responsibility for the well-being of their community.

Liz Lochhead's *Thebans*

Scottish playwright Liz Lochhead has reclaimed women's power from the men writers by rewriting the myth of Oedipus, Jocasta, and Antigone in her 2003 play *Thebans*. Through rewriting these plays, Lochhead can claim ownership rights, make the play her own, and empower other women to claim rights to these patriarchal myths. In the classroom, the close reading of her play will reveal the insidious ways the patriarchy has taught women to be damsel's in distress, helpless, and powerless.

Thebans is based on Sophocles's *Oedipus Rex* and *Antigone*, Euripides's *Phoenician Women*, and Aeschylus's *The Seven Against Thebes*. Lochhead states that "There is not a single word in *Thebans* that isn't merely my response to, my version of, something in these texts in one of the umpteen different translations I read" (2003, p. iii). Thus, she uses Euripides's unhanged Jocasta to give her voice in the myth. Jocasta commits suicide at the end of Sophocles' *Oedipus Rex*, which is the most prevalent version of the myth. However, in Lochhead's play Jocasta does not commit suicide although her husband/son states that death would be better "for her sake" (Lochhead, 2003, p. 29). Jocasta lives until her two sons, Eteocles and Polynices, kill each other fighting to claim the throne. She begs her sons to take her seriously with these words, "sons there is more to old age than aches and pains / and grey hairs experience grant me this at least if / you won't go so far as credit me with wisdom" (Lochhead, 2003, p. 43).

Lochhead's plain language and precise adaptation of the tragedies takes Jocasta away from her position as the "fulfillment of our own childhood dreams" (Freud, 1953, p. 262) as Freud defines her. Instead, Lochhead's Jocasta becomes the hysteric suffering from the Cassandra syndrome. In Greek mythology, Apollo loved Cassandra bestowed her with the power to foretell the future; however, when she refused Apollo's love, he cursed her, and no one believed in Cassandra's insights. As Laurie Layton Schapira states in *The Cassandra Complex, Living with Disbelief: A Modern Perspective on Hysteria*, "What the Cassandra woman sees is something dark and painful that may not be apparent on the surface of things or that objective facts do not corroborate. She may envision a negative or unexpected outcome; or something which would be difficult to deal with; or a truth which others, especially authority figures, would not accept" (1988, p. 65). Unfortunately, to the authority figures, "her words sound meaningless, disconnected and blown out of all proportion" (Schapira, 1988, p. 65). Jocasta's words are, similarly, meaningless to her sons as they cause civil strife and murder each other.

Lochhead's revival of the archetypal conflict between matriarchal and the patriarchal depictions of women like Jocasta and Antigone seeking to find their voice demonstrate to students how narratives of silencing women have been repeated for centuries. Remaining silent has become a learned behavior in many women. Schapira argues that the silenced turned hysterical woman "tends to be exploited or scapegoated. She learns early on to hide it or use it to shape-shift" (1988, p. 62). Jocasta and Antigone have not learned to hide their intuitions, and, thus, they become scapegoats for the patriarchy who wishes to silence women. Through punishing Jocasta and Antigone with death, the patriarchal authority silences all unwanted sounds by spreading the belief that no one will listen to a woman. The insistent message is "remain silent if you want to live."

Furthermore, the patriarchal myths of Jocasta, Antigone, and Cassandra also reinforce that women should learn to be helpless. Martin Seligman and Steven Maier coined "learned helplessness" in 1967 and the term has been associated with low self-esteem and depression. Many social scientists (Luchow et al., 1985) have defined learned helplessness "as a lack of persistence in tasks that could realistically be mastered, usually because of a lack of motivation which might be caused by repeatedly experienced failure" (Spence & Stan-Spence, 1990, p. 2). In "Meeting 'Learned Helplessness' Head on with 'Active Learning,'" Ian Spence and Aileen Stan-Spence explain the term as a condition in which one lacks executive functioning and persistence. Furthermore, "it is habitual, and unrecognized by the student. Good remedial teaching in most small class, diagnostic/prescriptive settings actually encourages continued learned helplessness, because the student is entirely dependent on the teacher to guide him, and the accent is on content, rather than learning strategies" (1990, p. 16). When applied to the relationships between men and women, dependency is the desired effect: women's dependence on men. Spence and Stan-Spence offer active learning as an empowering tool to help fight learned helplessness: "[active learning] is designed to break the learned helplessness habit by constantly making the student aware of his passive style and helping him develop concrete tasks to substitute in its place" (1990, p. 16). Furthermore, breaking students from their dependency on educators is also important in breaking the cycle. Making students aware of their passivity is the solution Freire gives in the *Pedagogy of the Oppressed*. In the same way, many appropriationist playwrights, like Lochhead, aim to make the audiences aware of their passivity.

Students are surprised by Lochhead's ability to link the struggle within these Greek myths to modern struggles for expression across the world. The Cassandra complex in Lochhead's play is not a psychoanalytic phenomenon associated with women, but she shows how humanity learns to equate silence and passivity with survival. Out of a fear of speaking, one chooses silence. The chorus in *Thebans* states this clearly, "when we should have spoken out we were silent / kept our heads down survived thus far" (Lochhead, 2003, p. 88). The learned helplessness overcomes the instinct to express oneself. The chorus attests to keeping silent, although they could have spoken to change the consequences. As Lochhead draws the parallels to the ongoing problems in the Middle East in her introduction to the play, she states that "it was hard not to feel that the Euripides who wrote Jocasta's great plea to her sons to step back from the brink was, uncannily, writing about and just for us, here, now" (2003, p. iv). She adds that "there's nothing pure or Sophoclean about this particular telling of the tale" (2003, p. iii). Students learn that the fear of expressing oneself is a curse that patriarchal society has implemented not only women. Citing Freire's thoughts about fear is useful for students to understand the duality experienced by the oppressed: "although [the oppressed] desire authentic existence, they fear it. They are at one and the same time themselves and the oppressor whose consciousness they have internalized" (2005, p. 48). Freire adds that "until they concretely 'discover' their oppressor and in turn their own consciousness, they nearly always express fatalistic attitudes towards their situation" (2005, p. 61). Therefore, unless the oppressed comes to understand the psychology of the oppressor and discover their own consciousness, they face the danger of fatalism. Under such a mindset, the oppressed comes to believe that humans are powerless to change social problems. For instance, if not in a powerful position, one might refrain from speaking because they believe they will inevitably be unheard like Cassandra. By teaching a critical pedagogy of reclaiming these ancient myths, students learn how to break the learned behavior and to believe that one's voice is powerful enough to transform the world.

Adopting Lochhead's play into one's curriculum can enable students to comprehend the social messages that negate their powers and suppress them. Such revisionist plays could be paired with a group project to discover similar messages from contemporary media. The damsel in distress trope is still a very prevalent and destructive myth that should be challenged. It perpetuates fatalism about one's ability to change. Using Lochhead's play to reflect on these disempowering myths will inspire students to liberate others and to seek collective transformation.

Rame and Fo's *A Woman Alone*

Like Lochhead, Franca Rame and Dario Fo have written a short performance piece on Medea, which is called *A Woman Alone* (1989) to break the myths that suppress women. The play can teach students how to spot the internalized oppression that leads individuals to value patriarchy. As Freire states, this is another version of fatalism he calls "duality." Self-depreciation is an outcome of the duality faced by the oppressed. He states that self-depreciation "derives from the internalization of the opinion the oppressors hold of [the oppressed]. So often do they hear that they are good for nothing, know nothing, and are incapable of learning anything—that they are sick, lazy, and unproductive—that in the end they become convinced of their own unfitness" (Freire, 2005, p. 63). The oppressed learn to devalue themselves and this would naturally lead to abhor the oppressor; however, this internalized oppression almost always leads the oppressed to crave to be like the oppressor (Freire, 2005, p. 46). As Freire states, "the oppressed feel an irresistible attraction towards the oppressors and their way of life" (2005, p. 62). This attraction leads the oppressed to imitate their oppressors. By internalizing the ideals of the oppressor, they treat others who are also oppressed worse than the oppressor. Moreover, siding with the oppressor will provide a false sense of comfort that leads to inaction. Rather than assume the responsibility that results from freedom, many individuals seek to protect the status quo (Freire, 2005, p. 47). Students are often guilty of protecting the status quo when faced with acknowledging the ramifications of their social privilege.

Rame and Fo's revisioned myth of Medea, however, reveals this tendency to fear one's freedom and one woman's fight to overturn the self-depreciation and misogyny of women. Lizbeth Goodman calls traditional depictions of Medea the "ultimate caricature of the sexual woman and 'bad mommy'" who has dared "to react to abandonment by her unfaithful husband, sacrificing the children she loves in the process" (2000, p. xv). Throughout the centuries, Medea has become the "selfish, spiteful woman scorned. Each new generation recreates her, each looking through the lens of a culture and a period with all its attendant expectations for 'motherly behavior'" (Goodman, 2000, p. xv). Rame and Fo have reinterpreted the myth of Medea "as a report on the state of mind and ravings of the 1970s housewife Medea, who is locked into the mythic story of the woman who kills her children, but within a modern setting" (Goodman, 2000, p. xxii). They have given perspective to this so-called child murderer, so that she can explain the rationale behind her actions. In the ancient myths, Medea was mysterious; everything she did seemed to be the cause of her jealousy. By demystifying her, Rame and Fo's Medea come to represent issues that many modern women encounter, thus making her highly relatable to students.

In the modern retelling, as her self-deprecating neighbors try to ease Medea's rage against her husband's deceit, they say, "You're not the only one who's been dumped by a husband – it's happened to us too. … it's just fate … women's destiny: men trade us in for younger flesh, younger skin, younger breasts, voices, lips … it's the law of nature" (Rame & Fo, 1989, p. 82). Medea immediately resists this emasculation. Students appreciate that this Medea questions her fellow women about the laws, which they believe to be natural laws. Medea asks, "What laws are you talking about? Who dreamed up this law? … It was men … men … men who dreamed it up … they wrote it down, they signed and sealed it and said it came down from Heaven on tablets of stone" (Rame & Fo, 1989, p. 83). After questioning the laws of nature recorded by men, Medea realizes that she cannot endure becoming invisible or forgotten by her children and her husband. Thus, she indicates, "I've got to kill my children. Oh sure, I know I'll always be remembered as a wicked mother, a woman who was driven out of her mind with jealousy … but it's better to be remembered as a wild animal than forgotten like a pet nanny goat!" (Rame & Fo, 1989, p. 83).

Medea also condemns the issue of mothering by stating that men have "chained our children round our necks like millstones to keep us in our places – just like you chain a hard-wooden yoke round a cow's neck to force her to stand docilely while she's milked and mounted" (Rame & Fo, 1989, p. 85). Through Medea's words, Rame and Fo deconstruct the myth of the monstrous mother and empower Medea by allowing her to name her experiences. They announce the birth of a new woman who will free herself from the clutches of masculine constructions of women and will awaken women from accepting as normal "a male system of values" (Fetterley, 1978, p. xx). Bringing Rame and Fo's short play into the classroom helps students draw connections between the self-depreciation they encounter in their everyday lives and that which women have endured for centuries. Students can apply what they have learned about the harms of duality and fatalism through an assignment in which they write their own creative stories.

Rame and Fo's revisioned Medea questions her acceptance of this fatalism and demands to change the message. Freire posits that "critical reflection is also action" (Freire, 2005, p. 128) that can only be achieved "if [one's] action encompasses a critical reflection which increasingly organizes their thinking and thus leads them to move from a purely naive knowledge of reality to a higher level, one which enables them to perceive the causes of reality" (Freire, 2005, p. 131). By encouraging students to rethink the reasons behind Medea's brutal actions, Rame and Fo encourage a more sophisticated reading of the text that considers all sides inherent to the problems facing women. Being open to understanding all sides of a problem is the first step in cultural synthesis. Cultural synthesis, therefore, could resolve many conflicts that women must endure even in the twenty-first century. Giving perspective to the struggles of women along with demanding critical inquiry can lead students to provide support to move beyond harmful stereotypes, bias, and prejudice. Discovering the multiple sides of an issue to reach a synthesis that could benefit all should be the aim in every class project.

Wertenbaker's *The Love of the Nightingale*

Another monstrous mother is represented in the myth of Philomela and Procne, where Procne kills her son after learning that her husband has raped and mutilated her sister. In *The Love of the Nightingale* (1988) Timberlake Wertenbaker discusses various feminist and theatrical issues simultaneously. By rewriting the myth of Philomela and Procne, Wertenbaker initially reminds her audience of the conventions of Greek culture, theatre, and myth, as she directs her audience to reinterpret these core aspects of Western civilization. As Wertenbaker reevaluates Greek culture and myth, she deconstructs Ovid's recorded version of the myth of Philomela and Procne, in order to reveal the persistent hegemonic masculinity power struggles and their consequences. Philomela's rapist, Tereus, becomes the ultimate figure of fear, the oppressor who silences all those around him, not just Philomela. Thus, very similar to Lochhead, Wertenbaker also reveals the constructed power structures within the myth that lead to fatalism. Due to their fear of Tereus, his men keep silent although they see his fondness of his sister-in-law, Philomela. However, this silence leads to Philomela's rape and mutilation, and eventually to the murder of Itys by his mother seeking revenge from Tereus. To end the violence, gods turn Tereus, Procne, and Philomela into birds. However, as Patricia Klindienst argues, this "metamorphosis preserves the distance necessary to the structure of dominance and submission … In such stasis, both order and conflict are preserved, but there is no hope of change" (1998, p. 621).

When the myth ends in this way in Ovid's version, Klindienst asserts that the status-quo will be preserved, and the sisters will always be remembered as more violent than the man, since they were the ones to kill and cook their own child in revenge. Also, by turning the characters into birds, Klindienst remarks that, "Culture hides from its own sacrificial violence" (1998, p. 621). The myth seems to stop the violence by turning the major characters into birds; however, it also suggests that the violence will forever continue, and the metamorphosis of the main characters remains the only transformation in the social structure of the myth. Transforming the characters to birds does not affect a change in society. Therefore, when Wertenbaker adds another scene to her version of the myth, she turns the myth into a force of healing for her society which amounts to the cultural synthesis Freire seeks to achieve.

In this last scene, Philomela regains her voice as a bird and interviews Itys. Although Itys wants Philomela to sing a song, Philomela urges him to ask questions first. When Itys asks if she likes being a nightingale, Philomela replies, "I never liked birds, but we were all so angry the bloodshed would have gone on forever. Thus, it is better to become a nightingale. You see the world differently" (Wertenbaker, 1988, p. 67). Then, Philomela asks Itys if he understands, "why it was wrong of Tereus to cut out [her] tongue" (1988, p. 68). However, Itys asks another question as a reply, "What does wrong mean?" (1988, p. 68). When Philomela says, "It is what isn't right" (1988, p. 68), Itys this time questions what right means. Unable to answer his questions, Philomela starts singing, as if to silence his questioning. Not merely men, but women are submerged in the teachings of the Symbolic Order that limit language to the binary oppositions. Binary oppositions, like right/wrong, white/black, civilized/primitive, male/female, demand valuing one side to the other. Unable to escape the binary language of the male-dominated world, Philomela asks Itys to understand the meaning of the two binary oppositions of right and wrong. Instead, Itys questions these binary oppositions, and Philomela, unable to avoid her sexist teachings, cannot find an answer to Itys's questions. When Philomela, devoid of words, begins to sing to avoid answering Itys's questions, Itys asks, "Didn't you want me to ask questions?" (1988, p. 68). These are the last words of the play. The need and the power to question is an instinct that is often removed from children mature into adulthood. By the time students reach the freshman classroom, most have learned to avoid asking questions. Educators must bring this instinct back into the classroom and normalize the need to ask questions for the sake of disrupting sexism and other forms of oppression.

Freire explains that oppressors often take away the power of the oppressed to question by prescribing their truths onto the oppressed. He states, "Every prescription represents the imposition of one individual's choice upon another, transforming the consciousness of the person prescribed to into one that conforms with the preserver's consciousness" (Freire, 2005, p. 47). Thus, very similar to internalized oppression, the behavior of the oppressed follows "the guidelines of the oppressor" (Freire, 2005, p. 47). After overcoming Tereus, Wertenbaker is suggesting that Philomela might fall into the trap of assuming the role of the oppressor. However, Wertenbaker makes sure that new generations negate Philomela's prescription. Therefore, Itys being the future is made to question, whereas the present, represented by Philomela, is unable to escape the teachings of patriarchal viewpoints. Most people remain ignorant to changing the old myths, which were defined as "unwanted truths" (Wertenbaker, 1988, p. 41) by the male chorus.

It is not only women, but also men, who are still under the control of the sexist world, and, for this reason, patriarchal worldview still determines what right and wrong is, and which truths/myths should be accepted. As educators, we must answer the following question: Whose truths do we teach our students? If educators feed them their own truths, then they corrupt their critical thinking abilities. If educators refrain from giving answers and support students in finding their own truths, educators may succumb to the fear that this will lead to anarchy. To repeat Freire's words, "People will be truly critical if they live the plenitude of the praxis, that is, if their action encompasses a critical reflection which increasingly organizes their thinking and thus leads them to move from a purely naive knowledge of reality to a higher level, one which enables them to perceive the causes of reality" (Freire, 2005, p. 131). Critical revisionist mythmaking pedagogy allows students to reflect on and question the truths/reality of the status-quo imposed upon them. As Wertenbaker believes, theater is "a space that allows us to understand, and (hopefully) to know more about ourselves (not just personally, but socially, culturally, politically)" (Aston, 2003, p. 168), and, therefore, to achieve change in the male-dominated world.

As Elaine Aston argues, "Wertenbaker has always been attracted to the idea of tackling 'big subjects,' frequently turning to classical myths or plays and giving them a contemporary twist" (2003, p. 150). The Greek myth "offers a way of resisting the received view of women's writing as somehow confined to and concerned only with domestic, 'female' environments" (Aston, 2003, p. 150). In her parody of the Greek tragedies, Wertenbaker demonstrates the patriarchal formulation of power, which only belongs to those who occupy the highest hierarchical positions in society. By rewriting the patriarchal myth of Philomela and Procne, she retells the narratives of silenced individuals, "in a way which empowers the feminist spectator/reader to participate in changing them, rather than endorsing the value-system of the 'father' text" (Aston, 1995, p. 23). Thus, Wertenbaker achieves Freire's cultural synthesis by parodying a well-known myth that helps students learn how to remodel the myth to suit contemporary requirements.

As Susan Bassnett explains, "the use of myth reinforces the notion of hybridity, since myths transcend national boundaries and become part of a shared inheritance" (2000, pp. 78–79). By using the well-known myth of Philomela and Procne and adding the inaction and voicelessness of the chorus representing Tereus's crew, Wertenbaker turns a female experience of rape and suppression into a universal experience. In her revision of the Philomela and Procne myth, she "is using a myth premised on an idea of metamorphosis that serves as a device for inviting the audience to think through questions of transformation and change" (Bassnett, 2000, p. 79). Thus, student audiences become involved in a re-interpretation process, where the myth is no longer a mere story of adultery and revenge. Rather, in Wertenbaker's production, it turns into a microcosm of a universal struggle between the dominant powers and the minoritized, the oppressors and the oppressed. Therefore, Wertenbaker can be perceived as a "representative of the post-colonial writer" (Bassnett, 2000, p. 79), since she is directing her audience "to consider the ways in which power relations in the world have been shaped by the language imposed by the dominant power" (Bassnett, 2000, p. 79).

In her appropriation of the Greek myth, Wertenbaker strips the conventions of the western male-dominated view to help students acknowledge the consequences of forceful restraint. Therefore, as she breaks the myth of Philomela and Procne, she constructs it to emphasize the persistent pattern that controlling one's language and forceful silencing will lead to unwanted consequences, and prescription of one's ideas to others is the repetition of this hierarchical system. Ending the play by interrogating one's right to ask questions, Wertenbaker demands the cultural synthesis Freire aspires. Pairing this play with a research project about the destructive nature of language could lead to fruitful discussions in the classroom. In such a project, students could discuss topics including gender bias and sexist language, racist language, language discrimination, profanity and gender, binary oppositions and discrimination, and Lacan's psychoanalytic order.

Conclusion

Many feminist writers are seeking ways to reclaim the power of women. The most effective strategy is to reclaim and create their own myths. In using female figures from mythology, feminist writers choose to represent these female villains or victims of classical mythology as characters who have their own motivations, which justify their actions. Lizbeth Goodman (2000) argues that as women writers give voice to female characters from mythology, the characters become more "real." As Goodman claims "The point is not to bring myth to life, nor to kill the stories, but to highlight the uneasy distinction between the two, and to show how many erroneous assumptions and gendered uses of language have traditionally defined and carried meaning from one text, culture and generation to the next" (Goodman, 2000, p. xvii). By presenting women of mythology as round characters, who are "explaining their motives and seeking sympathy and understanding often by exploring and critiquing the circumstances which have led to their fate" (de Gay & Goodman, 2003, p. 15), feminist writers repeatedly expose the oppressive and prescriptive ideology of the patriarchal society.

Further, feminist writers refrain from representing these classical women as victims of patriarchy, and they try to prevent their "audience from identifying themselves with the victims in a disempowering way" (de Gay & Goodman, 2003, p. 16). If one identifies intimately with the classical representation of these characters, then women will continue to be associated with learned helplessness and fatalism imposed on them by many prominent texts. The women of classical mythology were either pitiful victims of powerful men or these women were jealous crones who were as mad as to murder children like Medea, Philomela, and Procne, or to cause the death of their unrequited love object like Phaedra. Thus, identifying with such women would only result in the audiences' pitying of the women characters in the plays. However, these feminist writers aim to alienate their audience, for them to be able approach these issues dealt with on stage critically. Freire refers to this critical consciousness as *conscientização*: the term "refers to learning to perceive social, political and economic contradictions, and to take action against the oppressive elements of reality" (2005, p. 35). This ability to perceive contradictions will empower the audience to name and, therefore, to change the oppression they feel around them.

In addition to giving voice to the traditional victims of mythology, women writers also disclose the inherent power structures within these myths to present the suppression of not only women but all who remain outside the power constructs. This is evident in the *Thebans* and *The Love of the Nightingale*. Internalized oppression and the fear of raising one's voice leads to choosing silence and this results in further violence: such as civil war in *Thebans*, rape, mutilation, and child murder in *The Love of the Nightingale*. By revealing the suppression of all who remain outside the hierarchical constructs, these women writers also seem to be revealing the consistent pattern that patriarchal power structures are destroying all the members within their social formations through forceful restraint.

As implied in Alicia Ostriker's words, "revisionist mythmaking" is, in fact, the attempt to "revise and reconstitute" (Shurbutt, 1998, p. 43) the previously created myths in order for these myths to include women. Thus, revisionist mythmaking becomes an attempt to rewrite and to break those grounded myths to make way for women to establish their own myths. Sylvia Bailey Shurbutt declares that "Women have always been uniquely aware of the power of the printed word; and women writers, from Amelia Lanier to Virginia Woolf, have made a concerted attempt to rewrite or revise the myths and to seize for themselves the language that constructs and reconstructs the lives of women" (1998, p. 44). Shurbutt perceives revisionist mythmaking as women's "masking, encoding, and subversive use of language in order to create or recreate themselves through words, and in so doing, they are able to create not just a literature of their own but a mythic life of their own" (1998, p. 44). According to feminist archetypal theorists like Estella Lauter, signs of myth reveal themselves in repeated patterns of "images, narratives, ritual gestures, attitudes, or tones that might belong to a coherent story" (1984, p. 172). Thus, seeking the persistent patterns formed in women's writing and art is an attempt to expose the potential of women's mythmaking in its progressive stages. This will be the first step in unveiling the oppression: "Consequently, as myths are regarded as the source for collective experiences, analyzing how women have revised, devised, and originated myths would thus permit us to find out which of our experiences have been most critical or enduring" (Lauter, 1984, p. 8). Once we unveil the myths of the oppressed and listen to the problems from both sides, we will have the chance to reach the cultural synthesis Freire believes in. As he states, "Sooner or later, a true revolution must initiate a courageous dialogue with the people. Its very legitimacy lies in that dialogue. It cannot fear the people, their expression, their effective participation in power" (Freire, 2005, p. 128). Women's revisionist drama and critical revisionist pedagogy in the classroom seeks to open this door to courageous dialogue.

References

Aston, E. (1995). *An introduction to feminism and theatre.* New York: Routledge.

Aston, E. (2003). *Feminist views on the English stage: Women playwrights, 1990–2000.* Cambridge: Cambridge University Press.

Barthes, R. (1973). *Mythologies.* London: Paladin Books.

Bassnett, S. (2000). The politics of location. In E. Aston & J. Reinelt (Eds.), *The Cambridge companion to modern British women playwrights* (pp. 73–81). Cambridge: Cambridge University Press.

de Gay, J., & Goodman, L. (2003). *Languages of theatre shaped by women.* Bristol: Intellect.

Fetterley, J. (1978). *The resisting reader: A feminist approach to American fiction.* Bloomington: Indiana University Press.

Freire, P. (2005). *The pedagogy of the oppressed* (M. B. Ramos, Trans.). New York, NY: Continuum (Original work published 1970).

Freud, S. (1953). *The interpretation of dreams* (J. Strachey, Trans.). London: The Hogart Press (Original work published 1900).

Gilbert, S. M., & Gubar, S. (1979). *The madwoman in the attic: The woman writer and the nineteenth-century literary imagination.* New Haven: Yale University Press.

Goodman, L. (2000). *Mythic women / real women: Plays and performance pieces by women.* London: Faber and Faber.

Klindienst, P. (1998). The voice of the shuttle is ours. In J. Rivkin & M. Ryan (Eds.), *Literary theory: An anthology* (pp. 612–629). Massachusetts: Blackwell.

Lauter, E. (1984). *Women as mythmakers: Poetry and visual art by twentieth-century women.* Bloomington: Indiana University Press.

Lochhead, L. (2003). *Thebans.* Glasgow: Theatre Babel.

Luchow, J. P., Crowl, T. K., & Kahn, J. P. (1985). Learned helplessness: Perceived effects of ability and effort on academic performance among EH and LD/ED children. *Journal of Learning Disabilities, 18*(8), 470–474.

Lustig, M., & Koester, J. (1999). *Intercultural competence. Interpersonal communication across cultures* (3rd ed.). New York: Longman.

McNeill, W. H. (1986). *Mythistory and other essays.* Chicago: The University of Chicago Press.

Ostriker, A. (1985). The thieves of language: Women poets and revisionist mythmaking. In E. Showalter (Ed.), *The new feminist criticism: Essays on women, literature, and theory* (pp. 314–338). New York: Pantheon Books.

Rame, F., & Fo, D. (2000). A woman alone. In L. Goodman (Ed.), *Mythic women / real women: Plays and performance pieces by women* (pp. 79–86). London: Faber and Faber.

Schapira, L. L. (1988). *The Cassandra complex, living with disbelief: A modern perspective on hysteria.* New York: BookSurge.

Seligman, M., & Maier, S. (1967). Failure to escape traumatic shock. *Journal of Experimental Psychology, 74*, 1–9.

Sellers, S. (2001). *Myth and fairy tale in contemporary women's fiction.* New York: Palgrave.

Shurbutt, S. B. (1998). Writing lives and telling tales: Visions and revisions. In L. Longmire & L. Merill (Eds.), *Untying the tongue: Gender, power, and the word* (pp. 43–51). Connecticut: Greenwood Press.

Spence, I., & Stan-Spence, A. (1990, March). Meeting "learned helplessness" head on with "active learning" (pp. 1–16). Retrieved from https://eric.ed.gov/contentdelivery/servlet/ERICServlet?accno=ED318165

Walker, N. A. (1995). *The disobedient writer: Women and narrative tradition.* Austin: University of Texas Press.

Wertenbaker, T. (2000). *The love of the nightingale.* In L. Goodman (Ed.), *Mythic women/real women: Plays and performance pieces by women* (pp. 21–68). London: Faber and Faber.

CHAPTER FIVE

Implicit Attitudes and Explicit Harms: Combating Biases that Hinder Inclusivity

RUSSELL W. WALTZ

Introduction

It is essential to consider how implicit attitudes fuel exclusivity in the classroom. Critical thinking requires that individuals demonstrate a disposition toward maintaining critical engagement via sustained intellectual inquiry (Dewey, 1910, p. 6). There is reason to suggest that implicit attitudes work in tandem with hegemonic masculinity and heteronormativity to inhibit the critical engagement needed to create inclusivity in the classroom. A lack of critical engagement only serves to promulgate the status quo, which means that being unengaged leads to the further cementation of hegemonic masculinity and heteronormativity, both of which hinder efforts to create inclusivity in the classroom.

Attempts to use critical thinking instruction to transcend implicit attitudes have traditionally consisted of teaching informal logic and examining logical fallacies. eaching informal logic to develop students' critical thinking skills incorrectly assumes that implicit attitudes will be less prevalent in students, and when they are present, their impact will be weak (Paul, 1984). Central to overcoming implicit attitudes that can work in tandem with hegemonic masculinity and heteronormativity to perpetuate exclusivity is understanding the role that implicit attitudes play in inhibiting educators' efforts to make their classrooms spaces of inclusion. Since, in my view, implicit attitudes manifest as emotional, automatic appraisals not grounded on reason, teaching students informal logic is not enough to generate anti-biased implicit attitudes. Thus, this chapter demonstrates how generating an affective (i.e., emotional), rather than a cognitive (i.e., rational) approach to combating implicit attitudes can create an inclusive classroom by encouraging students to overcome their biases and the cloud of hegemonic masculinity and heteronormativity to appreciate the experiences of women and members of the LGBTQIA+ community.

Hegemonic Masculinity's Problematicity

"Hegemony" denotes "the process of influence where we learn to earnestly embrace a system of beliefs and practices that essentially harm us while working to uphold the interests of others who have power over us" (Davis & Kimmel, 2011, p. 9). A dominant construction of what it means to be masculine is held as an idealized archetype that individuals should strive to reach and maintain (Connell, 2005). Hegemonic masculinity is problematic since it works in tandem with implicit attitudes that act as exclusionary mechanisms. Situating an overtly masculine, heteronormative ideology as an ingrained, default framework makes students less likely to appreciate others' subjective experiences that fall outside the perceived norms of that hegemonic, heteronormative framework. As a result, the experiences of women and members of the LGBTQIA+ community are ignored and oppressed since their experiences fit outside the bounds of hegemonic masculinity. For example, let us consider out-group homogeneity bias, which denotes the tendency to exaggerate the sameness of those outside of one's peer group. In contrast, in-group heterogeneity bias fuels the opposite phenomenon. These biases help reinforce norms, values, and beliefs aligned with masculinity since this is the dominant societal framework. Those who do not manifest heteronormative, masculine traits are signaled as "other," and the differences between these individuals and the masculine status quo are considered stark. At the same time, those who manifest said heteronormative, masculine traits are considered "just one of the guys" and are given the freedom to "let boys be boys."

The pervasiveness of hegemonic masculinity hinders efforts to create inclusivity in the classroom since, when plagued with implicit biases, students are less able to critically think about the experiences of women and members of the LGBTQIA+ community. This is so because the salience of information about their experiences is distorted due to the irrational, affective implicit biases that students hold (e.g., confirmation bias, disconfirmation bias, the backfire effect, etc.). To think critically, one must gather as much information as possible. Inclusivity encourages the sharing of information that is typically distributed asymmetrically. Diversity enhanced through inclusion, rather than exclusion, helps ensure that information is pooled together in ways that best allow individuals to think about all individuals' experiences critically.

Critical Thinking

For this chapter, John Dewey's conception of critical thinking in *How We Think* (1910) serves as a sound foundation for what it means to think critically. As Dewey states: "active, persistent and careful consideration of a belief or supposed form of knowledge in the light of the grounds that support it and the further conclusions to which it tends" (Dewey, 1910, p. 6). Put another way, critical thinking consists of a dispositionally engaged mode of diligent inquiry where care is taken to examine the evidence supporting one's views and parse out their logical and practical entailment as a means of solving problems. Critical thinking has a two-fold structure that includes a distinction between a skill dimension and a disposition dimension. Critical thinking skills include interpretation, analysis, evaluation, inference, explanation, and self-regulation (Facione, 1984). A disposition that enhances critical engagement includes inquisitiveness, a concern about being knowledgeable and well-informed, and honesty about one's implicit attitudes (Facione, 1984).

The Traditional Approach to Critical Thinking Instruction

Traditional critical thinking instruction has typically focused on teaching critical thinking through the study of informal logic. Informal logic primarily consists of identifying, constructing, and evaluating arguments found within the scope of ordinary language (i.e., non-symbolic language), deductive and inductive reasoning, and logical fallacies (Ennis, 1987; Johnson, 1996; Lipman, 1988; McPeck, 1981; Paul, 1993; Siegel, 1988). As this chapter suggests, studying informal logic fails to eradicate implicit attitudes since, as discussed below, there is much evidence to suggest that implicit attitudes are grounded upon affective appraisals, and instead of existing as beliefs, they are best understood as aliefs rooted in affect and not higher-order cognition (Gendler, 2008; Madva, 2015). Further, aliefs are quite stubborn mental states. Even when exposed to rational argumentation that runs counter to their influence, we often fail to escape their grasp and seem powerless to resist them. When it comes to aliefs, we can listen to reasoned argumentation and work through reflective cognitive exercises, but their hold over us persists. Implicit attitudes impair one's ability to think critically about the information that enters their attention. Since implicit attitudes hinder critical thinking, efforts to develop critical thinking curriculum by way of rational, logical argumentation to lessen the prevalence and force of implicit attitudes fail.

Implicit Attitudes

Affective Appraisals

Robert Zajonc first popularized the concept of affective appraisals by claiming that the appraisals that we make about external stimuli are, at root, grounded upon unreflective, noncognitive assessments that occur automatically and without conscious thought (Zajonc, 1980, 1984). Zajonc theorized that the ability to make unreflective appraisals about our experiential environment's features increases our evolutionary fitness since escaping danger often leaves little room for reflective deliberation. In the case of a woman, for example, walking down a street who hears a shuffling of footsteps while passing by a darkened alleyway, Zajonc would claim that precortical processing in the amygdala makes it possible for automatic, unconscious appraisals to be made to escape perceived imminent threats (Zajonc, 1980). This shuffling of feet so close in proximity to her in lighting conditions that do not permit her to see who is lurking beside her could easily (and I would argue, should) be perceived as a threat.

Zajonc examined affective appraisal theory through studies involving the mere exposure effect (1980). In these studies, Zajonc exposed participants to a series of faces and symbols faster than the time necessary for these images to register consciously in his subjects' neocortices. Zajonc found that when participants were asked to appraise those faces and symbols after being reintroduced to them, the participants overwhelmingly reported a positive felt response to those faces and symbols they had been exposed to during the initial phase of the study (Zajonc, 1984). Put carefully, the participants had assigned positive valence markers (a term coined by Jesse Prinz) via affective appraisals to the faces and symbols that they had been exposed to for such a brief time that they did not even know that they had been exposed to them (Zajonc, 1984; Prinz, 2004).

Aliefs

Since the publication of the findings from Zajonc's experiments, scholars have toiled over the question of whether felt attractions and aversions are cognitive beliefs or are something entirely different. Tamar Gendler (2008) coined the term "alief" and presented convincing evidence for why we should not assume that the human tendency to feel specific ways about external stimuli are grounded in intentional belief. Gendler uses a series of cases to introduce and demonstrate aliefs that involve situations where interlocutors are in safe environments, such as a glass walkway over the Grand Canyon or an extraordinarily tall and fast roller coaster (Gendler, 2008). In both cases, it can be said that people hold cognitive beliefs that affirm their safety since the walkway and the roller coasters are vigorously tested and maintained to the highest standards. If the walkers and riders did not hold the belief that they were indeed safe, it is doubtful that they would allow themselves to occupy those contraptions. Also, in both cases, many people experience a sense of irrational dread and fear, to the point where some are unable to move their limbs and become visibly sick. Individuals allow themselves to occupy these spaces, given that many have such experiences because they hold the cognitive belief that they are relatively safe. Individuals who have obsessive-compulsive disorder also experience this phenomenon in the comfort of their own homes. While a person with OCD might hold the cognitive belief that no one will die if they fail to touch the doorknob five times in succession before entering a room, it is often difficult to ward off immediate feelings of dread when they realize that they have "entered without touching."

Moreover, implicit attitudes are insensitive to considerations of logical form (i.e., negation and conditional logical operators) though beliefs are (Madva, 2015). While the truth or falsity of belief states hinge upon logical operators, negation and conditional operators do not affect implicit attitudes, much in the same way that subjects holding aliefs consisting of dread fail to be assuaged by reflectively derived assurances of safety (Madva, 2015; Gendler, 2008). Rather than displaying sensitivity to logical form, implicit attitudes show sensitivity to "spatiotemporal relations in thought and perception" (Madva, 2015). The same could be said for aliefs since the precise manner that someone is introduced to an experience, whether that consists of walking across a sheet of glass hundreds of feet in the air or being persuaded that global warming is real and there is plenty of scientific evidence to prove it.

How one is introduced to new information is extremely important. This is especially so for those who are strongly affected by confirmation bias and disconfirmation bias. For example, individuals holding confirmation bias who are also homophobic might read a news story in their local paper about a gay man dying of AIDS. Since the news story's information would confirm their view that many gay men have AIDS, that information would resonate with the reader, and they would consider it highly significant. In turn, if the news story contained information claiming that gay men are statistically better fathers than heterosexual men, a reader holding disconfirmation bias would be apt to dismiss the information as either insignificant, tangential, or outright false since it fails to confirm his homophobic views. What is most troubling is that there is evidence to show that the more credible information given to individuals with confirmation bias, the more likely they are to reject the credible evidence and place greater significance on their previously held and erroneous bias laden views. This phenomenon was dubbed the "backfire effect" by Brendan Nyhan and Jason Reifler (2010). This is a case where an affective, irrationally grounded implicit attitude is made stronger by presenting factually justified, rational evidence. In this case, confirmation and disconfirmation biases are amplified to the point that attempts to present biased individuals factually justified and rational evidence would be futile. This is especially problematic when one examines how this phenomenon bears out, practically speaking. For instance, imagine a case where an individual holds the irrational belief that transwomen seek to use bathrooms designated for women solely because they desire to prey upon ciswomen. According to this phenomenon, even if they were presented with factually justified, rational evidence because such evidence ran contrary to their bigoted views, this information's presentation would cause them to dismiss such evidence as insignificant. Presenting such a person with information that directly and convincingly refutes their aliefs about transwomen grounded on affective appraisals would only reinforce those aliefs, no matter how bigoted or irrational they happen to be. Confirmation bias, disconfirmation bias, and the backfire effect make it extremely difficult for individuals to sort through evidence and think critically about information they are consuming and how it relates to their held aliefs. Due to the affective nature of aliefs influenced by implicit attitudes, distortion concerning how information is processed and given salience is likely to occur.

There is good reason to believe that implicit attitudes are at root, affective, and, therefore, noncognitive (Gendler, 2008; Madva, 2015). Because of this, traditional means of critical thinking instruction fails, since those means have traditionally involved having students work through logic problems or to practice reflective thinking. These techniques work well to help students revise and reformulate held beliefs. Still, since implicit attitudes seem more likely to be affective, unreflective aliefs, these cognitive measures, such as teaching critical thinking via informal logic curriculum, will continue to fail, thus hindering student's critical thinking development. Without modifying critical thinking instruction to account for the notion that implicit attitudes are aliefs that require a different strategy than what is used to eradicate pernicious beliefs, a hindrance to critical thinking will endure. As a result, students will continue to fall prey to their tendency to think about their world through a haze shaped by their implicit attitudes.

This is a serious problem since, as the example above showed, individuals who hold and promote values and norms steeped in hegemonic masculinity and heteronormativity will only continue to promulgate their flawed assertions rather than revise them, which will hinder educators' efforts to promote inclusivity in the classroom.

The Remedial Effects of Knowledge

Dewey's insistence that inquiry, arising from recognizing a problem to be solved, establishes the need to gather as much information as possible about one's environment (Dewey, 1910). This means that effective critical thinking requires that individuals gain as much knowledge as possible about themselves, their situation, and others around them. Rather than working in an exclusive environment created via hegemonic masculinity, heteronormativity, and implicit attitudes, an inclusive environment would best enable individuals to gather as much knowledge about others' experiences. To help students overcome implicit attitudes steeped in hegemonic masculinity and heteronormativity, which would foster inclusivity in the classroom, certain types of knowledge have been recognized as more helpful than others. Pedagogy must primarily feature first- and second-person knowledge and only secondarily feature third-person knowledge. To clarify, first-person knowledge is comprised of information concerning the subjective experiences of others. In contrast, second-person knowledge consists of normative claims that others issue in response to their circumstances. Third-person knowledge is impersonal, academic knowledge of the sort found in a textbook or encyclopedia.

As Elizabeth Anderson notes, third-person knowledge is insufficient to educate individuals adequately since it cannot help them overcome implicit attitudes (2007). This is so because third-person knowledge fails to resonate with individuals on an affective level, while first- and second-person knowledge more than adequately satisfy that condition. As a result, first- and second-person knowledge is better suited than third-person knowledge to help students overcome implicit biases that impede efforts to foster inclusivity in the classroom since doing so requires that information resonates with students on an affective level. In cases where first-hand first- and second-person knowledge is unavailable, an abundance of "the right kind" of second-hand first- and second-person knowledge bestowed via educators could encourage students to break free from the grips of implicit attitudes.

Considering affective engagement through the lens of a noncognitive, process-centered view will show that presenting students with mere third-person knowledge does not sufficiently overcome the grip of implicit attitudes, which harm students' ability to think critically. This is because presenting abstract, impersonal information about women and members of the LGBTQIA+ community is unlikely to resonate with students at an affective level, encouraging them to sympathize with women's and LGBTQIA+ individuals' experiences.

Knowledge's Role in Overcoming Implicit Attitudes

According to Anderson, third-person knowledge is academic knowledge and is "conscious, articulate, impersonal propositional knowledge" (Anderson, 2007, pp. 606–607). As she states, "academic knowledge covers only technical knowledge and, to a lesser extent, awareness of the problems and circumstances of people from different walks of life" (Anderson, 2007, pp. 606–607). Presenting students with third-person knowledge is insufficient for several reasons. First, in many cases, mere third-person knowledge does not hold information about individuals' subjective experiences associated with particular events (i.e., first-person knowledge). This is so in cases "when the knowledge needed concerns individuals' interpretations of and responses to what they see as the meanings of different actions and events" (Anderson, 2007, pp. 609–610). In such instances, "there is no substitute for taking up the first-person point of view" (Anderson, 2007, p. 610). Without aid, students cannot understand what it is like to live like individuals across sectoral lines (Anderson, 2007, pp. 608–614). Without being able to form even a vague appreciation of others' experiences of others, creating an inclusive classroom will be quite challenging to achieve.

In a classroom where hegemonic masculinity and heteronormativity are deeply entrenched, it may be difficult for students to understand the need for Feminism or rights for members of the LGBTQIA+ community. This is so because masculinity and heteronormativity work in tandem with implicit attitudes like confirmation and disconfirmation bias and the backfire effect. Students holding traditional, heteronormative views, for instance, will be prone to dismiss the experiences of their classmates or those of individuals studied in class if those experiences do not conform to the standards of hegemonic masculinity. For example, after the shooting in Orlando, FL at Pulse, statements made on news programs and the Internet intimated that, for some, the tragic experiences that victims shared were lost on unsympathetic ears which could not overcome their affectively-grounded appraisals of members of the LGBTQIA+ community to take their strife seriously. Moreover, those who dismiss the struggle of women in the face of rape culture, sexual harassment, catcalling, etc., often do so because of their implicit attitudes working in conjunction with the hegemonic masculinity that they embrace, whether they do so wittingly or not.

No matter how much factually justified and rational evidence educators could present to students affected by implicit attitudes about members of the LGBTQIA+ community, students who hold such implicit attitudes will not be moved to one day simply "get it." To be clear, abstract, impersonal information fails to motivate students to appreciate the experiences of others. Moreover, since mere third-person knowledge does not hold data about normative claims issued in response to events (i.e., second-person knowledge), it fails to motivate students to become critically engaged with such experiences in a normative light. Mere third-person knowledge's failure in these two respects is problematic as developing inclusivity requires that individuals be affectively engaged. The presentation of subjective experiences and normative claims is needed to motivate affective engagement (Anderson, 2007, pp. 608–614). In cases where mere third-person knowledge is presented, implicit biases are left unchecked, and it is difficult for students to become affectively engaged toward others' experiences.

Moreover, implicit biases foster incompetence because it causes students to develop distorted, stereotypical views of others' experiences (Anderson, 2007, p. 605). Anderson construes stereotypes to be schemas "for making inferences about the nature of a particular object once it has been recognized as a member of a class with an associated schema. Stereotypes are crude, typically unconsciously held heuristics that enable people to economize on information processing and react quickly to situations involving the object" (Anderson, 2007, p. 604). As she claims, stereotypes create implicit biases that leave individuals unable to become aware of others' problems (Anderson, 2007, p. 604).

Anderson argues that implicit attitudes grounded upon stereotypes foster incompetence in learners. Stereotypes distort our perception of new evidence, "making stereotype-confirming evidence highly salient, … leading [us] to overlook stereotype-disconfirming evidence" (Anderson, 2007, p. 604). The two implicit attitudes associated with this phenomenon are confirmation and disconfirmation bias. Imagine a case where a bigoted individual who holds the alief that most members of the LGBTQIA+ community are sexual deviants views a news story depicting a gay man as a rapist. According to Anderson's account, this story would resonate with this particular viewer more forcefully and for a more extended period than a narrative depicting a gay man as a good Samaritan.

Lastly, stereotypes change the causal explanations for the behavior of members of a class. In other words, implicit attitudes cause individuals to give accounts of the root causes of behaviors of members of a class, whether in their class or that of others. This is known as the "fundamental attribution error." As Anderson claims, "when an object's behavior conforms to the stereotype, those who hold the stereotype tend to attribute the behavior to the object's internal characteristics. When the object's behavior contradicts or fails to conform to the stereotype, those who hold the stereotype tend to attribute the behavior to circumstances external to the object" (Anderson, 2007, p. 604). For instance, upon viewing that same story, our bigoted viewer might attribute the subject's alleged criminal behavior to internal characteristics rather than believe that the subject's social environment influenced the life choices that the subject made quite considerably.

First- and second-person knowledge, coming directly from personal interactions between members across sectional lines, is best suited to help students overcome implicit biases. That said, direct contact between individuals across sectoral lines is not possible in some cases. Some localities could manage the task on a grand scale (e.g., Philadelphia, Chicago, etc.). For others, however, mere tokenism would be possible (e.g., various locales in Kansas, Alaska, etc.). Small-scale direct contact would prove counterintuitive, as such tokenism could reinforce cognitive biases perpetuated by stereotypes, a point that Anderson recognizes (Anderson, 2007, p. 617).

This presents a difficulty. How can students be educated in conditions where the only degree of contact possible would be considered a token effort? It is possible, and for it to work, educators must present students information about others' subjective experiences and the normative claims they issue. To avoid the distortive influence of implicit biases, students must be exposed to others' experiences and the normative claims they make in ways that encourage them to appreciate, as best that they can, the experiences of others (i.e., women and members of the LGBTQIA+ community). The presentation of first- and second-person accounts is valued above all else because such narratives represent "the world from the perspective of a particular agent[;] ... what it is like – for that agent, as the agent sees [the world]" (Anderson, 2007, p. 607).

To address the concern about tokenism mentioned above, when meaningful direct personal contact is not possible, mediators can present such narratives indirectly. As Anderson states, "the first-person point of view is immediately experienced by the agent, but it may also be communicated to others through testimony. For others to get access to the first-person point of view of another, they typically need personal contact, communicative competence, and rapport with the other, or else they need someone else with such social and cultural capital to mediate between the other and oneself" (Anderson, 2007, p. 607). Also, testimony must be "salient ... whenever it is normatively relevant to resolving the practical question at stake in deliberation and ... arouse, or be clothed in, some motivationally engaged feelings" (Anderson, 2007, p. 608).

To encourage students to overcome implicit attitudes, knowledge must invoke affective engagement (Anderson, 2007, p. 608). As noted above, in addition to first-person knowledge, second-person knowledge is required as it provides information about normative demands individuals issue upon others. As Anderson states, second-person "claims are demands for responsiveness to another's interests and evaluations[.] … They are embodied in normative judgments that purport to offer authoritative claims on others' actions and feelings" (Anderson, 2007, p. 607). Such claims are essential because they can motivate students to develop a disposition to sympathize with others' experiences.

Strategies for Combating Implicit Attitudes

Pedagogy of the Oppressed

The pedagogy of the oppressed, first made famous by Paulo Freire, largely inspired the rise of critical pedagogy, on which this chapter is grounded. While it is outside the scope of this chapter to offer a complete reiteration of Freire's views, one idea, in particular, could help us understand why first- and second-person knowledge is key to helping students overcome implicit attitudes steeped in hegemonic masculinity and heteronormativity. This idea is that all of the knowledge needed to overcome implicit attitudes is already held by the oppressed (Freire, 1970). Thus, it is necessary to create avenues through which first- and second-person knowledge about the experiences of the oppressed can be presented to students who hold implicit attitudes grounded in hegemonic masculinity and make appreciating others' experiences difficult.

The Tunnel of Oppression

At the University of Kansas, I taught a first-year seminar course titled: Psychology and Research in Education 101 (PRE 101). The course was designed to acclimate students to the university, enhance their critical thinking skills, and develop into conscientious citizens, able to sympathize with others, and understand the need for social justice. Since I am dedicated to raising my students' consciousness, I planned activities whose aim was to help them overcome their held implicit attitudes and abandon any lingering aliefs formed by hegemonic masculinity and heteronormativity. In doing so, I adopted a pedagogical strategy influenced by the pedagogy of the oppressed. The primary pedagogical activity that I used to encourage students to overcome their implicit biases was centered around a campus event called the Tunnel of Oppression sponsored by the Sabatini Multicultural Resource Center at the University of Kansas.

The event was housed in a unit of offices and hallways that were transformed into various learning spaces where students witnessed instances of sexism, bigotry, homophobia, transphobia as recounted by volunteers through live-action roleplaying exhibits (University of Kansas, 2008). For example, one learning space involved a Black woman reading emails that she received where the sender used sexist and racist language to refer to the woman. My students were predominantly white men between the ages of eighteen and nineteen who came from upper-middle-class families around the Kansas City, Missouri area, mostly attended private secondary schools with an almost all-white student body. For many, this was the first time they were presented with first-person knowledge about others' oppression experiences. During the event, they were also presented with second-person knowledge consisting of normative, affect-laden claims made about the cases of oppression that they witnessed. Instead of explaining what occurred using third-person academic knowledge, the exhibits presented affect-laden, emotion-driven information about others' experience facing oppression. Both first- and second-person knowledge are key to combating implicit biases. Before the activity, I presented third-person academic knowledge on various course readings students reviewed before the event's commencement. I also led them through a discussion on hegemonic masculinity, heteronormativity, and oppression to prime them for the transformative learning that was to occur during the activity.

Other learning spaces included first-hand, affect-laden accounts of experiences presented by members of the LGBTQIA+ community who had been the target of hate speech and other bigotry and survivors of sexual assault. In all cases, the look on my students' faces, faces that had most likely no prior familiarity with first-hand accounts of the type of experiences being presented to them by women and LGBTQIA+ individuals, held expressions of deep personal reflection.

At the end of the activity, a session was held by a professionally licensed counselor employed by the University of Kansas and assigned to this event. During the session, the counselor worked with my students to help them appreciate what they had witnessed, which included helping them work through the experiences of women and LGBTQIA+ individuals that they had been presented. After the event and debriefing session, I was approached by several of my students individually and thanked for enabling them to undergo such a transformative experience and opening their eyes to the oppression that others face. While I acknowledged their appreciation, I also reminded them that what they had witnessed was merely a glimpse of the experiences of women and members of the LGBTQIA+ community, and I encouraged them to continue to learn about others' experiences and become an ally for the oppressed.

In the weeks after the activity, I noticed several positive changes in my students. Once, during class, a student quipped, "that's gay," and before I could even open my mouth to call them out, one of their peers replied, "Dude. Not cool. Remember the Tunnel of Oppression event?" The offending student apologized to the class, and I used the opportunity to praise the student who called out the offender and launch into a discussion of privilege and heteronormativity. While I did not appreciate the verbal aggression being uttered in my class, I was glad to see that the Tunnel of Oppression activity has succeeded in getting some of my students to check their implicit attitudes and fight against heteronormativity.

The Implicit Association Test

Another activity that proved successful while teaching Psychology and Research in Education 101 (PRE 101) was the in-class administration of the Implicit Association Test (IAT) (Greenwald et al., 1998). The assessment is free to administer and complete and is available on the Internet. During a class session, I had students complete the assessment and discuss the results in a group setting. My students were surprised to learn that most of their scores on the assessment indicated they held moderate to strong implicit biases toward white, cisgender, heterosexual men. I used this opportunity to lead a group discussion on hegemonic masculinity and heteronormativity and the fact that I was far less surprised by their results than they were. This was not because I thought my students were pernicious-minded individuals, but simply because they were mostly white, affluent Midwestern families from Kansas and Missouri. My students grew up with privilege that most in the United States do not have, and I was sure to announce and check my privilege as well. I found it essential to help my students understand the connection between implicit attitudes and hegemonic masculinity, and the fact that the activity was not meant to demonize any particular individual but to raise their consciousness about how implicit attitudes work in tandem with hegemonic masculinity and heteronormativity to create spaces of oppression for others. Identifying and checking our implicit attitudes is a critical step in overcoming their affective hold over individuals. Activities like the Implicit Association Test could help encourage students to do this.

Conclusion

In this chapter, I have argued that implicit attitudes work in tandem with hegemonic masculinity to pose a serious challenge to educators in the higher education classroom. When such biases are present, creating and maintaining an inclusive learning environment is challenging. Students who exhibit implicit biases, such as confirmation bias and disconfirmation bias, while also harboring heteronormative views, struggle to participate in an inclusive classroom. The traditional pedagogical approach to counteracting these biases typically involves presenting students with critical thinking instruction grounded in informal logic. When this traditional approach to identifying and eradicating implicit biases fails, it is because such biases are affective rather than rational prejudices. Lastly, I explored pedagogical strategies that could enable students to reflect on implicit attitudes and hegemonic masculinity. I hope that when educators adopt an affective approach, rather than a purely rational approach to teaching course content, students will overcome their implicit attitudes that often thwart educators' efforts to create an inclusive classroom.

References

Anderson, E. (2006). The epistemology of democracy. *Episteme*, *3*(1–2), 8–22.

Anderson, E. (2007). Fair opportunity in education: A democratic equality perspective. *Ethics*, *117*(4), 595–622.

Connell, R. (2005). *Masculinities*. Berkeley, CA: University of California Press.

Davis, T., & Kimmel, M. (2011). Mapping guyland in college. In T. Davis & J. A. Laker (Eds.), *Masculinities in higher education: Theoretical and practical considerations* (pp. 3–15). New York, NY: Routledge.

Dewey, J. (1910). *How we think: A restatement of the relation of reflective thinking to the educative process*. Boston, MA: D.C. Heath & Co.

Ennis, R. H. (1987). A taxonomy of critical thinking dispositions and abilities. In J. Baron & R. Sternberg (Eds.), *Teaching thinking skills: Theory and practice* (pp. 9–26). New York: W. H. Freeman Co.

Facione, P. (1984). Toward a theory of critical thinking. *Liberal Education, 70*(3), 253–261.

Freire, P. (1970). *Pedagogy of the oppressed*. New York, NY: Herder and Herder.

Gendler, T. (2008). Alief and belief. *The Journal of Philosophy*, *105*(10), 634–663.

Greenwald, A. G., Mcghee, D. E., & Schwartz, J. L. (1998). Measuring individual differences in implicit cognition: The implicit association test. *Journal of Personality and Social Psychology, 74*(6), 1464–1480.

Johnson, R. H. (1996). *The rise of informal logic*. Newport News, VA: Vale Press.

Lipman, M. (1988). Critical thinking: What can it be? *Analytic Teaching, 8*, 5–12.

Madva, A. (2015). Why implicit attitudes are (probably) not beliefs. *Synthese, 193*(8), 2659–2684.

McPeck, J. (1981). *Critical thinking and education*. New York: St. Martin's Press.

Nyhan, B., & Reifler, J. (2010). When corrections fail: The persistence of political mispercep- tions. *Political Behavior, 32*(2), 303–330.

Paul, R. (1984). Critical thinking: Fundamental to education for a free society. *Educational Leadership, 42*(1), 4–14.

Paul, R. (1993). *Critical thinking: What every person needs to survive in a rapidly changing world.* Santa Rosa, CA: Foundation for Critical Thinking.

Prinz, J. (2004). *Gut reactions: A perceptual theory of emotion.* Oxford: Oxford University Press.

Siegel, H. (1988). *Educating reason: Rationality, critical thinking, and education.* New York, NY: Routledge.

University of Kansas, Sabatini Multicultural Resource Center. (2008, April 16). *Tunnel of Oppression* [Press release]. Retrieved March 1, 2020, from http://archive.news.ku.edu/ 2008/april/16/oppression.shtml

Zajonc, R. (1980). Feeling and thinking: Preferences need no inferences. *American Psycholo- gist, 35*(2), 151–175.

Zajonc, R. (1984). On the primacy of affect. *American Psychologist, 39*(2), 117–123.

PART TWO

ANTI-HETEROSEXIST APPROACHES TO DISRUPTING HEGEMONIC MASCULINITY AND SEXISM

"Sex≠Gender!" Reframing Cultural and Linguistic Assumptions in Undergraduate Courses

MÁRIA I. CIPRIANI

This chapter chronicles five years of teaching an undergraduate course called Women & Media at SUNY Old Westbury. The analysis, including anecdotes and general outlines of lessons, follows the Women & Media class. The class population is racially diverse as approximately 30 percent of the total class of thirty-five students is Black, 30 percent white, 30 percent Latinx or Hispanic, and 10 percent Asian or Native American. Ten percent of the students are non-traditional or returning students, and there is usually a three-to-one ratio of participants who identify as women to those who identify as men. Housed within the American Studies Department, lessons in history, representation, feminism, and the male gaze challenges undergraduates to become aware of the cultural, linguistic, and personal gendered assumptions that they make day by day, minute by minute, encouraging them to perceive the world differently. The stated learning objective is for each student to leave the course thinking differently about their relationship to one another and their consumption of media. This chapter uses course content and case studies to describe directed class discussions, specific key discomfiting questions, and challenges encountered by participants, both faculty and students, as they grapple with their lifelong assumptions, presumptions, and malfunctions. The description of course content includes considerations of inclusivity as pedagogical praxis and methods for maintaining professionalism while simultaneously modeling the concept that the political *is* personal.

Lesson #1 Definition of Feminism

The course begins by asking the Women & Media students a basic question: What is feminism? Answers typically fall into two categories: "promoting women as superior to men" (unfortunately, the common misconception) and "promoting equity among people of all sexes and genders" (the correct definition). From the outset, educators should strive to distinguish between sex and gender to model a framework for participants to conceptualize "sex and gender" as two separate linguistic terms.

After watching Emma Watson's 2014 speech to the United Nations promoting her #HeForShe project (United Nations), students can discuss whether they would take up the cause, join the campaign, and "come out" as feminists. The discussion is usually lively, and those who do not want to identify as feminists, for the most part, state that while they believe that no one sex or gender should be promoted over any other, they do not like the word "feminist." The question of why "feminist" is so objectionable to some leads to a variety of answers, with many objecting to the root "*fem-*" as being either too exclusive ("seems like it's only for females"), too closely related to femininity ("I'm a guy, not a 'fem'") to "having a negative history," or connected to the "man-hating" misconception that became associated with the word in the 1970s (Rensin, 2015). Words matter, and how words characterize people matters in a broad sense, not simply within the context of the classroom.

Lesson #2: Addressing Assumptions: Sex≠Gender

Next, the class can broach a significantly bigger hurdle for many, which is expanding upon the differentiation of sex and gender. For this lesson, the ubiquitous SmartBoard is replaced by an erasable whiteboard. Students arrive to see "Sex≠Gender" written on the board. After a discussion of what the students think this statement means, educators can conduct a mini lecture that describes "sex" as chromosomal sex, most commonly XX and XY and "gender" as masculinity and femininity. Students learn that gender is culturally constructed, meaning that what is considered "masculine" and "feminine" varies from culture to culture and changes within cultures over time (Halberstam, 1998; Paoletti, 2012). While some students shift a bit in their seats thinking that gender is culturally-defined, they have been inured to these ideas generally through other classes and their media consumption.

Next, students are encouraged to think about the binaries of male and female chromosomally and masculine and feminine culturally (Halberstam, 1998). Biology and mathematics are usually more easily digested in an academic setting, so they start with biology, discussing why the chromosomes are X and Y (because the actual chromosomes look like the letters), and what the XX and XY combinations signify (female and male, respectively).

Educators should also discuss statistics on sex and gender with students. For instance, we discuss the world's population size of 7.7 billion people, as well as the notion that it is statistically impossible for 7.7 billion of anything to fit neatly into two, and only two, categories (Fausto-Sterling, 1993). This is true of chromosomes, as more than two combinations of X and Y occur in humans, including XXX (trisomy X or Triple X Syndrome); XXY (Klinefelter's Syndrome); XO (Turner's Syndrome); and XYY (not viable in utero).

Care should be taken when discussing issues that are outside of one's expertise such as biology or statistical analysis. In this most basic of discussions, terms like intersex (having the characteristics of both sexes) and androgynous (having sex organs of both sexes) is not introduced unless a student asks a question or uses one or both terms. The introduction of these concepts is usually reserved for later, as this first discussion simply encourages students to think non-binarily. The ramifications of alternate chromosomal patterns, however, which are not taught in middle-school or secondary biology, are pertinent to the next part of the discussion about gender. If 7.7 billion things do not fit neatly into two categories biologically, it follows that the same number, 7.7 billion, also does not fit neatly into two, and only two, categories culturally. Thus, the categories of "masculinity" and "femininity" also cannot be so rigid as to designate everyone via a binary system.

"Right, gender is fluid" is a rote, almost bored response by millennials who have been hearing this for most of their lives. Such is not the case for their older, non-traditional student counterparts, who are usually quiet at this point, listening but not reacting, yet. "Yes." I say, "Gender is fluid. What does that mean?" I am typically met by blank stares, and if I am lucky, a shrug. The main premise of the discussion should be kept in view: sex does not equal gender. Mirroring is particularly useful when students self-disclose as part of their discussion of their experience with gender, both conforming and non-conforming. Mirroring acknowledges the speaker instead of letting a personal comment drop too quickly (Hendrix, 1990).

Educators should note that most traditional undergraduates will talk about "girls" and either "men" or "guys." This teaching moment provides an opportunity to talk about the disparity in the distinction between "girls" and "men," and even "girls" and "guys," as opposed to "boys." After the lesson, I say "women" whenever students say "girls" if they are not also saying "boys." Words matter, and this lesson must be modeled in each classroom discussion. In this case, the words that matter are comparative: "men" implies males who are masculine and adult with some authority, compared to "girls" which implies female and feminine but also young and unauthoritative, not-yet-adults, which makes "girls" a demeaning and diminishing term when used in tandem with, or in contrast to "men."

Educators can mark this linguistic point back to the terminological difference between sex and gender, which occurs not only in English. The second part of the "Sex≠Gender" discussion is about how the two terms came to be conflated, and why the conflation is a linguistic one initially: female≠feminine and male≠masculine, but cultural languages now use the terms interchangeably. This is as true in the United States and in other English-speaking countries where only the third-person pronouns are gendered as it is in countries whose nouns and corresponding adjectives are gendered. For example, German, which uses the masculine, feminine, and neuter declensions and the Romance languages (Italian, Spanish, French, Portuguese, Romanian) which feature masculine and feminine nouns, articles, and corresponding adjectival declensions.

Educators should inform their students that persons cannot be signified within language without the mark of gender. This discussion includes the use of "they" as a third-person singular pronoun to replace "he" and "she" as a means of examining whether gender-neutral pronouns reduce the mark of gender. To develop the discussion further, educators can ask: What bearing does this linguistic issue have on our study of women? The purpose of the question, and the discussion in general, is to focus students' thoughts on microaggressions, unconscious assumptions, and the idea of "so-called 'natural' gender" (Boroditsky et al., 2002).

Half of my students speak English as well as at least one other language. Many speak Spanish, and can understand and use gendered nouns, but often do not see their significance. To students, gendered nouns are a "natural" function of the language, nothing more. Educators should highlight the idea that unconscious assumptions emerging from the words used (or do not use) affect the ways they are read and judged. Examples to illustrate this abound. From the children's Harry Potter series, where only boys "bellow" and only girls are "shrill" and "shriek"(Cherland, 2008/2009; Clark, 2002; Galliardo & Smith, 2003; Fine, 2010); to politics where the adjectives used for women acting in the same way as men are pejorative, and the "likeability factor" creates a double-bind for women seeking power (Sundeep et al., 2018; Elsesser, 2019).

One example of the importance of words describes an ongoing fight in France that began in 2017 to make the French language less sexist. The grammatical rule in Romance languages is that if a group is comprised of all women, the feminine plural form of noun and corresponding adjective is used. If one man enters the group, the plural ending automatically becomes masculine, even if the man is one in a group of a thousand women. When asked, the Spanish- and French-speaking students in the class agree that this is the grammatical rule, often with a nod and a shrug. The teachers of French in France want to change the language that "summarizes the necessary subordination of the feminine to the masculine" (O'Brien, 2017) to make it less sexist, noting that the linguistic sexism has a profound effect on children's thoughts about gender (McCallum, 1999; McCoubrey, 2017). For example, when French school children are asked about their favorite author (*auteur* in French, which is a masculine noun), they only name authors who are men (Dauge-Roth, 2019). The assumptions that underpin the grammatical rule are themselves expressly sexist (Konishi, 1993): the grammatical rule was instituted in the eighteenth century; the French language itself has been in use since 1 BCE. The grammatical rule included in a 1767 grammar book said that the (grammatical) masculine is considered more "noble" than the (grammatical) feminine because of the superiority of men to women, which is a sexist statement.

Lest English speakers be too self-congratulatory about English's lack of linguistic sexism, while the English language may not be so blatantly sexist as French, until the 1970s, when a group of people was addressed, "he" was assumed, even when women were present, and this is still the case in many aspects of American culture. The "Smurfette Principle," a term coined by *The New York Times* writer, Katha Pollitt (1991), refers to the media practice of including one woman in group of men. Much like the French grammatical rule, the one woman Smurf, with her feminizing gendered signifiers (long hair, high heels, dress), gives girls the message that they exist only as ancillary to boys. The feminine suffix "ette" is itself insulting. Like the earlier example of "girls" compared to "men," the "ette" suffix is diminishing ("-ette" makes something smaller), and, again makes the default men and women a second, separate afterthought. To reinforce this important concept, educators can assign the Feminist Frequency video on feminizing gendered signifiers (Sarkeesian). Note that I say "important" rather than "seminal" because the latter word, having the same root as "semen" once again shows the ubiquity and the primacy given to masculine things.

Returning to the consideration of the linguistic conflation of "sex" and "gender," students again tackle the question: Why does the conflation matter? The linguistic conflation in French of grammatical and human gender leads to the reinforcement of the fallacious notion that men are superior to women. Likewise, the linguistic conflation in English of "sex" and "gender" leads to a false correlation of sex and gender that begins at birth, and therefore is seemingly "natural" to many, particularly those who are cisgender, that is, those whose chromosomal sex aligns with their culture's expectations of their assigned gender. To maintain an atmosphere of empowerment, using labels for everyone is a practice that should begin at the start of the course, with further explanation of the gendered cultural climate of living in a cis-, EuroAmerican, ableist, heteropatriarchy. Throughout the course, I endeavor to label both cis- and transpersons (where "cis" means on the same side of, and "trans" means across the sex-gender conflation); EuroAmerican and African-, Asian-, Native-American; abled and differently-abled; queer and straight/"hetero," and male and female to avoid a presumptive norm in the absence of identifiers. This puts students on notice that in this class, words truly are important, and what is said matters as much as what goes unsaid (Wickens, 2011).

The linguistic conflation of sex and gender leads to the false correlation that suggests that what is inescapably natural begins at birth or, now, with "gender reveal" parties, occurs even prior to birth. A gender reveal party is a social gathering of friends of a woman, or couple, expecting a child. At some point during the party, the gender of the fetus is revealed to the parent(s)-to-be and guests by a trusted friend who holds the "secret" until the appointed reveal time during the party. This new cultural phenomenon is a fitting example of the linguistic conflation of sex and gender. Gender reveal parties are technically "sex reveal" parties, because the ultrasound can only reveal observable genitalia and DNA tests can only reveal the biological X-Y chromosomal status of the fetus, demonstrating the ongoing conflation of sex and gender that is apparent in the culture. The gender reveal party phenomenon also provides a current, specific example of the myriad ways in which the culture determines, before a child is born, what the expected actions, color choices, apparel, toy/game choices, hairstyles, interest/career choices, and lifestyle (Konisi, 1993; Paoletti, 2012) in the cis-, Euro-American, ableist, heteropatriarchy of the United States. At this point, the class is accustomed to the description, and many have begun to form opinions of both the list and its professor. This list is used deliberately, to make the point about the unspoken cultural assumptions, particularly the ones that assume maleness when no feminizing gendered signifiers are present.

In 2019, with the advent of the #MeToo movement, the many women who ran for public office and won, and the ongoing strides that women appear to be making, one might wonder why gender reveal parties are popular now. As more women are becoming vocal about being abused by powerful men, and simultaneously more women are taking on powerful roles traditionally held by men, gender should be less, not more, of an issue for parents. This is yet another discussion topic educators might use, along with the creation of a list (on the board) of where strides have been made, and where the culture might be sliding backward or making no movement in terms of gender equity.

Lesson #3: Formally Introducing the Concept of the Male Gaze

The discussion of language and the conflation of sex and gender leads to further exploration of who creates (and benefits) from these linguistic assumptions, and whether students should do anything more than be aware of these sexist assumptions. Half of the participants in the Women & Media class have heard the term "the male gaze" prior to attending class. Of this half, one or two can offer an accurate definition. The male gaze is the act of looking at the world from a masculine and heterosexual perspective which results in objectifying women as sexual objects for the pleasure of the heterosexual male viewer (Mulvey, 1997). For example, a camera shot of a woman that moves from her knees up to her face, sexualizes her before identifying her. Students are assigned several readings prior to the discussion that include Laura Mulvey's (1997) "Visual Pleasure and Narrative Cinema," Marita Sturken and Lisa Cartwright's (2001) essay "The Gaze," bell hooks' (1996) "The Oppositional Gaze, Black Female Spectators," E. Ann Kaplan's (2000) "Is the Gaze Male?" and Megan Angelo's (2016) "Let's Rewrite Hollywood, Shall We?"

In the classroom, I guide students on an exploration of the ubiquity of the male gaze, not only in art, but also literature, popular music, from the Opera to the Opry, and religion. For instance, the Ancient Hebrew story of Adam and Eve (which is also the creation story for Christianity and Islam) is told from the male gaze perspective. Adam, given control of everything on Earth by a deity considered male in contemporary culture, becomes controlled by Eve, who tempts him to eat an apple from the Tree of Knowledge, which he does. This one-time subordination of Adam to Eve is not logical, particularly when the more egalitarian version that Adam and Eve ate the fruit *together* makes more sense, given the backstory. Students are invited to consider how the male-gendered version of the story has, throughout history, enabled religiously enforced the supremacy of men. This is an eventuality that seems to have happened in translation, however, as the original Ancient Hebraic version of the story does not feature a specifically masculine deity. The original text refers to god as a balance of masculine and feminine traits (Barton, 2015).

The original biblical text was first translated into Greek. The Greek patriarchy created democracy, though the only voting citizens in Greece were Athenian males. One of the Greeks' creation myths was the story of the first woman, Pandora, who, as the story is told by Hesiod (c. 700 BCE) in *Works and Days*, appeared on Earth after men had lived without women for a long time, and she, Pandora, brought to the world suffering, and death, along with hope (West, 2008, pp. 39–40). This mythology and the translation history leads to a discussion of whether the original biblical text of a story that, arguably, has influenced many religions and even more human interactions, from the Crusades through the present, would have had a different effect if the original understanding of the deity as multi-gendered or ungendered had been accurately translated. A secondary question about why antiquity's translators, who were men, would not have translated accurately also offers a chance to explore the concept of the male gaze.

Students are encouraged to identify the male gaze in current media through an analysis of popular music, media, art, and public discourse. To do this, students name their favorite form of entertainment, and as a group they analyze, by listening to lyrics, watching videos, and looking at images in art, how much or little the male gaze influences the entertainment they consume. For example, some students mentioned they really enjoyed the most recent version of *Wonder Woman* (2017). The group assessed whether the imagery in this film had moved past relying on the male gaze. An analysis of the costumes worn by the Amazons and (non-Amazon demigod) Wonder Woman led to their determination that with so much skin showing, and so few blemishes, including scars, this woman superhero (designed by a female director) is still scantily clad and thus not as well armored (and therefore not as well protected) as her men counterparts. The 2017 *Wonder Woman* still plays to the male gaze as the titular character and her "fellow" Amazons are still objectified for their flawless beauty. This results in women being objectified for the visual pleasure of the heterosexual male. Educators could contrast *Wonder Woman* (2017) with the 2016 *Ghostbusters* reboot in which the female heroes are dressed, like their 1984 male counterparts, for work, not beauty, in one-piece jumpsuits.

Students next revisit the consideration of representations of men and women political candidates, first in print, then in television and internet news. They are reminded of the prevalence of men, and therefore the cis-, EuroAmerican, ableist, heteropatriarchal male gaze, in much of media creation. We analyze Matt Lauer's interviews of 2016 presidential candidates Trump and Clinton along with the reading from *The New York Times*, "When Our Trusted Storytellers are Also the Abusers" (Rogers, 2017). Following this example of the male gaze, specifically the cis-, EuroAmerican, ableist, heteropatriarchal gaze, students find examples of current candidates' representations in print and digital media which are then discussed. As students watch the interviews, with the hindsight of Lauer's abuses, they begin to see the double standard of competence and likeability to which female, but not male, candidates are held (Elsesser, 2019). This is reinforced by Sheryl Sandberg's (2010) TED talk "Why we have too few women leaders" which supplies the perspective of women and power by one of the few COOs (Chief Operating Officer) of a top-tier company (Facebook). It is interesting to note that Facebook, which was launched in 2004 by Mark Zuckerberg and his four (male) college roommates, was started ostensibly as a social media networking service, and was, in fact, a male-gaze vehicle by which college men objectified college women on social media, through a "hot or not" game comparing two female students and deciding which was more attractive (Kaplan, 2003).

These considerations lead to an analysis of the #MeToo movement that made headlines in 2017, after allegations about Harvey Weinstein's decades of sexual abuse of women were made public (Kantor & Twohey, 2017; Farrow, 2017). The #MeToo movement is met with various reactions from students, and again brings to the forefront the idea of an individual's gaze and how the representation of an object as a function of that gaze distorts the object (Mack & Rock, 1998). When the object is a human being, a woman for example, that distortion dehumanizes the person (Lewinsky, 2018), making her (for the heterosexual male gaze) seem inferior to the one who is gazing. The inferiority of the objectified person is what makes it wrong, particularly from a feminist perspective. In the years since the Weinstein accusations brought #MeToo to the social media forefront, students, particularly male students, have slowly found the confidence to question the assumptions and perceived dangers of this media-generated social movement. They speak from the anxiety of being unjustly accused and voice fear of a mob or vigilante mentality and the possibility of revenge rather than justice. One example of a conversation that highlights the perceived dangers of the #MeToo movement came from a male student who noted that as a man, he enjoys looking at beautiful women, and he said that he feels he cannot do that anymore without fear that #MeToo will accuse him. He went on to ask, if he is accused, how does he protect himself, noting that sex sells, and #MeToo makes that wrong.

To address comments like this, educators should lead students in a discussion of what is wrong with trying to make "sex sells" frowned upon. If making sex sell without objectifying one sex or the other, and certainly without objectifying one sex 90% more than another (Kozlowska, 2014), were possible, it would not be the type of problem that it is today, when the majority of those objectified are women, and the ones doing the objectifying are men. This is because, theoretically, everyone's body would be equally gazed at as an object of beauty and commerce. The fact is that making sex sell without objectification is not possible, and when only one sex is objectified, sexual misconduct, sexual abuses, and the use of sex as power is bound to follow. The conversation moves to discussing ways to change this situation so that sex sells equally for everyone, or other concepts than sex (e.g., happiness, fun, empowerment) might be selling points instead (Kozlowska, 2014).

Another way to address this issue is to suggest that if the public were not opposed to seeing a male or female half naked, or both fully frontally naked (not just women), there would be less of a problem because the representation, and objectification, would be equal. But think of it this way: How many women must walk by images of scantily clad women on the sides of busses or on billboards? Make no mistake: the lack of an equal number of representations of naked or underdressed males shows an unequal number of times that women, but not men, are undermined in this way. In this context, everyday advertising and its constant objectification of women has the same subtle derogatory effect (Plakoyiannaki et al., 2008; Capella et al., 2010; Sturken & Cartwright, 2001). Students are inclined to make blanket statements such as "But that's art" or "It's just an ad." My response is that art has been created as a function of the male gaze for at least two thousand years, and longer (Berger, 1972). Advertising, for instance, has followed the example of art. The point here is to take the first step, to recognize the objectification, to acknowledge the prevalence of the male gaze, and to become more conscious of sexism that has been, up to now, the unconscious byproduct of a cis-, EuroAmerican, ableist, heteropatriarchy.

Lesson #4: Addressing Homophobia, Sexism, Transphobia, Misogyny in Media and the Classroom— Inclusivity as Pedagogical Praxis

The Women & Media class focuses on thoughtful media consumption, and the message is that the words, and by extension, the images, that we use matter in the representation of subjects, including the subject of one's ideology. The deliberate use of the phrase, "cis-, EuroAmerican, ableist, heteropatriarchy" is intended to model the use of labels, and to serve as a continuous reminder of the attributes that are unlabeled, or "unmarked" in our culture as described in Anita Sarkeesian's (2013) video, "Feminist Frequency's Tropes versus Women in Video Games," which underscores the idea of gendered signifiers and what is marked, and what is not, in our culture. After watching the video, a class discussion ensues about marking misogyny and the male gaze. This discussion is often introduced in the online learning management system (Blackboard) first, so that participants can express their initial thoughts online after watching the video and then continue the discussion in the face-to-face class. This way students can view the video, reflect a bit, then formulate their first thoughts before coming to class. This method also saves class time and ensures that everyone can respond to the video. The focus of the discussion starts with the use of the concepts "tropes," "gendered signifiers," and "labeling" and moves on to an exploration of the reaction that Sarkeesian received in connection with her Feminist Frequency videos (Rensin, 2015). This leads to another interrogation of the male gaze, and how labeling works to reinforce a set of norms within our culture, specifically, those of the cis-, EuroAmerican, ableist, heteropatriarchy to the detriment of those who do not fit into any or all those categories. The result is culturally-, religiously-, and linguistically-reinforced transphobia, homophobia, sexism, and misogyny as any combination of trans/fluid, non-EuroAmerican, differently-abled, and non-hetero (queer), non-patriarchal (but not necessarily matriarchal) prerogatives challenge the existing norms and bring into question the culturally- and religiously-held beliefs that have, over time, been linguistically inculcated. Individual students' final projects might document the ways that the norms are reinforced within the culture and try to answer the question: How might the language and culture be different if these norms were not enforced so absolutely?

At some point in the class, the continued use of the phrase cis-, EuroAmerican, ableist, heteropatriarchy brings up the following question: Why are women so angry about the things we talk about in this class? The first time I was asked that question directly, it surprised me. I had been talking about the women's march on Washington after the 2016 election. We watched Ashley Judd's (2014) "Nasty Woman" recitation on YouTube, and I had made a comment about it being an example of a counter-gaze to the cis-, EuroAmerican, ableist, heteropatriarchy because it is the statement of a clearly female point of view written by a poet who is speaking objection (if not truth) to power. Judd's recitation is controversial because of its language, the subjects it touches on, and, for some, because it is presented in an angry female tone. The subjects addressed underscore the inequity within the culture, and thus, the angry tone is appropriate, even if discomfiting for some.

Lesson #4A: Projection, Prejudices, and Professionalism—Passionate Professor or Another Angry Feminist?

A non-traditional student, about mid-age, who had been vocal in class all along, spoke up and asked, "Okay, but why are you so angry when you talk about it?" It was an interesting mirror for me, and I asked what made me seem angry. "Your voice is raised, you're pacing around while you're talking, I guess." There is an art to asking an elegant question and to walking a fine line between curiosity and defensiveness. I did not want to be defensive on this issue, and I was curious about his experience of me in class. I asked what the difference was for him, and the rest of the class, between passion and anger. Could a person be passionate without being angry? When Marines yell "HUAA!" are they angry? When football players spike the ball in the end zone after scoring a touchdown, are they angry? How do we know? If women are feminists, are they automatically angry? If feminists are animated, excited, or passionate about something, does that make them angry? Does my repeated cis-, EuroAmerican, ableist, hetero-patriarchy statement, because I have been repeating it, make me seem angry when I am feeling passionate? There are two things to consider regarding how passion and anger are perceived in relation to women. One is that yes, being confronted, or assaulted even, by sexism daily can make one angry. The other is that women who are feeling, and acting passionately, animatedly, and excitedly about something are not necessarily angry, though often they are accused of being angry when they are not. It's important that educators stress that labeling women who are passionate as being angry is dismissive and is related to the concept of projection.

Projection is a psychological term that parallels the film technology of the same name. Psychologically, a person projects onto another an unverified set of experiences, events, and likeability factors. This is a fun mini lesson to present because during the presentation, educators will witness students experience "aha moments," particularly when they observe that everyone tells stories about everyone else all the time. I ask students, when they first walked into the classroom, looked at me, what story about me came into their mind? Sideways glances or downward gazes accompanied by subtle smiles indicate acknowledgment of the storytelling. I tell them that the story, whatever it was, came from their experiences, unconnected to anything about me. I go on to guess aloud that when I opened my mouth, the story shifted, or became enhanced. Students are surprised to learn that I also told myself a story about each student when they walked in. When people are aware that it is a story they made up, they can put it aside after a while. That story is a projection. With awareness, anyone can more easily hear facts that are less distorted by projection. Educators can ask: how does this discussion of projection affect the consideration of passion versus anger?

The discussion that follows in intended to enable students to interrogate their own projections and realize that for anyone to know whether someone is angry or passionate, they must ask. I also ask students to substitute "passionate" for "angry" to determine whether that changes anything in their understanding about what I am communicating. A discussion about the male gaze and how it influences projections may or may not be part of this discussion. The two concepts are connected because the male gaze is often the defining gaze, and thus it determines how the objects of that gaze are interpreted, or if they are even worthy of notice (and "worthiness" is itself an interpretation, recall the origins of Facebook).

Modeling that "the political is personal," and addressing questions of prejudice, microaggressions, and projections can lead to one being either inauthentic on the one hand, or too personal (read: unprofessional) on the other. The ways to avoid these pitfalls can vary among individuals and institutions. One starts with awareness of the goal (in this case, to teach about feminism, the male gaze, and labels in media), and of one's own vicissitudes. As one to whom at least some parts of the cis-, EuroAmerican, ableist, heteropatriarchal label applies, educators must remember that in their classroom, "inclusivity" also includes those to whom the entire label applies, those who, perhaps for the first time, are realizing that they are not necessarily in the majority. Educators must include everyone, normative/mainstream and non-normative/queer, or else learning will not occur. One cannot assume everyone experiences the world the way they do, and questioning one's personal prejudices, microaggressions, and projections provides the model for promoting greater understanding among people, which is a goal for media studies and media generally, and therefore also a political goal.

Lesson #5: What's in a Name? Of Ladies, Madams, and Title IX

For some, the concept of masculinity as the unmarked norm (Sarkeesian, 2013) is difficult, so educators might supply an example from sports. Title IX of the Education Amendments act of 1972 is a federal law that states: "No person in the United States shall, on the basis of sex, be excluded from participation in, be denied the benefits of, or be subjected to discrimination under any education program or activity receiving Federal financial assistance" (US Department of Justice, 1972). In college sports, that means that if a school provides a men's team in a sport, there must be an equivalent women's team, with equivalent playing conditions, so that if there is a men's lacrosse team, there must be a women's lacrosse team, men's and women's track, men's baseball and women's softball. At this point we stop and have a brief discussion of why women are excluded from playing baseball, and the idea that "soft" ball is (a) not really soft (but is contrasted with "hard" ball), and (b) considered "appropriate" for women as an outgrowth of the male gaze which expects women to be soft and "lady-like."

Additionally, professional softball does not offer the same income opportunities as professional baseball (Berri, 2018), so does the baseball-softball pairing really follow the Title IX guidelines? In fact, thirty-seven years after the enactment of Title IX, in 2009, the NCAA ruled that baseball and softball are two different sports, and under Title IX women cannot be denied a tryout on the baseball team (Baseballforall.com). Also, and pertinent for the class, educators might discuss whether Title IX includes equal media coverage of men's and women's college team games, with most students reporting that their school's men's and women's basketball games get equal air time, unlike the 4% coverage that women's sports gets in mainstream media reporting, according to the Tucker Center (2014) and Neiman Reports (2019).

The next question is more difficult because it challenges an existing practice at many colleges: Does Title IX coverage also mean not prioritizing (by not marking) men in team names as in "The Bulls" and "The Lady Bulls"? What exactly is a "Lady Bull"? When I ask whether the women's team should be called "The Cows," this usually gets a laugh, which leads us to a discussion of the difference in nomenclature and imagery between fire-snorting, seeing-red "Bulls" (intended to inspire fear) and cud-chewing, placid "Cows" (which inspires laughter). Is "Lady Bulls" a better choice of team name than "Cows"?

It is worth considering the word "lady" and the historically oppressive, now-unspoken cultural imperatives that accompany it. Why are women athletes, for example, called "lady"? Calling women athletes "lady" evokes misogynist, homophobic, and patriarchal assumptions that inform the use of "lady" in front of the team name. This is so, because culturally speaking, "ladies" were expected to be quiet, well-bred, genteel, well-behaved, subordinate, weak, and not outspoken, assertive, competitive, or athletic and thus strong.

A brief aside about the word "Madam" follows in this context, from the French translation "my lady." While some might view it as an intended honorific, it also signifies a woman who runs a brothel, and this suggests possible contingent issues for the use of "Madam" as in "Madam President." In the classroom, educators accompany this discussion with a video clip from Episode 66 of the Netflix series, *House of Cards* (Dobbs & Davies, 2018) that underscores this point. In the scene, President Clare Underwood (Robin Wright) notes that, "'Madam President' makes me sound like I'm running a brothel, not a country." After playing the clip, transitioning back to the discussion about adopting more egalitarian method of naming teams is ideal.

In the Olympics, as in professional soccer, the men's and women's teams are both labeled according to gender. In contrast, as emphasized earlier, professional basketball still affords prioritization to men since the WNBA must add a gender-signifying label. The egalitarian solution would be to label both leagues the MNBA and WNBA, respectively. While most basketball fans would not be open to the idea, the discussion offers opportunities to indicate the workings of projection, the male gaze, and media coverage (and the lack thereof) in public perception and monetization. The question of why women's sports are considered less exciting, paired with the 4% mainstream sports coverage of women's sports, challenges participants to reconsider their presumptions in terms of media coverage. The UConn Huskies women's basketball team is much more successful (16–0 win-loss record in 2018) than the men's (7–11 in 2016) team, but a Google search of "UConn Huskies" reports on the men's team only. To find the women's team, one must add the word 'women.' Similarly, while the United States women's soccer team is more successful and exciting, and, in 2019, more watched than its U.S. male counterpart, women's soccer is covered less in mainstream news. Additionally, the women are paid much less than the men, even after winning their fourth World Cup title, like they did in 2019 (Baker, 2019). Also discussed in class is whether increasing the reportage of women's teams would combat both the pay disparity and the effects of the male gaze. Educators should discuss these forms of oppression in semesters to come, continually adapting its contents based on media, current events, and students' needs.

Conclusion

The classroom pedagogy set out in this chapter aims to counter the male gaze by, for example, presenting statistics pertinent to women, distinguishing between the sex term female and the cultural term woman, and by using, as much as possible, descriptive labels for all, including repeating the "cis-, EuroAmerican, ableist, heteropatriarchy" descriptor to highlight the exclusivity implied when not everyone is labeled.

At the end of the course, after we talk about the cultural assumption of "male" as the norm, I ask the final question: Does it matter the gender of the person teaching this course? On an exam, this question would ask students to respond in terms of labels, projections, the male gaze, and the cis-, EuroAmerican, ableist, heteropatriarchy. Readers of this chapter might consider whether my gender impacts how they read the essay, or whether they assumed that I was a specific gender, and whether it affects their attributions of authority to the author.

References

Angelo, M. (2016, January 21). Let's rewrite Hollywood, shall we? *Glamour.com*. Retrieved from https://www.glamour.com/story/female-directors-and-writers-rewrite-male-dominated-movies.

Baker, N. (2019, July 9). What explains the pay gap in women's soccer? *BigThink.com*. Retrieved from https://bigthink.com/politics-current-affairs/womens-soccer-pay.

Barton, M. (2015, April 21). Gender-bender god: Masculine or feminine? *Black Theology*, 7(2), 142–166. doi:10.1558/blth.u712142.

Baseballforall.com. (2019). First she was denied then she made the team: A parent's story. *Baseballforall.com*. Retrieved from https://www.baseballforall.com/right-to-play

Berger, J. (1972). *Ways of seeing*. New York, NY: Penguin.

Berri, D. (2018, August 20). National pro fastpitch after 15 years is like major league baseball a century ago. *Forbes*. Retrieved from https://www.forbes.com/sites/davidberri/2018/08/20/national-pro-fastpitch-after-15-years-is-like-major-league-baseball-a-century-ago/#13e3c1ab60b7.

Boroditsky, L., Schmidt, L., & Phillips W. (2002). Sex, syntax, and semantics. In D. Gentener & S. Goldin-Meadow (Eds.), *Language in mind: Advances in the study of language and cognition* (pp. 61–80). Cambridge, UK: Cambridge University Press.

Capella, M., Hill, R., Rapp, J., & Kees, J. (2010). The impact of violence against women in advertisements. *Journal of Advertising*, 39(4), 37–51. Retrieved from www.jstor.org/stable/25780658.

Cherland, M. (2008/2009). Commentary: Harry's girls: Harry Potter and the discourse of gender. *Journal of Adolescent & Adult Literacy*, 52(4), 273–82.

Clark, B., & Higonnet, M. (1999). *Girls, boys, books, toys: Gender in children's literature and culture*. Baltimore, MD: Johns Hopkins University Press.

Dauge-Roth, C. (2019, August 1). France claims its language is already gender-inclusive. History shows it's not. *Frenchly*. Retrieved from https://frenchly.us/france-claims-its-language-is-already-gender-inclusive-history-shows-its-not/.

Dobbs, M., & Davies, A. (writers) & Sakarhov, A. (director). (2018, November 2). Episode 66. [Television series episode]. In B. Willmon (creator) *House of cards*. Netflix.

Elsesser, K. (2019, January 8). The truth about likeability and female presidential candidates. *Forbes*. Retrieved from https://www.forbes.com/sites/kimelsesser/2019/01/08/the-truth-about-likability-and-female-presidential-candidates/#5e35862c646d.

Farrow, R. (2017, October 10). From aggressive overtures to sexual assault: Harvey Weinstein's accusers tell their stories. *The New Yorker*. Retrieved from https://www.newyorker.com/news/news-desk/from-aggressive-overtures-to-sexual-assault-harvey-weinsteins-accusers-tell-their-stories.

Fausto-Sterling, A. (1993). The five sexes: Why male and female are not enough. *The Sciences*. March/April, 20–24.

Fine, C. (2010). *Delusions of gender how our minds, society, and neurosexism create difference.* New York, NY: Norton.

Galliardo, X., & Smith, C. J. (2003). Cinderfella: J.K. Rowling's wily web of gender. In G. L. Anatol (Ed.), *Reading Harry Potter: Critical essays* (pp. 191–206). NY: Praeger.

Halberstam, J. J. (1998). *Female masculinity.* NC: Duke University Press.

Hendrix, H. (1990). *Getting the love you want.* NY: Harper Perennial.

Hesiod. (2008). *Theogony; and, works and days* (M. L. West, Trans.). Oxford World's Classics (Original work published ca 700 B.C.E.).

hooks, b. (1996). The oppositional gaze black female spectators. In J. Belton (Ed.), *Movies and mass culture* (pp. 247–265). NJ: Rutgers University Press.

Judd, A. (2014, January 21). "I am a nasty woman" YouTube [Video]. Retrieved from https://www.youtube.com/watch?v=w8IApUwjHU8.

Kantor, J., & Twohey, M. (2017, October 5). Harvey Weinstein paid off sexual harassment accusers for decades. *The New York Times.* Retrieved from https://www.nytimes.com/2017/10/05/us/harvey-weinstein-harassment-allegations.html?auth=login-email&login=email.

Kaplan, E. A. (2000). Is the gaze male? In E. A. Kaplan (Ed.), *Feminism and film* (pp. 119–138). UK: Oxford University Press.

Kaplan, K. A. (2003, November 19). Facemash creator survives ad board. *Harvard crimson.* Retrieved from https://www.thecrimson.com/article/2003/11/19/facemash-creator-survives-ad-board-the/.

Konishi, T. (1993). The semantics of grammatical gender: A cross-cultural study. *Journal of Psycholinguistic Research, 22*(5), 519–534.

Kozlowska, H. (2014, August 14). What sells better: Sexy or empowered? *The New York Times.* Retrieved from https://op-talk.blogs.nytimes.com/2014/08/14/what-sells-better-sexy-or-empowered/?_php=true&_type=blogs&_r=1

Lewinsky, M. (2018, March 2). Emerging from the "The house of the gaslight" in the age of #MeToo. *Vanity Fair.* Retrieved from https://www.vanityfair.com/news/2018/02/monica-lewinsky-in-the-age-of-metoo.

Mack, A., & Rock, I. (1998). *Inattentional blindness.* MI: MIT Press.

McCallum, R. (1999). *Ideologies of identity in adolescent fiction the dialogic construction of subjectivity.* NJ: Garland Press.

McCoubrey, C. (2017, November 16). Opinion; Toppling the grammar patriarchy. *The New York Times.* Retrieved from https://www.nytimes.com/2017/11/16/opinion/french-sexism-grammar-everybody.html.

Mulvey, L. (1997). Visual pleasure and narrative cinema. In R. Warhol & D. P. Herndl (Eds.), *Feminisms* (pp. 438–48). NJ: Rutgers University Press.

Nieman Reports. (2019). 7 Ways to improve coverage of women's sports. *NeimanReports.org.* Retrieved from https://niemanreports.org/articles/covering-womens-sports/.

O'Brien, C. (2017, December 6). The battle to make French a gender-neutral language is emphasizing the country's inherent sexism. *Medium.com*. Retrieved from https://medium.com/au-milieu/war-of-the-words-the-battle-to-make-the-french-language-gender-neutral-7c2329003c9d.

Paoletti, J. (2012). *Pink and blue: Telling the boys from the girls in America*. IN: Indiana University Press.

Plakoyiannaki, E., Mathioudaki, K., Dimitratos, P., & Zotos, Y. (2008). Images of women in online advertisements of global products: Does sexism exist? *Journal of Business Ethics, 83*(1), 101–112.

Pollitt, K. (1991, April 7). Hers; The Smurfette principle. *The New York Times*. Retrieved from https://www.nytimes.com/1991/04/07/magazine/hers-the-smurfette-principle.html.

Pulitzer. (2017, February 12). GAP: Gender and the Pulitzer prize. *Pulitzer.org*. Retrieved from https://www.pulitzer.org/event/gap-gender-and-pulitzer-prize.

Rensin, E. (2015, August 18). The internet is full of men who hate feminism. Here's what they're like in person. *Vox.com*. Retrieved from https://www.vox.com/2015/2/5/7942623/mens-rights-movement.

Rogers, K. (2017, November 30). When our trusted storytellers are also the abusers. *The New York Times*. Retrieved from https://www.nytimes.com/2017/11/30/us/politics/sexual-harassment-media-politics-lauer.html.

Sandberg, S. (2010, December 21). Why we have too few women leaders [Video]. TED.com. Retrieved from https://www.ted.com/talks/sheryl_sandberg_why_we_have_too_few_women_leaders?language=en.

Sarkeesian, A. (2013, November 18). Ms. Male character—tropes vs women [Video]. Feminist Frequency. Retrieved from https://feministfrequency.com/video/ms-male-character-tropes-vs-women/.

Sundeep, B., Goodwin, G., & Walasek, L. (2018). Trait associations for Hillary Clinton and Donald Trump in news media a computational analysis. *Social, Psychological, and Personality Science, 9*(2) 123–130. doi:10.1177/1948550617751584.

Sturken, M., & Cartwright, L. (2001). Spectatorship, power & knowledge. In *The practices of looking: An introduction to visual culture* (pp. 72–108). Oxford, UK: Oxford University Press.

Tucker Center. (2014). Media coverage & female athletes. *University of Minnesota*. Retrieved from https://www.cehd.umn.edu/tuckercenter/projects/mediacoverage.html

United Nations. (2014, September 22). *Emma Watson at the HeForShe campaign 2014 – Official UN* [Video]. YouTube. Retrieved from https://www.youtube.com/watch?v=gkjW9PZ-BRfk.

US Department of Justice. (1972). Title IX of the education amendments of 1972. *Justice.gov*. Retrieved from https://www.justice.gov/crt/title-ix-education-amendments-1972.

Wickens, C. M. (2011). Codes, silences, and homophobia: Challenging normative assumptions about gender and sexuality in contemporary LGBTQ young adult literature. *Children's Literature in Education, 42*(2), 148–164.

WNBA. (2019). The official rules of the WNBA. *WNBA.com.* Retrieved from https://www.wnba.com/wnba-rule-book/

Women's Media Center (2019, February 21). The status of women in the U.S. media 2019. *Women's Media Center.* Retrieved from https://tools.womensmediacenter.com/page/-/WMCStatusofWomeninUSMedia2019.pdf.

CHAPTER SEVEN

Grammatical Gender Trouble: Counteracting the Discriminatory Nature of Grammatically Gendered Languages

ZUZANNA A. JUSIŃSKA

Introduction

The extensive debate about pronoun and neopronoun use in sociopolitical literature and the philosophy of language disciplines signals the importance of conveying gender-related information in language. In English-speaking countries, nonbinary people are gaining increasingly more recognition. Correlated with this increased recognition is the popularization of using the singular "they" as a personal pronoun. Missing from the debate, however, is the consideration of how to speak about nonbinary, gender non-conforming and intersex individuals in grammatically gendered languages. This chapter sets out to explain the difference between grammatically gendered languages and languages with natural gender. The differences between these languages cause the divergence between feminist strategies and reveal unequal possibilities for using gender-neutral language. Next, the analysis explores utterances with grammatically gendered expressions within a Gricean framework and speech act theory. It is followed by a discussion of analysis outcomes and a modified approach to information about sex/gender conveyed in language. In the last section of this chapter, a framework for how this modified approach can account for alternative ways of expressing oneself in grammatically gendered languages practiced by nonbinary users is presented. Examples of alternative linguistic practices of nonbinary Polish speakers are shared and strategies for teaching grammatically gendered languages that can enhance critical thinking about language are proposed.

This chapter targets dual audiences. First, it is aimed at educators teaching language courses in grammatically gendered languages in which case the analysis part of this chapter may seem less practical than the last part featuring inclusive strategies for teaching language courses. Nonetheless, it is the analysis and approach to sex/gender-related information proposed in this chapter that explain how linguistic practices are tied to the social reality of hegemonic masculinity, and why these ties are bound in grammatically gendered languages. Second, it is aimed at educators teaching philosophy of language and linguistics courses, both in languages with grammatical gender and those without it. Those who teach in grammatically gendered languages may find the inclusive strategies for teaching language courses helpful since they include some general remarks about addressing students in ways that avoid reinforcing gendered stereotypes. Most philosophy of language and linguistics courses usually examine Gricean pragmatics, speech act theory, as well as presupposition and common ground. That said, these courses usually do not cover how to model sex/gender-related information in a way that includes transgender, nonbinary, gender non-conforming, and intersex people. Courses taught in languages without grammatical gender often do not address sex/gender-related information in any manner what-so-ever. This chapter provides educators teaching philosophy of language and linguistics courses with a step-by-step analysis of grammatically gendered utterances making use of Gricean pragmatics, speech act theory, presupposition, and common ground.

Grammatical Gender, Natural Gender and Gender-Neutrality in Language

Grammatical gender is a noun class system which divides nouns into two or three classes (e.g., feminine, masculine, and, in some languages, neuter), but it also manifests itself in other parts of speech such as pronouns, adjectives, and verbs. Further, these parts of speech are required to agree with the gender of the noun they refer to, which usually is said to reflect the gender of the noun's referent when the referent is a person or, in some languages, a nonhuman animal. With inanimate nouns, the grammatical gender is conventional and depends on the formal qualities of the noun rather than its semantic qualities. In some grammatically gendered languages (e.g., German, Polish, Bulgarian), there is a neuter gender but there is no one way of categorizing an animate noun as one of neuter gender. For example, in Polish, nouns referring to babies such as dziecko (child), niemowlę (infant), szczenię (puppy) are of neuter gender, while in German there are several types of nouns marked as neuter (e.g., das Mädchen, meaning girl).

Not every language has grammatical gender. Despite there being genderless languages, this chapter compares grammatically gendered languages to those that only have natural gender. Since this work is written in English, grammatically gendered languages are compared using the English language, a language with natural gender which can be found in pronouns (e.g., he, she) and gender-specific nouns (e.g., brother, stewardess). The English language is easy to use in a gender-neutral manner. Levi Hord (2016) compared how gender-neutral language developed and is used in grammatically gendered languages (French and German) and those of natural gender (English and Swedish). Grammatically gendered languages are more challenging to use in a gender-neutral way. This happens because every animate noun has a grammatical gender that corresponds to the sex/gender of the referent and because the forms of distinct parts of speech must agree with the gender of the noun used. In effect, the sex/gender of the referent is indicated not only by the noun used but by the forms of adjectives, verbs, and pronouns that refer to it. Before exploring this further, I wish to make clear that the phrase "sex/gender" will be used throughout this chapter, since the category of "biological sex" is as socially constructed as the category of "gender" (Butler, 1990; Fausto-Sterling, 2008; Ziemińska, 2018).

Natural gender languages have far fewer expressions indicating sex/gender of the referent than grammatically gendered ones, and because of this difference, feminist strategies in these two types of languages diverge. Within grammatically gendered languages, these strategies focus on creating and popularizing feminine versions of professions, positions, and titles. Feminine versions seek to fight the invisibility of women in professional fields and stereotypes concerning "typically male" social roles. On the other hand, feminist strategies within natural gender languages have two main focuses: working against the usage of masculine pronouns and nouns as generic, as well as against the feminization of titles and positions. Both are sexist linguistic practices which strengthen the patriarchal social structure. The usage of the generic "he" erases women from discourse and reinforces treating masculinity as a norm which marginalizes women. The feminization of titles and positions creates a sex/gender distinction in professional and social fields, which has a less obvious (but fundamental for hegemonic masculinity) effect of normalizing and reinforcing the sex/gender binary.

English guidelines for non-sexist language usually include eliminating the use of the generic "he," using "Ms." instead of "Miss" and "Mrs.," using gender-neutral forms when we do not know the gender of the referent (e.g., writing "Dear Colleague," "Professor" instead of "Dear Sir or Madam") and when gender is not relevant (e.g., using "chairperson" instead of "chairman" or "chairwoman") (Warren, 1986). Using the singular "they" is increasing in popularity when referring to a person whose gender is unknown (e.g., "someone left their wallet at the table") and when referring to those of nonbinary, gender non-conforming, and intersex persons who prefer gender-neutral pronouns (e.g., "this is Alex"). Even though the singular "they" has appeared in texts written by Jane Austen, Walter Scott, and even William Shakespeare, there are still many voices deeming the singular "they" incorrect (Bodine, 1975). In September 2019, the debate concerning the correctness of "they" was clarified when the Merriam-Webster dictionary added its forth definition which is "used to refer to a single person whose gender identity is nonbinary" and posted a note explaining this decision ("A Note on the Nonbinary They," 2019). The note stated that all new words entered in Merriam-Webster must meet the following three criteria: meaningful use, sustained use, and widespread use. The singular pronoun "they" used to refer to nonbinary persons meets all three criteria.

Conversely, there are compelling arguments for making "they," or a different gender-neutral pronoun, even more widespread by adopting it for everyone, thus moving towards genderless English (Wayne, 2005; Dembrof & Wodak, 2018; Saguy et al., 2019). As Robin Demobrof & Daniel Wodak (2018) claim, pronouns are problematic since they indicate the sex/gender of the referent. Grammatically gendered languages have expressions that indicate the sex/gender of the referent, since all nouns have grammatical gender and various parts of speech must accord with that gender.

In English, it is easy to refrain from using gender-specific nouns, ask individuals what pronouns they prefer, or to avoid pronouns by repeating a person's name. Unfortunately, speakers of grammatically gendered languages must gender themselves and others with most utterances. Even when the information about one's gender is not what they want to communicate, the language they speak forces them to do so. Why is this important in terms of resisting the hegemonic masculinity? Linguistic practices, especially in languages that somehow convey information about referents' sex/gender, are closely interwind with the social reality of hegemonic masculinity. Many languages have grammatical rules, such as generic "he" or using the masculine plural when there is at least one man in a group, which treats maleness as norm. Most of grammatically gendered languages make it almost impossible to speak in a gender-neutral manner, which imposes obligatory gender binary. Discursive mechanisms of imposing obligatory gender binary and treating maleness as norm both serve the patriarchal system by reinforcing two of its main axioms. The first is that there are only two genders (understood as two sets of character traits) tied by nature to two biological sexes (understood as two sets of physical traits). The second one is that the traits, either character or physical, displayed by males is superior by nature. As the relationship between linguistic practices and social reality is reciprocal, choosing, and often inventing, linguistic practices alternative to the traditional patriarchal and cisnormative ones, is one of the ways of fighting the hegemonic masculinity.

The Analysis

Feminist philosophy of language has primarily focused on critiquing the maleness of the English language (Moulton, 1981; Penelope, 1990; Spender, 1980) and analyzing pornography and rape within the framework of the speech act theory (Langton, 1993; McGowan, 2003; MacKinnon, 1993). There is also a rather wide literature about language and gender, and language and sexuality, although it focuses mainly on the way we speak about ourselves and others (Livia & Hall, 1997; Vitanova, 2010; McConnell-Ginet, 2011; Litoselliti, 2013), and not about the grammatical forms of language itself. The focus here will be on the ways in which grammar limits speakers' communicative ability and forces them to communicate more than they wish to. This is done by comparing English sentences to their Polish translation, since Polish, besides being this author's native language, is a perfect example of a grammatically gendered one.

The Analysis within Gricean Framework

A fundamental distinction in Grice's (1975) theory is one of "what is said" versus "what is communicated." The notion of what is said is connected to lexical meanings of expressions used and does not require appealing to conversational implicatures or intentions of interlocutors, without which identifying what is communicated is impossible. How does one identify what is communicated? Grice claims that a conversation is, at least on some level, an act of cooperation that has a purpose, with adequate and inadequate conversational moves. Grice formulates the Cooperative Principle (CP), which is supposed to be ceteris paribus observed by interlocutors: "Make your conversational contribution such as is required, at the stage at which it occurs, by the accepted purpose or direction of the talk exchange in which you are engaged" (1975, p. 45). The overall Cooperative Principle consists of conversational maxims which fall into four categories: Quantity ('Be as informative as required'), Quality ('Be truthful'), Relation ('Be relevant') and Manner ('Be perspicuous') (Grice, 1975; Levinson,

1983). For example, if A asks their friend B, "What time is it?" and B replies, "It is night" or "It is eleven, fourteen minutes, and six-seconds PM" both of these answers violate the quantity maxims. The first reply is not informative enough, and the second is too informative. If B would lie, say something unrelated to the question, or answer poetically or vaguely, they would then violate the Quality, Relation, and Manner maxims. According to Grice, when a speaker violates a conversational maxim, the hearer is faced with a minor problem: "How can [their] saying what [they] did say be reconciled with the supposition that [they are] observing the overall Cooperative Principle?" (1975, p. 49) The answer to this question is the notion of conversational implicature defined by Grice (1975). S (the speaker) saying (or making as if to say) that p conversationally implicates that q if and only if:

(i) S is to be presumed to be observing the conversational maxims, or at least the Cooperative Principle
(ii) the supposition that S thinks that q is required in order to make their saying (or making as if to say) p consistent with the Cooperative Principle
(iii) S thinks (and would expect the hearer to think that S thinks) that it is within the competence of the hearer to work out, or grasp intuitively, that the supposition mentioned in (ii) is required.

In everyday communication, speakers often violate conversational maxims. For example, when A asks B, "Do you want to have dinner tonight?" and B says, "I have an exam tomorrow," they violate a maxim of relation. However, assuming that they are observing CP, A understands that they conversationally implicate that, "I have to study for the exam, so I can't have dinner with you tonight." Considering utterances with grammatically gendered expressions within the Gricean framework, one can notice the unexpectedly common, violations of maxims of Relation and Quantity, whose combination will be called the "RQ maxim" throughout this chapter. Such utterances often violate the RQ maxim because they contain information about a person's sex/gender which is a part of what is said. Grice gives an example of a sentence: "[He is] in the grip of a vice" and states what we know about what was said:

One would know that he had said, about some particular male person or animal x, that at the time of the utterance (whatever that was), either (1) x was unable to rid himself of a certain kind of bad character trait or (2) some part of x' s person was caught in a certain kind of tool or instrument (approximate account, of course) (1975, p. 44).

Thus, we see that according to Grice, the information about the referent's sex/gender (in Grice's example conveyed in the pronoun "he") is a part of "what is said." Of course, in Grice's example this information may be relevant; for example, it can help us identify the referent. However, in the case of grammatical gender, expressions that convey information about sex/gender occur much more often, and it is grammatically impossible to avoid them. To reconcile the information about a person's sex/gender (the violation of the RQ maxim) with CP, we have to assume that this information is relevant in every context which would mean that being of a certain sex/gender is relevant in every situation.

Analyzing utterances with grammatically gendered expressions within the Gricean framework requires bringing "context" and "intentions" into account. Consider (1) uttered by the Speaker (S) to the Hearer (H), where the context of this utterance is that S is a very important person at a big law firm and says (1) as a response to H's remark about an ongoing case. Square brackets are used to explain the meaning behind foreign words.

(1) You are my assistant.

Following Grice, one can now identify "what is said" by fixing the referent of the indexical "you." "What is said" in (1):

(1.1) H assists someone.
(1.2) H assists S.

As a response to an idea about how to proceed with a case, (1) seems irrelevant, which is why H must resort to S's intentions to make sense of this utterance. S's intention is for it to be clear that H is a subordinate and their ideas will not be taken into consideration. "What is communicated" in (1):

(1) You are my subordinate, and I will not listen to your remarks.

The conversation above was an example of an ordinary conversation. Again, speakers violate conversational maxims every day, yet manage to communicate well with others. While Grice's framework accounts for that easily and elegantly, when applied to grammatically gendered languages, things become complicated. Let us see what happens when, in this same scenario, we translate the utterance into Polish:

(2) Jesteś [You are] moim [my, masculine] asystentem [assistant, masculine].

When identifying "what is said," we find another information:

(2.1) H assists someone.
(2.2) H assists S.
(2.3) H is a man.

The main reasoning that leads H to identify what was communicated is the same as in the English example. However, in this case (2.3) is not something that S wanted to communicate; it is forced by grammatical rules of the language. But that is not the only problem – (2.3) is also a violation of the RQ Maxim. Apart from identifying their boss' criticism, H has to deal with the unnecessary (2.3). What happens is that H assumes that S observes general CP and understands the intended criticism, but since (2.3) is a violation of the RQ Maxim, H also assumes that S believes that information about one's sex/gender is relevant in every context to reconcile this violation with CP.

Analyzing utterances with grammatically gendered expressions within a Gricean framework, one finds that the grammatical features of a language often force speakers to communicate something that they do not intend to communicate. Furthermore, when the information about one's sex/gender is not a part of what the speaker wants to communicate but is considered a part of "what is said," this information is a violation of the RQ maxim. According to Grice, when the hearer encounters a maxim violation on the side of the speaker, they must reconcile this with the assumption that the speaker observes the general Cooperative Principle. In the case of information about one's sex/gender, the hearer must assume that the speaker conversationally implicates that information about one's sex/gender is relevant in every context. If one analyzes utterances with grammatically gendered expressions within a Gricean framework, the result is that each of them conversationally implicates that being of a certain sex/gender is relevant in every situation.

The Analysis within Speech Act Theory

When considering utterances with grammatically gendered expressions as speech acts, they add something to each layer of a speech act. Austin (1962) distinguishes three layers of a speech act: locution, illocution, and perlocution. There are many proponents of the speech act theory whose definitions and developments of Austin's original idea often diverge (Strawson, 1964; Searle, 1969; Hare, 1970; Bach & Harnish, 1979); only. Austin's original view is briefly presented here, which is enough to see how grammatical gender affects utterances.

A locutionary act is an act of "saying something" that focuses on the semantic level of the utterance; it is an utterance of a meaningful sentence. If I say, "Bobby will lose," the meaning of the sentence itself is only that Bobby will lose, but one cannot know whether it is a prediction, a threat, or a promise from the content of the utterance. However, whenever one performs a locutionary act, one necessarily does it with an illocutionary force, which means we "do something by saying something," such as asking, asserting, and warning. The third level of a speech act is its perlocutionary effect which influences the hearer's thoughts, actions, or feelings. What is important is that the content of the speech act does not determine its illocutionary force and vice versa. Though there are many conventionalized ways of doing things with words (usually we make a promise using an expression "I promise that …" or a bet using an expression "I bet you that …"), any sentence can be used with any illocutionary force, for example, "I will come back" can be used to make a threat, a joke, or a promise.

Consider utterance (3), uttered by S to H. Throughout this section (X) will be used for utterances, (X.X) for illocutions and (X.X.X) for perlocutions.

(3) I need my 50 thousand dollars.
    (3.1) S asserts that they want their 50 thousand dollars back.
    (3.2) S orders H to give them back their 50 thousand dollars.
        (3.1.2) S causes H to be scared.
        (3.1.2) S causes H to decide to leave the country.

The meaning of the sentence uttered by S ("locutionary content") is usually considered to be a proposition expressed by said sentence (Green, 2017). (3) expresses a proposition that S needs their 50 thousand dollars. Propositions are bearers of logical value which resist translation and substitution of synonyms. Assuming we accept this view, (3) and (4) express the same proposition because (4) is a translation of (3) into Polish, and (5) and (6) express the same proposition because "bachelor" is synonymous to "unmarried man."

(4) Potrzebuję moich 50 tysięcy dolarów.
(5) John is a bachelor.
(6) John is an unmarried man.

Unfortunately, this is not so easy in every case. What happens with a proposition expressed by (7) after we translate it into Polish?

(7) I went to school.
(8) Poszłam [I went, feminine] do [to] szkoły [school].

In the case of Polish verbs, gender agreement is required in the past tense as well as in conditionals, which is why the speaker must choose one of the grammatically gendered forms: poszłam [I went, feminine] or poszedłem [I went, masculine]. The question is whether (8) expresses the same proposition as (7)? It seems impossible for (7) and (8) to express the same proposition since we can draw different inferences from them—the proposition expressed by (8) includes information about the speaker's sex/gender, while the proposition expressed by (7) does not.

When considering utterances with grammatically gendered expressions, one might wonder whether the information about the sex/gender of the referent being a part of the speech act's content does not affect its illocutionary force. Analyzing utterances with grammatically gendered expressions within speech act theory shows that the grammatically forced information about one's sex/gender affects every layer of a speech act. Using the prior examples of (8) and (9) shows the difference between them. An asterisk is used for propositions expressed by the said sentence.

(8) I went to school.
(8*) S went to school.
    (8.1) S asserts that S went to school.
    (8.2) S informs H about what S did.
        (8.1.1) S compels H to talk about what H did.
(9) Poszłam [I went, feminine] do [to] szkoły [school].
(9*) S went to school, and S is a woman.

    (9.1) S asserts that S went to school.
    (9.2) S informs H about what S did.
    (9.3) S genders S as a woman.
        (9.1.1) S compels H to talk about what H.
        (9.1.2) S compels H to have a stance on the fact of the gendering.

As already noted, the proposition expressed by (9) contains additional information about S's sex/gender, which is not a part of the proposition expressed by (8). Thus (8) and (9) do not express the same proposition. One may say that this seems like a problem for the theory of propositions assumed here and not for the actual language users, but this is not that important. What is important is that even if the speaker of (9) does not want to perform (9.3) and (9.1.2), they still occur as they are consequences of the grammatically gendered expression used in (9).

In the following examples, the focus is on the illocutionary and perlocutionary acts. Let us assume that S and H are friends studying together for a math test and S is nonbinary; after a while S sighs, hands H their notebook and says:

(10) I am so stupid!
    (10.1) S asserts that S is stupid.
    (10.2) S asks H for help with math.
        (10.1.1) S makes H laugh.
        (10.1.2) S makes H help S with math.
(11) Jestem [I am] tak [so] głupi [stupid, masculine]!
    (11.1) S asserts that S is stupid.
    (11.2) S asks H for help with math.
    (11.3) S genders S as a man.
        (11.1.1) S makes H laugh.
        (11.1.2) S makes H help S with math.
        (11.1.3) S makes H have a stance on the fact of the gendering.

Similarly, to the example before, in the English version of the utterance the illocutionary and perlocutionary acts connected to information about sex/gender do not occur. Using Polish S, intending to ask for help, must choose between a feminine or a masculine form of the adjective. Moreover, the lack of nongender-specific grammatical forms within grammatically gendered languages is the most problematic for those of nonbinary, gender non-conforming, and intersex people who want to refer to themselves using gender-neutral language. For many people, using feminine or masculine forms is simply inadequate, and it often triggers dysphoric feelings. Further, the lack of gender-neutral forms makes it impossible to express their identities in a given language (Rzeczkowski, 2010; Hord, 2016). The consequence of having to use a grammatically gendered expression is an unwanted and inadequate gendering of oneself as a man/woman.

Consider (12) and (13), the context being that S and H are at a party where J, a friend of H was supposed to be. S says to H:

(12) Will this friend of yours eventually come?
    (12.1) S asks H a question
    (12.2) S expresses irritation
        (12.1.1) S makes H respond
        (12.1.2) S makes H angry
(13) Czy ta [this, feminine] twoja [your, feminine] przyjaciółka [friend, feminine], czy tam [or] twój [your, masculine] przyjaciel [friend, masculine], wreszcie [finally] przyjdzie [will come]?
    (13.1) S asks H a question
    (13.2) S expresses irritation
    (13.3) S genders J as either a woman or a man
        (13.1.1) S makes H respond

(13.1.2) S makes H angry
(13.1.3) S compels H to say whether J is a woman or a man

Again, when the utterance is made in English, the illocutionary and perlocutionary acts connected to gendered expressions do not occur, which is why
(12) and (13) can differ in terms of their perlocutionary effects. Perlocutionary
effects can be connected with certain speech acts (e.g., making someone answer a
question or following an order), but not all of them are. Sally McConnell-Ginet
(2014) distinguishes "basic perlocutionary effects" and "expanded perlocutionary
effects." Expanded effects are, for example, frightening someone, making someone feel better, impressing someone. These effects depend on the hearer's reaction
to the speech act which is something the speaker cannot control. In the case of
(13), even if S did not have any intention of making H reveal the sex/gender of
the referent, the fact that S used both feminine and masculine forms could cause
(13.1.3). This is not only the case with alternatives: S might assume that J is a
man and use the masculine version which would compel H to correct them and
therefore informs them about J's sex/gender. In both cases, the grammatically
gendered expressions shift the focus toward sex/gender to make it more visible
in the conversation and to make conversational moves dependent on whether the
speaker knows the sex/gender of the referent.

One could say that it is not that different from English. If one changes the
construction of (12) into two sentences: "What about your friend? Is she coming?", the pronoun usage triggers the same effects as the feminine grammatical
form. The important difference is that: (i) in English, one can easily avoid gendered expressions by using "your friend" as in (12), (ii) to split the speech act into
two sentences, one can use singular "they," (iii) pronouns (and gender-specific
nouns) occur in English conversations much less than grammatically gendered
expressions in Polish conversations.

One might question whether every utterance in which a grammatically gendered expression occurs has an expanded perlocutionary effect of reinforcing a
binary way of thinking about gender. The fact that grammatically gendered languages force their speakers to include information about their (or others') sex/
gender in almost every utterance, and the fact that there are only two possible
choices, masculine and feminine, have the effect of imposing obligatory gender
binary onto their speakers.

The analysis of the utterances with grammatically gendered expressions
within speech act theory prompts us to observe that their occurrence affects every
layer of the speech act. At the locutionary layer, it adds information about one's
sex/gender to the proposition expressed. Including this information generates

another illocutionary act of gendering someone as either male or female and can have perlocutionary effects of shifting the focus of the conversation onto one's gender and, more widely speaking, of reinforcing a binary way of thinking about gender.

Objections and a Modified Approach

Starting with Gricean analysis, an obvious objection one could raise would involve treating the information about one's sex/gender conveyed by a grammatically gendered expression as a part of "what is said." As it was noted at the beginning of section 3.1, Grice (1975) treats such information, in his example conveyed by a pronoun, as a part of "what is said,". There are two possibilities: i) information about one's sex/gender conveyed by grammatically gendered expressions behaves differently than those conveyed by pronouns (or gender-specific nouns) in English; ii) Grice is wrong and information about sex/gender conveyed by pronouns is also not a part of "what is said." The latter is assumed to be true here. Of course, there are many different notions of "what is said" developed by neoGricean scholars (Recanati, 2001; Bach, 1994; Saul, 2002; Carston, 2004), but searching for a better one is not a solution. Instead, focus should rest on how the sex/gender conveyed both by grammatically gendered expressions and pronouns/gender-specific nouns is not explicitly said but presupposed by the speaker.

Regarding the analysis conducted within speech act theory, the main objection concerns the illocutionary level of the speech act. It can be controversial whether the act of gendering indeed happens every time a grammatically gendered expression is used. Such perspective would treat each speech act as an isolated event and ignore the wider context in which it occurs. The alternative is to consider entire conversations and speech acts (or "conversational moves") within them. It will make possible to treat the act of gendering someone as an information which, after being accepted by all participants, enters the "common ground."

A modified approach would categorize the information about one's sex/gender conveyed by grammatically gendered expressions as presupposition that is a part of the common ground of the conversation. As Robert Stalnaker writes: "to presuppose something is to take it for granted, or at least to act as if one takes it for granted, as background information, as common ground among the participants in the conversation" (2002, p. 701). Intuitively, we can distinguish what is asserted and what is presupposed in a statement. If someone says, "John stopped smoking" they presuppose that John used to smoke, and they are asserting that he stopped smoking. Presuppositions differ from entailments in their behavior in embedded contexts, both "John didn't stop smoking" and "Did John stop smoking?" presuppose that John used to smoke as well while they do not entail it (Schlenker, 2016). Pronouns are also said to trigger presuppositions, for example "she is magnificent" presupposes that the person referred to is a woman.

Common ground is usually said to consist of beliefs (and assumptions, presumptions) shared by all interlocutors. Common ground constantly changes during a conversation because with each utterance the beliefs shared by participants will change even if only to state that the utterance has occurred (Haslanger, 2012, p. 455; cf. Lewis, 1979). For example, if S says (14), during a dinner with friends and everyone accepts their utterance a belief that S is tired will enter into the common ground of the conversation, but a supposition that after the meeting S will go to sleep, or that S's day was tiring may enter into it as well (XCG refers to possible beliefs inferred from X that enter the common ground).

(14) Sorry, I won't stay long because I'm very tired.
(14CG.1) S is tired.
(14CG.2) S will go to sleep after the meeting.
(14CG.3) S's day was tiring.

Now, let us assume that another friend H comes to dinner late and someone updates them on the conversation saying (15) while pointing at S (Xp refers to a presupposition carried by X):

(15) She will not stay long because she is tired.
(15p.1) S is a woman.

If (15p.1) already was in the common ground the use of pronoun "she" does not convey any added information, it is just consistent with the information already shared by all participants. If there was no prior information concerning S's gender in the common ground, (15 p.1) will be accommodated. David Lewis formulated "the rule of accommodation for presuppositions:" "If at time t something is said that requires presupposition P to be acceptable, and if P is not presupposed just before t, then (ceteris paribus and within certain limits), presupposition P comes into existence at t." (1979, p. 340). The same is true for utterances with grammatically gendered expressions, barring that many more expressions aside from pronouns/gender-specific nouns will trigger presuppositions about one's sex/gender.

(16) Przepraszam [I am sorry], nie zostanę [I will not stay] długo [long], bo [because] jestem [I am] bardzo [very] zmęczona [tired, feminine].
(16p.1) S is a woman.

The difference is that in (16) it is the grammatical form of an adjective that triggers a presupposition that S is a woman and not a pronoun. In English, one rarely inexplicably genders oneself or the person they are addressing because it usually happens via a pronoun. In grammatically gendered languages, one must gender oneself in almost every utterance which on one hand makes it harder to express nonbinary identities and generally reinforces the gender binary, but on the other hand makes it easier to inexplicably inform interlocutors about one's gender. In a different context, for example, a multiplayer online game where most players are men and they assume that S is a man as well, (16) could be used to inform others that their shared belief is wrong.

This is an idealization. People constantly make assumptions about others' genders and the fact that one cannot know what someone's gender is until they disclose that, does not change that. Depriving languages of their grammatical (or natural) gender would not suddenly erase stereotypes about sex/gender, in grammatically gendered languages information about sex/gender is presupposed more often than in natural gender languages. It may not be the case that the common grounds of analogous conversations conducted in English and Polish vary, the belief about someone's gender can be shared by all participants of the conversation without ever being said or accommodated. Rather, the distinguishing feature of using a grammatically gendered language is that it is always mentioned.

Thinking about information about sex/gender, whether conveyed in natural gender languages or grammatically gendered ones, in terms of presuppositions entering the common ground captures common sense intuitions about how successful communication works (cases of (14), (15), and (16)). It can also account for phenomena such as misgendering and correcting oneself, and the way nonbinary users of grammatically gendered languages express their identity.

Queering Language in Life and in the Classroom

We can distinguish two types of misgendering: intentional and unintentional. Unintentional misgendering usually happens because of the speaker's presumptions and stereotypes. Here are a few examples. S sees a skateboarding teenager with short hair and shouts "Stop it, boy!". S calls a company, demands to speak to the manager and calls them "Sir"; S's daughter tells them that she is going on a date and S asks, "Is he nice?" A misgendered person (or someone else) can either straightforwardly correct the person (S's daughter can say "Actually, I'm dating a girl") or by saying something to show that they presuppose the correct gender (S's daughter can say "She is very nice!"), which makes the misgenderer accommodate.

Again, this works similarly in grammatically gendered languages except for the fact that more expressions trigger presuppositions about one's sex/gender, and because of that misgendering happens more often.

Intentional misgendering usually happens when the speaker either wants to insult a person (e.g., calling a gay man "she" or a "lady") or when the speaker does not accept a person's gender identity (e.g., calling a trans woman "he" or "guy,") and is a type of derogatory speech (Tirrel, 1999; Hornsby, 2001). In the first scenario, the speaker expresses their homophobic belief that "gay men are not real men" which is either accepted into the common ground if the interlocutors are also homophobic, or rejected if an interlocutor retorts, "you can't say that, this is not true." In the second scenario of intentional misgendering, when a speaker is transphobic and rejects the gender identity of the referent, there should be a shared correct belief about the referent's gender in the common ground, but the transphobic interlocutor holds a different belief that "trans women are not real women."

It might seem that in grammatically gendered languages, it is impossible to express nonbinary identities, but this is false. Before showing some of the ways that nonbinary speakers use the Polish language it must be noted that even if a nonbinary person uses feminine or masculine forms exclusively, this does not erase the presupposition about their nonbinary identity from the common ground. Many nonbinary people prefer using binary pronouns which does not invalidate their nonbinary identities (Sanders, 2019). If there already is a shared belief about S's nonbinary identity and they say (16), it is not the case that we have two clashing presuppositions about S's gender but a presupposition that S uses grammatically feminine forms. Nonetheless, many nonbinary speakers of grammatically gendered languages do not feel comfortable using either feminine of masculine forms, and instead, adopt alternative ways of expressing their identity (Hord, 2016; Berger, 2019). In Polish, there are two main linguistic strategies that can be adopted for this end: (i) using standard grammatical forms in nonstandard ways; (ii) creating new grammatical forms.

The first strategy is used much more often in practices such as: using both masculine and feminine forms, sometimes in the same sentence, Byłam [I was, feminine] tam [there] i [and] zobaczyłem [I saw, masculine], Jestem [I am] mądrym [smart, masculine] studentką [student, feminine]); using neuter grammatical gender in the first and second person (considered grammatically incorrect) and neuter pronouns, Poszłom [I went, neuter], Jestem [I am] piękne [beautiful, neuter], ono poszło [literally: it went, neuter]; changing generics into neutral descriptive forms, osoba studiująca [studying person] instead of student [student, masculine] or studentka [student, feminine], osoba przewodnicząca [chairing person] instead of przewodniczący [chairperson, masculine] or przewodnicząca [chairperson, feminine]; using passive voice to avoid gendering in past tenses, Szło mi się [I was going, in a passive voice], Jadło mi się [I was eating, in a passive voice]. Nonbinary Polish speakers create different grammatical forms to refer to themselves pf which the most popular are: a "new" neutral grammatical gender, taken from Dukaj's (2004) novel with nonbinary themes, Poszłum [I went, new neutral], Jestem [I am] pięknu [beautiful, new neutral], Onu poszłu [new neutral pronoun, went]; different spellings, Byłm, Byłæm, Byłxm instead of Byłem [I was, masculine] or Byłam [I was, feminine].

Some of these practices, like using a passive voice or changing generics into neutral descriptive forms, merely avoid presupposing a binary gender of the referent, but most of them do presuppose that the referent is nonbinary. Whether such presupposition will enter the common ground, however, depends on how much knowledge interlocutors have about nonbinary identities and ways of expressing them. It is crucial to respect the way nonbinary speakers refer to themselves, even though there is no one way of speaking Polish in a gender-neutral manner. Using neuter gender is becoming more popular throughout the nonbinary community, however, it is criticized as being dehumanizing since it is mostly used for babies (as "sexless beings") inanimate nouns, or to derogatorily refer to gender non-conforming people ("this thing") (Rzeczkowski, 2010). Even though the approach to information about one's sex/gender presented in this chapter may be too formal and complicated for younger students, it can be helpful in teaching a grammatically gendered language. The key feature of this approach is that it does not treat grammatical gender as limiting in terms of communication.

There are several tips that educators can use to create an inclusive approach to teaching languages. First, educators aim to avoid addressing students in a sexist (using a masculine form as a generic) or binary way ("Ladies and Gentlemen") by instead using gender-neutral ways of addressing people ("Dear All, Drogie Osoby" [dear persons]). Next, educators should avoid reinforcing gender stereotypes in exercises (e.g., teaching words for women's clothes and men's clothes or asking about girl's activities and boy's activities). Another useful recommendation is deterring from teaching to assume a person's gender based on how they look (e.g., exercises in which students are supposed to identify people in pictures or cartoons and describe what they are doing with correct grammatical gender). And finally, educators can be more inclusive by actively mentioning nonbinary, gender non-conforming and intersex people, and their linguistic practices in course content. Teaching a grammatically gendered language does not have to reinforce gender stereotypes and gender binary, on the contrary, it can bring awareness. While it is impossible for a chapter to supply gender-neutral strategies for every grammatically gendered language, it is a much-needed enterprise. It is also not a requirement for teachers to know linguistic practices of nonbinary, gender non-conforming and intersex people, but to raise this issue in the classroom. Educators can contact their local LGBTQIA+ organizations to request resources about how to speak in an inclusive manner in the classroom. Educators should try to create linguistic constructions that include all individuals, not just men and women. There is still much to be done in terms of gender-neutrality in grammatically gendered languages, but for it to be done, more people must recognize its need.

References

Austin, J. L. (1962). *How to do things with words.* U.K.: Clarendon Press.

Bach, K. (1994). Conversational impliciture. *Mind & Language, 9*(2), 124–162.

Bach, K., & Harnish, R. M. (1979). *Linguistic communication and speech acts.* Cambridge, MA: MIT Press.

Berger, M. (2019, December 15). A guide to how gender-neutral language is developing around the world. Retrieved from https://www.washingtonpost.com/world/2019/12/15/ guide-how-gender-neutral-language-is-developing-around-world/.

Bodine, A. (1975). Androcentrism in prescriptive grammar: Singular 'they,' sex-indefinite 'he,' and 'he or she.' *Language in Society, 4*(2), 129–146.

Butler, J. (1990). *Gender trouble: Feminism and the subversion of identity.* New York: Routledge.

Carston, R. (2004). Truth-conditional content and conversational implicature. In C. Bianchi (Ed.), *The semantics/pragmatics distinction* (pp. 65–100). Stanford, CT: CSLI Publications.

Dembroff, R., & Wodak, D. (2018). He/She/They/Ze. *Ergo: An Open Access Journal of Philosophy, 5.* doi:10.3998/ergo.12405314.0005.014.

Dukaj, J. (2004). *Perfekcyjna niedoskonałość.* Kraków: Wydawnictwo Literackie.

Fausto-Sterling, A. (2008). Should there only be two sexes? In A. Bailey & C. Cuomo (Eds.), *The feminist philosophy reader* (pp. 97–107). Boston, MA: McGraw Hill.

Green, M. (2017). Speech acts. In E. N. Zalta (Ed.), *The Stanford encyclopedia of philosophy* (Winter 2017). Retrieved from https://plato.stanford.edu/

Grice, H. P. (1975). Logic and conversation. In P. Cole & J. L. Morgan (Eds.), *Syntax and semantics, Vol. 3, speech acts* (pp. 41–58). New York: Academic Press.

Hare, R. M. (1970). Meaning and speech acts. *The Philosophical Review, 79*(1), 3–24. doi:10.2307/2184066.

Haslanger, S. (2012). Ideology, generics, common ground. In Witt, C. (Ed.), *Feminist metaphysics* (pp. 179–207). Boston, MA: Springer Verlag.

Hord, L. C. R. (2016). Bucking the linguistic binary: Gender neutral language in English, Swedish, German, and French. *Western Papers in Linguistics, 3*(4).

Hornsby, J. (2001). Meaning and uselessness: How to think about derogatory words. *Midwest Studies in Philosophy, 25*(1), 128–141. doi:10.1111/1475-4975.00042.

Langton, R. (1993). Speech acts and unspeakable acts. *Philosophy and Public Affairs, 22*(4), 293–330.

Levinson, S. C. (1983). *Pragmatics.* Cambridge, England: Cambridge University Press.

Lewis, D. (1979). Scorekeeping in a language game. *Journal of Philosophical Logic, 6,* 339–359. doi:10.1007/BF00258436.

Litoselliti, L. (2013). *Gender and language: Theory and practice.* New York: Routledge.

Livia, A., & Hall, K. (Eds.). (1997). *Queerly phrased: Language, gender and sexuality.* U.K.: Oxford University Press.

MacKinnon, C. (1993). *Only words.* Boston, MA: Harvard University Press.

McConnell-Ginet, S. (2011). *Gender, sexuality, and meaning: Linguistic practice and politics.* U.K.: Oxford University Press.

McConnell-Ginet, S. (2014). Meaning-making and ideologies of gender and sexuality. In S. Ehrlich, M. Meyerhoff, & J. Holmes (Eds.), *The handbook of language, gender, and sexuality* (2nd ed., pp. 316–334). New Jersey: John Wiley & Sons.

McGowan, M. K. (2003). Conversational exercitives and the force of pornography. *Philosophy and Public Affairs, 31*(2), 155–189. doi:10.1111/j.1088-4963.2003.00155.x.

Moulton, J. (1981). The myth of the neutral 'man.' In M. Vetterling-Braggin (Ed.), *Sexist language: A modern philosophical analysis* (pp. 100–116). New Jersey: Littlefield Adams and Co.

A Note on the Nonbinary 'They'. (2019, September 19). Retrieved from https://www.merriam-webster.com

Penelope, J. (1990). *Speaking freely: Unlearning the lies of the fathers' tongues.* New York: Pergamon.

Recanati, F. (2001). What is said. *Synthese, 128*(1/2), 75–91. doi:10.1023/A:1010383405105.

Rzeczkowski, M. (2010). Poza rodzajami męskim i żeńskim – trzecie płcie a język polski. In A. Gumowska, M. Kraska, & J. Wróbel (Eds.), *Między nieobecnością a nadmiarem.* Wydawnictwo Uniwersytetu Gdańskiego.

Saguy, A. C., Williams, J. A., Dembroff, R., & Wodak, D. (2019, May 30). We should all use they/them pronouns … eventually. Retrieved from https://www.scientificamerican.com/

Sanders, W. (2019, October 11). What people get wrong about they/them pronouns. Retrieved from https://www.them.us/

Saul, J. (2002). Speaker meaning, what is said, and what is implicated. *Nous, 36*(2), 228–248.

Schlenker, P. (2016). The semantics–pragmatics interface. In M. Aloni & P. Dekker (Eds.), *The Cambridge handbook of formal semantics* (pp. 664–727). U.K.: Cambridge University Press. doi:10.1017/CBO9781139236157.023.

Searle, J. R. (1969). *Speech acts.* U.K.: Cambridge University Press.

Spender, D. (1980). *Man made language.* U.K.: Pandora.

Stalnaker, R. (2002). Common ground. *Linguistics and Philosophy, 25*(5/6), 701–721. doi:10.1023/A:1020867916902.

Strawson, P. F. (1964). Intention and convention in speech acts. *The Philosophical Review, 73*(4), 439–460. doi:10.2307/2183301.

Tirrel, L. (1999). Derogatory terms: Racism, sexism and the inferential role theory of meaning. In K. Oliver & C. Hendricks (Eds.), *Language and liberation: Feminism, philosophy and language* (pp. 41–79). New York: SUNY Press.

Vitanova, G. (2010). *Authoring the dialogic self.* Amsterdam, The Netherlands: John Benjamins Publishing Company.

Warren, V. L. (1986). Guidelines for non-sexist use of language. *Proceedings and Addresses of the American Philosophical Association, 59*(3), 471–482.

Wayne, L. D. (2005). Neutral pronouns: A modest proposal whose time has come. *Canadian Woman Studies, 24*(2/3), 85–91.

Ziemińska, R. (2018). Beyond dimorphism: Intersex persons and the continuum of sex characteristics. *International Journal of Gender and Women's Studies, 6*(1), 176–184.

CHAPTER EIGHT

Putting the T and the Q into First-Year Composition: Using Queer Theory to Make Courses Trans-inclusive

EMILY DONOVAN

In 1973 at the Christopher Street Liberation Day Rally in New York City, Sylvia Rivera fought her way through the crowd. Rivera, a trans woman, was a local gay rights leader and co-founder of a group that provided services to homeless queer youth. It has been rumored that Rivera threw the first brick in the Stonewall Riots, which the Christopher Street Liberation Day Rally was supposed to commemorate. Still, organizers snubbed Rivera and other activists, and some even passed out flyers that accused them of making fun of women for entertainment (Osorio, 2017). The crowd was hostile. Some reports say Rivera was beaten and bloodied by the time she reached the stage, climbed onto it, and wrested a microphone from the hands of the emcee (Osorio, 2017). "Y'all better quiet down," Rivera began in what is now an iconic line. She tore into the crowd, accusing gay leaders of leaving behind vulnerable queer people, and then reminded the crowd that she and other vulnerable queer people are part of the same community. In a rhetorically impressive four-minute period, Rivera turned a crowd that had attempted to physically silence her into a rally repeating her words: "Gay power."

Too often, when trans people are excluded from a space, they themselves are the only ones willing to fight to better that space by making it more inclusive. Not unlike the Christopher Street Liberation Day Rally nearly 50 years ago, when educators attempt to make spaces accessible for queer students they have often addressed the concerns of gay, lesbian, and to some degree, bisexual students, but they have failed to ameliorate concerns for trans. "Queer" in this sense is the accepted umbrella term for all LGBTQIA+ people, although it is also used as a shorthand for genderqueer people, and "trans" refers to people who identify as a gender different from the gender that has been socially associated with the sex that they were identified as at birth, which will include transgender women, transgender men, and nonbinary, genderqueer, and Two Spirit individuals. As Kristen A. Renn points out, "Although colleges and universities are the source of much queer theory, they have remained substantially untouched by the queer agenda" (2010, p. 132). While theories from scholars like Judith Butler have helped to boost trans political and social movements, dormitories, restrooms, and sports remain sex-segregated, class rosters, online learning management systems, and degrees list names assigned at birth, and too many educators and classmates act as if trans people have no place on their campuses. This chapter will discuss recent research that explores the dire needs of trans college students, will assess best practices regarding how educators run their classrooms, and will suggest advocacy that educators can pursue on campus and in politics to improve the lives of trans students so they can better succeed in and beyond the classroom.

English composition pedagogy has fumbled with queer students and queer theory alike. In a review of queer scholarship in composition, Jonathan Alexander and David Wallace argue that "the particular critical power of queerness remains an under-explored and under-utilized modality in composition studies" (2009, p. 301). However, while Alexander and Wallace criticize theorists and researchers who fail to address "sexuality and sexual orientation" as "oddly out of step with the larger field of English studies," they and the scholars they discuss often fail to include gender identity along with sexuality and sexual orientation (p. 302). This conflates queerness with LGB people and ignores the trans parts of the acronym. If Alexander and Wallace consider who a person is attracted to as a valuable part of identity, they should also find what gender a person is and how they express that as crucial to study.

Trans students comprise an important part of our classrooms. A 2017 study conducted by Ellen B. Stolzenberg and Bryce Hughes found that 0.5% of incoming college first-year students identified themselves as transgender. An accurate numerical tally of college students who identify as trans might be greater than 0.5%, though it is difficult to determine this given the self-reported nature of this study and others like it.

More students are coming out as trans before they reach our classrooms than in past generations. Mid-life crises used to be a common age for trans people to accept and begin to express their gender identities, but today, larger numbers of queer and trans people are coming out as youths than in decades past (Beemyn &

Rankin, 2011). One survey commissioned by the queer advocacy organization GLAAD found that 20% of millennials identified as something other than strictly straight and cisgender, compared to only 7% of boomers (Steinmetz, 2017). Most Generation Z members (38% strongly agreed and 40% somewhat agreed) do not believe that gender defines a person as much as it used to, and most (56%) personally know someone who uses gender-neutral pronouns (Laughlin, 2016). Still, perhaps due at least in part to the fact that these identities were treated like mental illnesses in the United States until the 1980s and some still are, the empirical data is underwhelming.

These emerging numbers indicate that trans-inclusive pedagogy needs to become more common, and it also can enrich the student experience. In first-year composition classrooms, educators teach students to reexamine what they think they know (such as the understanding of gender based on one's reproductive capabilities) and to open their eyes to other perspectives (such as their classmates' varying identities and experiences). First-year composition aims to make students critical thinkers, and that should include thinking critically about their own and others' identities. Alexander and Wallace advocate for this when they say that "paying attention to queerness in composition studies is much more than just including yet another set of marginalized voices in the composition classroom" but instead "provides unique opportunities to engage students in challenging discussions about how the most seemingly personal parts of our lives are densely and intimately wrapped up in larger sociocultural and political narratives that organize desire and condition how we think of ourselves" (2009, pp. 302–303). Critical thinking skills can be gained by learning about how growing up "cisgender," or with a gender identity that matches the sex they were assigned at birth, has shielded some students from many forms of discrimination, and recognizing that being cisgender does not make someone inherently superior to trans peers. Additionally, Butler argues that recognizing the existence of trans people could expand "the framework of accepted intelligibility" (2004, p. 73), perhaps leading more people to recognize that supposedly incorrectly masculine men, incorrectly feminine women, and all trans people are indeed autonomous human beings who deserve basic human rights as much as any more-traditional cisgender person.

Even though English composition instructors and researchers struggle to accomplish Alexander and Wallace's goals, there are scholars in the field of feminist studies (e.g., Judith Butler) that have better realized the potential of trans-inclusive theory. Queer feminist theory is not merely an examination of how queer identities have been excluded. Instead, for example, Butler offers a direct attack on gender itself, as well as all socially constructed binaries, in *Undoing Gender* (2004). Butler theorizes that "we do or do not recognize animate others as persons depending on whether or not we recognize a certain norm manifested in and by the body of that other" (2004, p. 58) and that "the unrecognizability of one's gender" directly causes "the unrecognizability of one's personhood" (p. 58). Butler argues that we are so fixated on gender when we meet someone, that we may not consider that individual equally human if we cannot immediately categorize them as a man or woman based on their appearance. These socially constructed gender norms cause trouble for cisgender men who do not present traditionally masculinely enough, for cisgender women who do not present traditionally femininely enough, and for trans people whose gender presentation does not match up with what other expect from them based on these traditions. Butler's understanding of the dehumanization of trans people could help explain why trans students are more likely to have been bullied throughout their lives, more likely to face financial problems, and are more likely than their cisgender peers to have low emotional health. Additionally, discrimination due to being trans can compound racism, sexism, homophobia, ableism, xenophobia, and other forms of discrimination.

Standardizing trans-inclusive practices and applying a more inclusive queer theory to first-year composition classes could intervene at a critical time to create a generation of scholars, both trans and cisgender alike, who can resist binary thinking and also understand just how deeply political and socially constructed the personal can be.

Dire Needs

At present, it is safe to say that educators and administrators are increasingly encountering a student demographic of trans students whose needs they have largely failed to meet. School is far from a sanctuary for most trans students. The exact findings vary, but studies consistently report alarming rates of verbal, physical, and sexual harassment of trans students (Grant et al., 2011; Kosciw et al., 2014; Rankin et al., 2010; Stolzenberg & Hughes, 2017). Kosciw et al. (2014) reported that almost all of the 709 transgender students in their study had been verbally harassed at school within the past year, and more than half had been physically assaulted. Meanwhile, the National Transgender Discrimination Survey found that 78% of trans kindergarten through 12th-grade students are harassed, 35% are physically assaulted, and 12% experience sexual violence (Grant et al., 2011). Not only do adults in schools fail to ensure trans students' safety, but many contribute to or create the problem: A staggering 31% of trans people report having been harassed by teachers or staff, 5% report having been physically assaulted by them, and 3% report having been sexually assaulted by them (Grant et al., 2011). These numbers explain why transgender students report that attending school was "the most traumatic aspect of growing up" (Stolzenberg & Hughes, 2017, p. 38). It does not get better for everyone in college, as one study found that about one-third of trans respondents reported experiencing harassment or violence on college campuses because of their sexuality or gender identity (Rankin et al., 2010). Harassment in schools from kindergarten through college is so severe that 15% of trans people report having had to drop out of school due to it (Grant et al., 2011).

For those who attend college, trans students are more frequently financially stressed in ways that could negatively impact their performance. Employment discrimination, housing discrimination, costly medical expenses and medical discrimination, parental financial disownment, and homelessness are all more likely to affect transgender youth than cisgender. According to Jamie M. Grant and colleagues (2011), almost half (47%) of trans people report being fired, not hired, or denied a promotion due to being trans. Many (19%) reported being denied housing and some (11%) reported being evicted explicitly due to being trans (2011). Nearly half (48%) report having postponed medical care because they cannot afford it (2011). Most (57%) report significant family rejection and about one-fifth (19%) report having been homeless at some point in their lives (2011). Discrimination helps explain why 19% of transgender students report major concerns about financing their higher education, with some being unsure if they can afford to finish their degrees (Stolzenberg & Hughes, 2017). This makes transgender students more than 50 percent more likely than their peers to face major financial concerns. In addition to the 15% of trans people who report dropping out of school due to harassment, another 15% of trans people report having dropped out of school due to transition-related financial reasons (Grant et al., 2011).

These forms of discrimination help contextualize studies that report dire mental health for trans people and trans incoming college students. More than half (52.1%) of trans incoming college first-year students reported their emotional health as below average or in the worst 10% of all incoming first-year students; in comparison, about half (50.6%) of all incoming first-year students report themselves as being above average or in the top 10% (Stolzenberg & Hughes, 2017). In fact, 47.2% of trans incoming first-year students reported feeling frequently depressed, compared to only 9.5% of all incoming students (Stolzenberg & Hughes, 2017). Most alarmingly, Arnold H. Grossman, Jung Yeon Park, and Stephen Russell (2016) found that 49.5% of transgender youth ages 15 to 21 have had suicidal ideation at some point in their lives and 24.4% have attempted suicide once or more. In comparison, one study found that 12.1% of adolescents nationwide have had suicidal ideations and 4.1% have attempted suicide (Nock et al., 2013). Every trans person's life experience is different, but these statistics indicate an alarming pattern.

One theorization of suicide can help us understand how bullying at school and financial stressors contribute to the high rates of suicidal ideation and attempts for transgender youth. The interpersonal psychological theory of suicide posits that three factors, when combined, indicate that an individual may be at risk of suicide. First, an individual possesses the capability to enact self-harm due to a high tolerance for physical pain that is acquired by being exposed to painful events over time. Second, a person experiences perceived burdensomeness, or a sense of being so flawed as to be a burden on others who are important. Third, an individual perceives thwarted belongingness, or a lack of reciprocally caring relationships and having few to no social supports (Van Orden et al., 2010). Transgender and gender-nonconforming youth are more likely to be exposed to issues that can lead to these three factors than their peers (Hendricks & Testa, 2012). Harassment, violence, and discrimination can lead to the capability to enact self-harm. Unemployment or homelessness can result in feelings of perceived burdensomeness. Rejection from family, friends, and peers can lead to social isolation, which can create a feeling of thwarted belongingness.

Stolzenberg and Hughes' research (2017) indicates that trans students are financially and emotionally stressed and that histories of anti-trans bullying at school means they are more likely to view the college classroom as a source of danger. The interpersonal psychological theory of suicide can be used to argue that educators accommodating transgender and gender-nonconforming students in the classroom could be lifesaving. Classroom practices that create a hostile atmosphere such as forcing trans students to be called their "dead name," an outdated legal name that generally stirs up negative emotions, could prevent them from feeling like themselves around their peers and contribute to feelings of thwarted belonging. Classroom practices that, while not hostile, are not already informed on how to accommodate trans students, such as forcing trans students to educate the educator and peers on pronouns and fight an uphill battle to make the educator or peers use their pronouns, could contribute to feelings of perceived burdensomeness. While classroom practices alone cannot heal major contributors to these feelings such as family rejection or employment discrimination, their potential to exacerbate or partially compensate for these stressors is worth consideration.

Trans and gender-nonconforming people have not taken these blows lying down. Resiliency and activist engagement should also be considered when characterizing trans students and their needs. While trans people ages 18–24 are less likely to be in school than the general population (37% compared to 45%), older trans people are more likely to be in school (22% compared to 7% for ages 25–44 and 5% compared to 2% for ages 45–54) (Grant et al., 2011). Importantly, despite high levels of workplace harassment, the vast majority of trans people (78%) report that transitioning improved their performance at work and their comfort. Furthermore, Stolzenberg and Hughes (2017) found that trans students are about twice as likely to be politically engaged than their peers. Trans students were more than twice as likely as their peers to be involved in activism as their peers, as 47.4% of trans students reported they had participated in any type of activism in the year before entering college, compared to 20.8% of students nationwide. Trans students are almost three times as likely to frequently discuss issues, as 43% of trans students reported that they frequently share their opinions on important causes compared to only 14.5% of students nationwide. Trans students were also more than twice as likely to protest on campus, as 68.7% of trans students reported they expected to participate in a campus protest, compared to 33.1% of students nationwide. However, this highly anticipated engagement is likely because trans students generally reported that they "come to college anticipating the need to resist a hostile climate" (Stolzenberg & Hughes, 2017, p. 43). Students should not have to protest to have their humanity recognized.

Accommodations in the Classroom

Educators may not know when they have a trans student in their classes. Skyler Jay, a trans man whose appearance on a *Queer Eye* episode put him into the public eye, famously said that when someone tells him that he is the first trans person they have ever met, he responds, "That you know of" (Kaspar, 2018, para. 10). Trans and gender-nonconforming people are everywhere, and only some might explicitly introduce themselves as trans. Some trans students may have transitioned and updated their legal names before entering the classroom, meaning that educators may only learn that students are transgender if those students decide to disclose.

There are also trans and gender-nonconforming students who have recognized and begun to express their gender identities before a class starts but for whom the university's registrar has outdated names listed and who may use pronouns that educators might not assume for them. University registrars generally only change a student's name and gender in their systems if the student legally changes these items by following proper procedures to request the change. The process for a legal name change or sex marker change is determined at the state level. In some states, it is a "byzantine" (Barrios, 2016, para. 5) process that can be confusing to navigate without legal or parental help and too expensive for some. Many states still require proof of gender affirmation surgery in order to change one's sex marker on legal documents, and these surgeries are often unattainable or undesirable for many trans people, which helps explain why 41% of trans people have not updated their driver's license or other state identification (Grant et al., 2011). Furthermore, most states still do not legally recognize nonbinary gender. These procedures mean that the legal name listed on an attendance sheet might be a student's dead name. An educator who spends the semester calling such a student by their dead name will make that student feel uncomfortable in the classroom. These deterrents also mean that the student's gender identity may be different from what one might assume. Many trans people first recognize, accept, and express their authentic gender identities during college and some others do not until after (Beemyn & Rankin, 2011). Across all categories, most trans college students report avoiding coming out at times because they fear being mistreated (Rankin et al., 2010). This means that many trans and gender-nonconforming students do not yet privately or publicly identify as trans but may take a special interest in choices regarding trans accommodations or content.

The following tips are designed to accommodate trans students who use a different name and pronouns than their official registration and wish to come out in the classroom. Adopting these measures signals not only that the educator has done their homework but also models behavior for cisgender students on how to accommodate trans and gender-nonconforming students. For these reasons, educators should adopt these practices regardless of whether there is a trans or gender-nonconforming student in the classroom.

Educators should complete two tasks before passing out a syllabus on the first day. First, students' names should be double-checked and, second, every student should be asked for their pronouns. Ravel specifically recommends finding ways to "*support* rather than *draw attention to*" trans and gender-nonconforming students (2017, para. 8). She has students write their names and pronouns on a loose piece of paper that they hand in on the first day. Spade (2011) also recommends against reading students' names from the roster in order to avoid outing a student who may want to use their chosen name but who does not feel comfortable confronting an instructor in front of their peers.

On the first day of class, educators can combine these suggestions by projecting the following on the board:

Please answer the following questions on a piece of paper and make a stack of papers up front when you're done:

1. What name would you like to be called?
2. What are your pronouns? (she/her, he/him, they/them, etc.)
3. What is your major?
4. What are your goals for this course?
5. Do you have any concerns about this course?

Since I do not have time to read these papers before I must begin class, when I call roll for the first time, I call on listed last names instead of first names and ask students to tell me what they want me to call them. I record names that do not match the roster's listed first names and also write down pronunciation notes as necessary. These practices mean that a trans student in my class whose legal name is outdated never has to hear their dead name read out loud or respond to it if they do not want to. These practices also benefit those who wish to be called nicknames along with helping me learn pronunciation for easily mispronounced names.

Another way I signal that my course is a safe space is by displaying these questions to students as soon as they enter the classroom. Students who are unaccustomed to reading an inclusive list of pronouns may realize that including "they/them" along "she/her" and "he/his" demonstrates that gender-nonconforming people are as equally valid as women and men. Sometimes students ask myself or other students to explain the pronouns. Whenever either of these scenarios occurs, I explain to students the use of pronouns in grammar and that gender-neutral pronouns like "they" or "their" exist because gender-nonconforming and genderqueer people exist. As Gail Hawisher phrases it, making space for queerness could "elicit in students a critical awareness of that which was once invisible" (Alexander & Wallace, 2009, p. 304). I explicitly tell my students that by asking for them to list their pronouns, I am making it clear that if anyone who happens to be trans wants me to call them a different name or use certain pronouns for them, I am willing to do that.

Educators must be consistent about using a student's chosen name and their pronouns and should also be prepared to correct that student's classmates if they make a pronoun mistake. Even if the trans student is not present, allowing the mistake to go uncorrected will encourage that speaker and anyone who overheard the mistake to misidentify the trans student in the future (Spade, 2011). It also can make a big difference to the trans student. One trans student named Christopher who participated in a case study said that "nobody says crap when the teacher backs you up" about pronouns (Pryor, 2015, p. 448). In comparison to Christopher, a student named Aimee reported dropping out of a class because she felt disrespected and miserable when an instructor continued to use her dead name after she asked him not to and she was unable to focus when it caused her classmates to look at her funny.

Additionally, educators should be sensitive to the fact that trans and gender-nonconforming students may be out in some contexts and not in others. Coming and being out should always be on an individual's own terms. As Dean Spade gives as an example, a comment such as "I knew Gina when she was Bill" (2011, p. 57) about a student who has completed a legal name change may be well-intended, but revealing a student's dead name or identifying a student as trans is an intrusion on their privacy. Similarly, if one encounters a student in public who is out in their classroom as trans or gender-nonconforming, one should not assume that they are out in all settings or out to all people. Spade (2011) recommends avoiding using any pronouns at all for a trans student in settings or with people where it is unknown if the student is out. Sometimes educators avoid pronoun use by using one's proper name, saying, for example, "It is Jesse's turn." However, this solution can be problematic for a trans student who has asked to be called a different name than what some others know them as. When in doubt, it is a best practice to follow the student's lead.

Tips for Teaching Trans Content

In addition to these simple trans-inclusive accommodations, lessons could include trans subject matter. In first-year composition courses, a queer pedagogy could be smoothly incorporated to use queer examples to accomplish the same course goals. Barrios (2016) offers several reading suggestions that could lead to useful discussions: "Why Nice Guys Finish Last" by Julia Serano, a feminist essay discussing gender norms that benefits from Serano's perspective as a trans writer but that is not focused on trans issues, "Sisterhood Is Complicated" by Ruth Padawer, an article discussing trans students at an all-female school, and "Preface" and "The New Civil Rights" by Kenji Yoshino and "Making Conversation" and "The Primacy of Practice" by Kwame Anthony Appiah, chapters which offer frameworks to think about different forms of discrimination and oppression that are not focused on but could be applied to trans issues. Queer pedagogy could include, as Ravel (2017) suggests, making conversations about gender a regular part of the classroom discussions or assignments.

An educator using these readings to remind students that trans people exist and have valuable perspectives on other issues also worthy of study can normalize trans people and help students unlearn internalized transphobia. Furthermore, teaching students to become more aware of trans people and subject matter has been shown to get results. Kim A. Case and Briana Stewart (2013) found that class readings by and about transsexual people significantly improved how students thought about trans people. (That said, the more positive thinking did not impact predictions for how participants treat trans people.)

Educators should make every effort to ensure they are familiar enough with inclusive course material in order to talk about gender and trans subject matter in a way that will avoid harming trans students. Scholar Catherine Fox saw that the sudden appearance of safe space stickers on office doors was not accompanied by substantive training for faculty members, which "actually served to create a safe space for folks to feel free from the guilt of homophobia and heterosexism" without having to do any actual work to better accommodate or improve queer lives (Alexander & Wallace, 2009, p. 317). Educators must educate themselves and take care that they do not inadvertently force their trans students to explain or justify their existences to their peers.

Furthermore, as Tre Wentling and colleagues discuss (2008), an educator who wants to bring in content related to trans people should be prepared to have to determine which questions about trans bodies and topics are valid and which are exoticizing or voyeuristic. Educators should also be prepared to intervene. A trans student named Bob reported feeling uncomfortable and unable to respond when another student drew a comparison between their bipolar disorder and his experiences as a transgender person. He said the comparison was "loaded, because there's a violent history of trans people being deemed mentally unstable" and that he felt the instructor should have been equipped to intervene (Pryor, 2015, p. 448). Seeking out trans writers writing about trans subjects, such as Susan Stryker's historical *Transgender History: The Roots of Today's Revolution* (2017) or Amy D. Ronner's theoretical "Let's Get the 'Trans' and 'Sex' Out of It and Free Us All" (2013) could help educators anticipate issues.

Beyond the Classroom

So many aspects of pursuing a college degree are gendered in ways that cisgender students, educators, and administrators may not realize until they are pointed out, from physical locations like showers, restrooms, and sports teams to electronic data like student academic records. These are things that those of us who are not trans must consider. Much English rhetoric and composition scholarship, including Mary Elliot's 1996 *College English* article, has framed queerness in the classroom as an issue for queer educators and queer students to deal with rather than a valuable framework for educators and students of all identities. Accommodating trans students should not be left for affected people to figure out alone. Then again, trans students and staff do need to be involved. D.A. Dirks (2016) finds that some university policy initiatives that intend to welcome trans students actually undermine themselves by not including trans voices in policy discussions and by depicting trans people as disabled and vulnerable.

Fixing a problem begins with understanding the problem and then holding oneself publicly accountable. The Campus Pride Index, which has been around since 2001, ranks colleges and universities on institutional commitment to LGBTQIA-inclusive policy, program, and practice. It can be used by potential students deciding where to apply and by anyone wishing to look closer at which practices colleges and universities are pursuing. Colleges and universities are listed and updated on voluntary bases, meaning many but not all are listed. Campus officials can add their institution by logging in and filling out an assessment which, according to the FAQ, takes an average of 30 to 45 minutes. Many universities have a multicultural center, and some have a designated staff member in charge of LGBTQIA initiatives, who would be the most natural person to take charge of the Campus Pride assessment.

Best practices to make campuses more trans-inclusive are well established. Campus Pride's criteria were developed in part by Genny Beemyn and Sue Rankin, leading scholars in queer inclusion in higher education. Criteria include creating social opportunities on campus like queer student organizations and queer alumni groups, institutional policies like non-discrimination statements and a standing advisory committee that deals with queer issues, having designated paid queer support services staff, providing trainings for campus police on issues related to sexuality and gender identity, and trans-inclusive health care policies. For college and university administrators looking for additional guidance on how to enact these policies, the Consortium of Higher Education LGBT Resource Professionals' Trans Policy Working Group published a list of best practices in 2014 that includes specific language recommendations related to campus records, housing, sports, facilities, fraternities and sororities, hiring policies, health centers, and counseling centers.

Some policies are also worth considering on a departmental level. Beemyn and Rankin (2016) suggest that seeking out trans or gender-nonconforming speakers, performers, and other trans-focused programming to sponsor can lead to important events alongside or in lieu of other events. While waiting for university-wide actions, nondiscrimination policy statements can be added to departmental syllabi and trainings on issues related to sexuality and gender identity can be added to mandatory departmental trainings.

Many of these best practices are filling in gaps while American federal law lags. As of this writing, the United States still does not have any federal legislation that would protect LGBTQIA people from discrimination. In thirty states, it is legal to discriminate against trans people based on their gender identity in public employment, private employment, housing, public accommodations, credit, or some combination of the above (Movement Advancement Project, 2017). Furthermore, some states have passed laws that prevent non-discrimination policies from applying to religious exemptions, and some have banned counties or cities within the state from passing local nondiscrimination laws. Stolzenberg and Hughes (2017) and other scholars recommend that universities adopt formal non-discrimination policies specifically to protect trans students and faculty at least within the campus setting. However, creating learning environments that are as open to trans students as to their cisgender peers requires that we as educators advocate for protections on local, state, and federal levels.

Thirty-four states have failed to prohibit discrimination in healthcare or to promote the safety of trans people (Movement Advancement Project, 2017). These states allow private insurers, state employee insurers, and Medicaid to discriminate against covering hormones or surgeries for transitioning people. Some of these states have made it a criminal offense to expose others to HIV, which actually discourages people from getting tested and therefore has negative health outcomes for the public and for trans people especially, since trans people are infected with HIV at four times the national average rate (Grant et al., 2011). It is also common for healthcare providers to be uninformed about trans issues, as 50% of trans people report having to teach their medical providers about transgender care (Grant et al., 2011). Administrators could double-check that the student health insurance policy accepts trans students just like their cisgender peers and covers trans-specific health needs. Again, we as educators can and should also advocate for changes to state and federal laws to right these wrongs.

Some states have passed laws that actively discriminate against trans people on the basis of their gender identities, including North Carolina's law to prevent trans people from safely using bathrooms in public (Movement Advancement Project, 2017). Student housing and locker-room and bathroom facilities could be made co-educational to accommodate trans students' needs on campuses. According to Campus Pride's Trans Clearinghouse in 2014, more than 150 colleges and universities already offer options for students to live with a roommate of any gender (Beemyn & Rankin, 2016). If not co-educational, separate facilities can be designed as gender-inclusive so long as they are not more expensive to live in or less conveniently located than residence halls and bathrooms available to cisgender students.

Several U.S. states and one federal district (i.e., California, Oregon, Washington, D.C., Vermont, and Washington) have started allowing for a third gender option to appear on birth certifications, state identification, or other legal documents (Nowicki, 2019). These policies allow for gender-nonconforming people, including people who are gender-neutral, genderqueer, agender, and Two Spirit, to have their genders recognized legally. Meanwhile, however, federal government requirements for student data reporting have not updated to include this option, and many universities struggle to create procedures even for trans students of a binary gender. As more states recognize nonbinary genders, more students will expect their online tools and their educators to respect gender-neutral pronouns. Student information systems will need to accommodate gender-neutral pronouns, including "they" and "ze."

Until U.S. Department of Education reporting requirements are updated to better accommodate students who use gender-neutral pronouns, wish to change their names, and are waiting for their gender identities to match the sexes they were assigned at birth, Ewa Nowicki (2019) recommends that student information systems retain dead names and legal sex markers. This initiative will also allow students to hide their dead names in outward records and have a chosen name and set of pronouns released instead. According to Campus Pride's Trans Clearinghouse in 2014, more than 115 colleges and universities already allow some version of this process (Beemyn & Rankin, 2016). Allowing educators to know only the chosen names and not the different legal names eliminates stress for students like Aimee, who said in a case study, that roll call with her dead name provided a major and unavoidable stress, and for Lucas, who answered to his legal name because he "[didn't] want to deal with it, especially if they are just going to keep messing it up" (Pryor, 2015, p. 448).

Without a push from faculty as well as students, administrations are not likely to take proactive actions to welcome queer students. Rather than wait to have a rally interrupted, I propose English rhetoric and composition educators heed Rivera's and trans scholars' words to re-examine their vision of queerness and their application of queer theory. For educators, that means making space for trans people who use different pronouns, educating themselves on trans issues, never allowing trans people's existence be questioned, and taking concrete steps discussed above to make campuses and communities safer for trans people. For all students, this means reading about trans issues, considering trans perspectives on not-specifically-trans issues, and reflecting on their own experiences. Unlike Rivera who had to fight through a hostile crowd, this generation of trans scholars could be welcomed onto the English academic stage.

Centering trans and gender-nonconforming people in our ideation of queerness can start to provide much-needed and easy-to-provide support to trans and gender-nonconforming students and create a radical new framework for all. For trans and gender-nonconforming students, easy additions to icebreaker activities can combat a decade of harassment in classrooms. For cisgender students and faculty, learning how easy it is to welcome trans and gender-nonconforming people is a vital life skill. Failing to envision queer theory as a direct attack on the gender binary itself rather than simply a critique of heteronormativity fails to equip scholars and students with tools that they could use to deconstruct all binaries, which is a power that has not been sufficiently tapped in English academia. If the personal is political, and we owe it to our trans and cisgender students alike to give them these skills from day one of first-year composition.

References

Alexander, J., & Wallace, D. (2009). The queer turn in composition studies: Reviewing and assessing an emerging scholarship. *College Composition and Communication, 61*, 300–320.

Barrios, B. (2016). Transgender students in the classroom. *Macmillan Community*. Retrieved from community.macmillan.com/community/the-english-community/bedford-bits/blog/2016/08/31/transgender-students-in-the-classroom.

Beemyn, G., & Rankin, S. R. (2011). Introduction to the special issue on 'LGBTQ campus experiences.' *Journal of Homosexuality, 58*, 1159–1164.

Beemyn, G., & Rankin, S. R. (2016). Creating a gender-inclusive campus. In Y. Martínez-San Miguel & S. Tobias (Eds.), *Trans studies: The challenge to hetero/homo normativities* (pp. 21–32). New Brunswick, NJ: Rutgers University Press.

Butler, J. (2004). *Undoing gender*. New York, NY: Routledge.

Case, K. A., & Stewart, B. (2013). Intervention effectiveness in reducing prejudice against transsexuals. *Journal of LGBT Youth, 10*, 140–158.

Dirks, D. A. (2016). Transgender people at four big ten campuses: A policy discourse analysis. *Review of Higher Education, 39*(3), 371–393.

Grant, J. M., Mottet, L. A., Tanis, J., Harrison, J., Herman, J. L., & Keisling, M. (2011). *Injustice at every turn: A report of the national transgender discrimination survey*. Washington, DC: National Center for Transgender Equality and National Gay and Lesbian Task Force.

Grossman, A. H., Park, J. Y., & Russell, S. T. (2016). Transgender youth and suicidal behaviors: Applying the interpersonal psychological theory of suicide. *Journal of Gay & Lesbian Mental Health, 20*(4), 329–349. doi:10.1080/19359705.2016.1207581.

Hendricks, M. L., & Testa, R. J. (2012). A conceptual framework for clinical work with transgender and gender nonconforming clients: An adaptation of the minority stress model. *Professional Psychology: Research and Practice, 43*, 460–467.

Kaspar, B. (2018). Skyler Jay reveals his true feelings on *Queer Eye*'s trans makeover episode. *Them*. Retrieved from https://www.them.us/story/skyler-jay-reveals-his-true-feelings-on-queer-eyes-trans-makeover-episode

Kosciw, J. G., Greytak, E. A., Palmer, N. A., & Boesen, M. J. (2014). *The 2013 National School Climate Survey: The experiences of lesbian, gay, bisexual and transgender youth in our nation's schools*. New York: GLSEN.

Laughlin, S. (2016). *Gen Z goes beyond binaries in new innovation group data*. New York, NY: J. Walter Thompson Intelligence. Retrieved from www.jwtintelligence.com/2016/03/gen-z-goes-beyond-gender-binaries-in-new-innovation-group-data

Movement Advancement Project. (2017). *Mapping transgender equality in the United States*. Denver, CO: Movement Advancement Project & National Center for Transgender Equality.

Nock, M. K., Green, J. G., Hwang, I., McLaughlin, K. A., Sampson, N. A., & Kessler, R. C. (2013). Prevalence, correlates, and treatment of lifetime suicidal behavior among adolescents: Results from the national comorbidity survey replication adolescent supplement. *JAMA Psychiatry, 70*, 300–310.

Nowicki, E. (2019). Supporting trans and nonbinary community success in higher education: A new paradigm. *College and University, 94*, 3–9.

Osorio, R. (2017). Embodying truth: Sylvia Rivera's delivery of parrhesia at the 1973 Christopher Street Liberation Day Rally. *Rhetoric Review, 36*(2), 151–163.

Pryor, J. T. (2015). Out in the classroom: Transgender student experiences at a large public university. *Journal of College Student Development, 56*(5), 440–455.

Rankin, S., Weber, G. N., Blumenfeld, W. J., & Frazer, S. (2010). *2010 state of higher education for lesbian, gay, bisexual and transgender people*. Charlotte, NC: Campus Pride.

Ravel, K. (2017). Supporting transgender and gender non-conforming students in the first-year writing class. *Macmillan Community*. Retrived from community.macmillan. com/community/the-english-community/bedford-bits/blog/2017/09/27/supporting-transgender-and-gender-non-conforming-students-in-the-first-year-writing-class.

Renn, K. A. (2010). LGBT and queer research in higher education: The state and status of the field. *Educational Researcher, 39*(2), 132–141.

Ronner, A. D. (2013). Let's get the 'trans' and 'sex' out of it and free us all. *The Journal of Gender, Race and Justice, 16*, 859–916.

Spade, D. (2011). Some very basic tips for making higher education more accessible to trans students and rethinking how we talk about gendered bodies. *Radical Teacher, 92*(3), 57–62.

Steinmetz, K. (2017). Beyond 'he' or 'she': The changing meaning of gender and sexuality. *Time*. Retrieved from time.com/4703309/gender-sexuality-changing

Stolzenberg, E. B., & Hughes, B. (2017). The experiences of incoming transgender college students: New data on gender identity. *Liberal Education, 103*(2), 38–43.

Stryker, S. (2017). *Transgender history: The roots of today's revolution* (2nd ed.). New York, NY: Seal Press.

Van Orden, K. A., Witte, T. K., Cukrowicz, K. C., Braithwaite, S. R., Selby, E. A., & Joiner Jr., T. E. (2010). The interpersonal theory of suicide. *Psychological Review, 117,* 575–600.

Wentling, T., Windsor, E., Schilt, K., & Lucal, B. (2008). Teaching transgender. *Teaching Sociology, 36,* 49–57.

CHAPTER NINE

Disrupting Hegemonic Masculinity: An Argument for Restructuring the Undergraduate Literature Classroom

CAMILLE S. ALEXANDER

Academia has long been plagued with accusations of bias—that faculty rarely project an accurate depiction of the population or student body and curricula represent a white, western, masculine discourse. Michelle Jay notes that while "the ethnic makeup of the United States over the last century" has changed, the nation's "mainstream curriculum of its schools, colleges, and universities remains organized around concepts, events, and paradigms" reflecting "the experiences of Anglo-Saxon Protestant men" (2003, p. 3). To that claim, another could be added that mainstream curricula also reflect heteronormative experiences exclusive of members of the LGBTQIA+ community. Although colleges and universities in the United States have attempted to rectify the lack of faculty diversity, a review of literature anthologies indicates that undergraduate reading material continues to, unwittingly or not, promote a hegemonic discourse. The texts used in under-graduate literature classrooms often support hegemonic principles, which are demonstrated in displays of toxic masculinity, heterosexism, racism, and xeno-phobia, disseminating these ideas and beliefs to college and university students, who are rarely exposed to works representing races, cultures, sexual orientations, or genders divergent from the white, western, heterosexual, masculine narrative norm. Essentially, "schools, through their organization, structure, and curriculum (both formal and hidden)," maintain hegemony "by acculturating students to the interest of the dominant group and ... students are encouraged and instructed, both explicitly and implicitly, to make those interests their own" (Jay, 2003, p. 7). Limited diversity in undergraduate reading selections promotes a hegemonic discourse, subverting any attempts at challenging these imposed norms.

To rectify this issue of absence, exclusion, and silence, literature faculty can incorporate authors whose texts diverge from the canonical norm. While texts from the canon are used for instruction, the inclusion of more diverse reading selections could improve the classroom experience for undergraduates. Acknowledging differences is the first step to disrupting hegemonic dominance of masculinity and other pervasive and biased beliefs in undergraduate literature classrooms. This chapter proposes four pedagogical approaches to accomplish this goal. First, literature courses should incorporate texts by women—particularly non-Euro-American, writers of color in conjunction with traditional, canonical, typically white, male, European and American, selections. Second, literary theories challenging hegemonic masculinity should be included in literature courses in conjunction with primary texts. Third, instructors should place more emphasis on classroom discussions of reading material and literary theory; this practice allows students to carefully examine their biases through more active engagement with texts. Additionally, students must engage with theories that identify bias to challenge the influence of hegemonic masculinity on their verbal and written responses. The discussion of disrupting hegemonic masculinity in literature classrooms begins with an examination of hegemony.

Defining and Identifying Hegemonic Masculinity in Academia

Hegemony was first defined by Antonio Gramsci in *Prison Notebooks* (1971/2011) written during his incarceration from 1926 to 1937. Mike Donaldson, referencing Gramsci's initial definition, believes that hegemony "is about winning and holding power and the formation (and destruction) of social groups in that process" (1993, p. 645). Hegemony "refers to the cultural dynamic by which a group claims and sustains a leading position in social life" (Connell, 2005, p. 77). This dynamic is effective on a mass scale because it involves persuading "the greater part of the population, particularly through the media, and the organization of social institutions in ways that appear 'natural,' 'ordinary:' 'normal'" (Donaldson, 1993, p. 645). Hegemony promotes the masculine, white, Euro-American, Christian, and heterosexual as sought-after norms. Because of its silent influence, hegemony is embedded into institutions, like colleges and universities, governing how they function by guiding pedagogical approaches and incorporating hegemonic practices. Such biased methods can hinder students' ability to think critically, limit classroom experiences, and restrict students' exposure to ideas differing from the norm. For example, non-white racial affiliation becomes a marker establishing those classified as "white" as representative of the norm. This implied difference places students of color in positions of contestation and self-defense rather than of learning in classrooms.

Gregory Jay and Sandra Elaine Jones note that because students of color transition "from high school classrooms with few or no white faces to college classrooms overwhelming white in enrollment," they begin to feel "isolated and marginalized" (2005, p. 104). Curricula geared towards what many students of color may view as "white culture" only deepen these feelings of isolation in predominantly white institutions. The converse is that white students resist "antiracist or multicultural education" largely because they believe that "it is not about them" and that "they are being made to feel guilty" (Jay & Jones, 2005, p. 104). There may be resistance from white liberals in the classroom "who do not see their own complicity in a racist system" (Cannon, 2017, p. 47). This resistance can take the milder form of complaining or by openly defying the authority, for example, of a Black woman teaching the course (Jay and Jones, 2005, p. 104). In other instances, some white students may become so frustrated with multicultural readings that they stage a silent boycott, refusing to read the material or engage in discussions, making meaningful discussions about the text difficult (Cannon, 2017, p. 41). This silent rebellion, or the backfire effect, involves strengthening a misinformed belief although attempts are made to correct or refute that misinformation (Trevors, 2016, p. 341). While the backfire effect from white students is likely based on their own, individual discomforts, the influence of hegemony and masculinity on these behaviors is clear. Hegemony promotes the white, western, cisgender-heterosexual, man's dominance, making this position the norm, intentionally or unintentionally, in literature classrooms.

Hegemonic masculinity is a series of gendered and racially biased practices embodying common beliefs legitimating patriarchy and guaranteeing men's dominant position and women's subordination (Connell, 2005, p. 77). Hegemonic masculinity is not fixed; rather it "occupies the hegemonic position in a given pattern of gender relations," which remains contestable (Connell, 2005, p. 76). Gender relations are based on the position that "'[m]asculinity' does not exist except in contrast with 'femininity'" (Connell, 2005, p. 68). For masculinity to occupy a position of power, there must be a femininity to occupy a subordinate position. As a result, the "history of gender is necessarily a history of power" (Griffin, 2018, p. 377).

Hegemonic masculinity also works to implement racial biases by promoting a white, western narrative. One of the issues with identifying the impact of hegemony on promoting racism is first defining race. Steven J. Gold observes that race is a social construct "but one that has very real implications in shaping life chances and the distribution and denial of privileges to individuals and groups" (2004, p. 953). Essentially, race is typically based on phenotypical markers, separating and classifying groups based on physical attributes. In western nations, a "Black-white or bipolar model" helps to establish and maintain racial hierarchies (Gold, 2004, p. 953). This hierarchy places "white" in a position of dominance and "Black" in the contestable position of subservience. In the literature classroom, racial hierarchies influence text selection, leaning towards writings by white authors, which are promoted as the norm, and establishing a canon that is largely exclusive of non-white voices.

In academia, these positions of power are enacted daily in the pedagogical approaches of faculty worldwide because, as a global society, hegemonic masculinity is interwoven into the social fabric. The preference for all-things white, Euro-American, and masculine permeates academia, maintaining the status quo. While there have been many changes in academe in the past thirty years, reflecting a contemporary, international, open, and accepting global society, there is still much to be accomplished, particularly in literature classrooms.

Literature Classrooms

Literature classrooms can become ideal spaces to contest white, Euro-American masculinity's implied dominance, as well as the various notions governing its demonstrations. These spaces can evolve into contact zones, or "social spaces where cultures meet, clash, and grapple with each other, often in contexts of highly asymmetrical relations to power" (Pratt, 1991, p. 34). In these spaces, students can use literary texts to challenge their worldviews, explore new cultures and histories, and wrestle with these concepts using literature. Canonical literature can contribute to students critically challenging embedded ideas about the white, western, masculinized norm.

Literature appears to be the tool of the elite and the source of maintaining patriarchal structures is often supported by the canon. Charles Alteri states that there is somehow a "manifest power of various canonical works to transcend any single structure of social interest" (1983, p. 38). This statement implies an intercultural or perhaps socially open angle to the literary canon, whereas the canon is imbued with an inherent bias that typically favors white, masculine,

Euro-American, and Christian perspectives. Catherine Belsey refers to the canon as "great (moral) works by great authors, whose qualities are fully appreciated only by readers possessed of fine sensibilities, seen as innate though enhanced by correct training" (1982, p. 176). This rather satirical approach to the literary canon outlines what many contemporary readers may experience when engaging with the material. The canon excludes them, and they do not see themselves in the texts. Furthermore, Alteri's reference to "self-interest" when analyzing canonical texts implies that culture, class, race, ethnicity, religious beliefs, and sexual orientation should be set aside, and the past should be viewed "as a set of challenges and models" (1983, p. 40). There is some validity to this statement as the past, often troubling, can be used as a model of imperfection.

Literature classrooms can be sites of resistance and literary texts the tools of resistance. Ancient works like Euripides' *Medea* provide examples of literature challenging norms, such as the gendered mage of the ideal wife: quiet, forgiving, and accepting of her husband's hostile, public rejection. Modernist and late modernist novels, like *Mrs. Dalloway* (1925/1992) and *Wide Sargasso Sea* (1966/1985), respectively, while considered canonical today, were initially not included in the literary canon. First, both narratives disrupted hegemonic masculinity because they were authored by women. Second, the novels depicted women's lives as varied and complex rather than mundane or tragic. These novels, when examined individually, critically address the cultural impact of masculinity; however, when viewed as contributions to western, women's literature, the novels still fall short of challenging hegemonic masculinity. Both texts promote a white, western, middle class, or elite narrative that supports rather than disrupts the colonial narrative, which many other white, European, women writers promoted in a "subordinate role" (Brereton, 1998, p. 145). Therefore, incorporating texts such as these that inadvertently disrupt the inherently biased hegemonic masculine narrative represents a shift in literary studies toward inclusivity.

Incorporating the Other into Literature Curricula

While anthologies have become more inclusive in the past thirty years, they remain exclusive while wielding considerable influence over literature curricula. Often, textbooks are selected by committees that promote hegemonic masculinity in their coursework through ignorance of the available options or by willfully clinging to the notion that only certain texts are "worthy." Given this shift and technological advances promoting global interconnectedness, ignorance can no longer be used as an excuse for insensitivity. The long-term solution would be for academic publishing firms to hire more diverse editorial staff, particularly women of color; however, in the short term, college and university instructors could supplement anthologies with global readings. Mark Schaub, observing that university-level composition courses are largely centered "on the American context," proposes internationalizing the composition classroom by moving away from this narrow focus on American material and exposing students to global writers (2003, p. 86). Schaub also notes that focusing on the American instructional style and material can be an issue as the emphasis on the "phrase *American style* carries with it the baggage of linguistic and cultural imperialism," which is problematic in a globalized society still reeling from the impact of colonization (2003, p. 89).

Camille Alexander, building on Schaub's (2003) research, proposes that the "composition classroom … undergo a transformation in which the Other's voice is allowed to articulate more than it has in the past" (2011, p. 70). To that end, the composition classroom should include "essays penned by authors expressing opinions that challenge assumptions of power relations" (Alexander, 2011, p. 71). The same can be said of literature classrooms, which have long been held in the sway of deceased, white, Euro-American men. In many literature classrooms, the norm is to include writings by authors such as Jamaica Kincaid (1978/ 1983), representing the Caribbean, and the late Chinua Achebe (1958) from Nigeria. These selections are appropriate, exhibiting a positive, albeit delayed, shift in pedagogical practices towards women and writers of color from formerly colonized regions. However, these writers are also so well-known and anthologized that it is highly likely that students have already read "Girl" or *Things Fall Apart* at some point in their academic careers. However, one can be certain that, unless the students are from Trinidad, they have not read Merle Hodge's *Crick Crack Monkey* (1970) or the late Buchi Emecheta's *The Joys of Motherhood* (1979) unless they are familiar with contemporary African or Black British writing. Caribbean, African, or Feminist scholars are typically well-acquainted with both novels, but, outside of these highly specialized fields, the novels are less recognized. Including lesser-known but critical texts by women writers of color, such as these, should not be relegated to specialized literature courses but should become the norm in every undergraduate literature course. These texts offer a differing perspective from the normative narrative long permeating academia while exposing students to the voice of the Other, who remains marginalized and silenced. While it is critical that literature classrooms radically shift to include the Other's voice, it is not being suggested that canonical authors like William Shakespeare or Thomas Hardy be removed from literature curricula. The goal is to incorporate lesser-known authors whose work presents anti-imperialist, anti-masculinist narratives into general literature curricula to provide students with a more balanced and globalized worldview.

In addition to Emecheta and Hodge, several other texts could be included in literature courses to give students a globalized reading list. Late Nobel laureate Naguib Mahfouz (1962/1988) from Egypt is rarely included in literature courses or anthologies. However, as an anti-imperialist writer, his work adds an important perspective to this subject. Mahfouz's (1962/1988) "Zaabalawi" provides a glimpse into Islamic mysticism and existentialism, merging religion, culture, and philosophy. However, Nawal El-Saadawi's autobiography *A Daughter of Isis* (1999/2009) offers a more comprehensive depiction of a Muslim girl's upbringing during the decline of the British Empire in colonial Egypt while navigating a society in flux and preoccupied with differentiating itself from its colonial masters.

Jean Rhys' *Wide Sargasso Sea* (1966/1982), written in response to the colonial position taken in Charlotte Brontë's *Jane Eyre* (1847), is popular among postcolonial scholars. However, her other work, such as *Leaving Mr. McKenzie* (1930/ 1985) and her unfinished autobiography *Smile Please* (1979/1981) are not usually included in undergraduate literature courses. The exclusion of Rhys' other texts is disappointing as they fill historical gaps on colonial Caribbean, the British Empire, and Caribbean immigrant studies while also addressing the issue of being a white, Caribbean woman in the pre-independence era. These subjects are rarely broached with undergraduates, yet they remain critical to understanding the impacts of colonization and globalization on the region. Furthermore, novels like *Mr. McKenzie* tackle the subject of women's financial dependence, mirroring the reality of the post-WWI era and the modern period on traditional Victorian values and family structures. An autobiography like *Smile Please* offers a perspective on the social position and personal lives of women from the former Caribbean planter class in the century following abolition in the British Empire.

In addition to Rhys, late Black British author, Andrea Levy, produced the seminal work *Small Island* (2004), which, while critically acclaimed, may not have made its way into undergraduate literature classrooms. Highlighting the Black British experience through the Caribbean lens, *Small Island* is a novel that should be included in undergraduate literature courses as it foregrounds some social issues the UK currently faces, such as gender, race, and immigration. Trinidadian Lakshmi Persaud's *Daughters of Empire* (2012) is one of the writer's many texts examining the Indo-Caribbean woman's experience. As an emergent field of research, fiction and narratives focusing on Indo-Caribbean women could provide undergraduates with a literary experience that is both contemporary and crucial. Autobiographies, particularly those written by women of color, should be included in undergraduate literature courses for a similar reason. While many literary theorists might disagree with the inclusion of autobiographies in literary studies, autobiographies, particularly those authored by writers considered Others, provide insight into a lived experience that fiction may not convey. These narratives offer some understanding of lived experiences differing from the white, Euro-American, Christian, male master narrative. Therefore, the inclusion of El Saadawi's (1999/2009) or Rhys' (1979/1981) autobiographies, and others like bell hooks' (1997), Paule Marshall's (2009), and Maya Angelou's (1969/1997) help connect undergraduate students to the lived experiences of women writers who also represent the Other and disrupt the continued presence of hegemonic masculinity on literature classrooms.

In addition to incorporating readings that acknowledge non-western, non-Christian, women's, and voices of color, literature courses should also include readings addressing topics relevant to the LGBTQIA+ community and challenging heteronormative gendered notions. Several texts incorporate LGBTQIA+ characters while providing non-members of the community with a more multifaceted view of this group. Perhaps the most well-known, modernist LGBTQIA+ text is Woolf's *Orlando* (1928). This text presents the narrative of a gender-fluid protagonist whose story spans centuries and challenges hegemonic masculinity while demonstrating that sociocultural notions about gender are always in flux. In this novel, Woolf (1928) implies, through the title character's gender fluidity, that gender is a social construct at the mercy of a culture entrenched in hegemonic masculinity. That Orlando loses property bestowed on the character when he was a man because he suddenly transformed into a woman provides an admirable commentary on one of the issues that many women from Woolf's time faced—the codification of women's gender inferiority. Shani Mootoo's *Moving Forward Like a Crab* (2014), like *Orlando*, depicts a transgender protagonist, Sid (woman)/Sydney (man), who, while living as an immigrant, lesbian woman in Canada, identifies an incompleteness that can only be resolved by Sid's return to Trinidad but as Sydney. Through Sydney, and with the help of his adopted son Jonathan, Mootoo's audience connects with the internal struggles of transitioning, the finality of this decision, and the availability of support, both familial and community, for people in transition.

Thani Al-Suwaidi's *The Diesel* discusses the life of "a transgender person, who houses a woman's soul in a man's body" (1994/2012, p. 9). The novella, written in stream-of-consciousness, addresses the complexities of living as a woman while being a biological man in a society closed to non-heteronormative gender orientations. While *The Diesel* challenges the norms of societies steeped in tradition and patriarchy, it also provides a thoughtful depiction of navigating those social spaces. James Baldwin's *Giovanni's Room* (1956/2013) also falls into the category of social critique as the novel, through protagonist David, a white, wealthy, closeted gay man who engages in same-sex relationships while viewing these interactions with anger, regret, and disappointment. The impact of hegemonic masculinity is apparent in David's cruelty towards Joey, his first same-sex partner, as well as his abrupt abandonment of Giovanni, his lover after becoming engaged to a woman, Hella. David feels very little compassion towards either man because they are male, and, because they are gay, he has feminized them. The novel implies that Joey and Giovanni are somehow not men because they each have an emotional attachment to him, showing him love and affection and receiving only cruelty, unkindness, and distance in return. Texts like *Orlando*, *Moving forward Like a Crab*, *Giovanni's Room*, and *The Diesel* help undergraduate students connect with non-heteronormative characters who disrupt hegemonic masculine discourses. These protagonists are Others, and the texts work to humanize them in a globalized society that is often unsympathetic people whose sexual orientations disrupt masculine heteronormative discourses.

Separating the Author from the Text

When using texts, such as the examples provided, in undergraduate literature courses, one of the most effective approaches to instruction is to apply literary theory. Some literary theory, while necessary, can alienate readers with highly technical and academic language. The texts listed prior are likely to engage students because they have a strong connection to a specific theoretical mode (some to multiple modes). When selecting literary theory for undergraduates, instructors might consider authors who employ approaches that are less technical, though neither less academic nor accurate. Roland Barthes' "The Death of the Author" offers a sound introduction to literary theory as Barthes states that once a text (symbol) is produced, "the voice loses its origin, the author enters into his own death, writing begins" (1967/2001, p. 1466). Barthes' (1967/2001) suggests that an author is separate from the contents of a fictional text whether prose, poetry, or drama, stressing that authors are not their texts. While undergraduate scholars are heavily inclined to associate the author's lived experiences with the text's contents, in fiction, this connection is not always valid. The author's biography may have little connection to text content, and, by stressing the importance of separating the two, instructors can guide undergraduates into more critical readings and, in some cases, a new critical reading that looks at each text as a whole and not subject to external factors. Although new criticism ignores the author's subjectivity, avoiding this is becoming increasingly problematic in contemporary criticism; therefore, presenting new criticism as a theoretical approach may encourage students to explore other critical approaches or develop their own. This method of fostering student criticism could provide a starting point for challenging hegemonic masculinity in literature classrooms using other forms of criticism.

Race and Ethnicity

Henry Louis Gates Jr. states "that the teaching of Afro-American literature is being institutionalized," yet, in the decades following this observation, African American literature remains marginalized (1988/2001, p. 2427). A broader-scaled examination of undergraduate literature programs reveals that representing voices diverging from the white, middle-class, Protestant, Euro-American male subjectivity is viewed with distrust, polite humor, or outright avoidance. Gates notes that "the Afro-American literary tradition was generated as a response to allegations that its authors did not and *could not* create literature, considered the single measure of a race's innate 'humanity'" (1988/2001, p. 2427). Incorporating Gates (1988/2001) into an examination of, for example, Alice Walker's *The Color Purple* (1982/1985) or Jessie Redmon Fauset's *Plum Bun* (1928) can help undergraduates situate the challenge of writing with the content, which, in both texts, addresses race and gender. Furthermore, "it is necessary to create distance between reader and texts in order to go beyond reflexive responses and achieve critical insight into and intimacy with their formal workings" (Gates, 1988/2001, p. 2429). The reflexive response of a white, masculine reader to *The Color Purple* might be pity for the protagonist, Celie. However, it is more helpful to social justice causes to examine the various domestic pressures exerted on Celie, first by her stepfather and later by her husband; to note the economic, gendered, and racial biases she faces in domestic and social settings; and, finally, to mark the multiple ways Celie transgresses norms to overcome these obstacles. To fully examine a character like Celie, a theorist like Gates (1988/2001) is more helpful in disrupting hegemonic masculinity in the literature classroom than, for example, a white Feminist like Judith Butler (1990/2006), who, while a critical voice in Feminist theory, is also alienated from the experiences of African American women. Critical readings written by authors of color disrupt Western masculine narratives and encourage students to think critically about the texts, voices, and narratives they represent both in the past and present.

Feminism Studies

Llana Carroll, incorporating Rita Felski (2003), notes that if Feminist literary criticism fails to "uphold an imagined Feminist standard of 'positive images' of women," it "can end up undermining other Feminist goals, including helping students claim or recover their own agency and their own readings of literary texts" (2011, p. 153). When "less-than-positive images of women" are denounced or instructors guard "against such criticism by offering equally narrow alternatives," these actions "suggest that critics and texts are one-dimensional" (Carroll, 2011, p. 156). Despite this criticism, Feminism remains an important tool in challenging hegemonic masculinity in literature classrooms, including in pedagogical practices. Carroll (2011) notes that of the readings she selected for an existentialist literature course, only one text was by a woman writer, thus perpetuating the stereotype that women only produce popular fiction and nothing of substance. However, Hélène Cixous (1975/2001) believes that the problem of women's representation in writing lies in women fearing judgment when they write and, therefore, choosing not to write. As a result, the issue of woman writer representation in the literature remains a pressing concern. Cixous' observation that "writing is precisely *the very possibility of change*" demands that women use writing as a "space that can serve as a springboard of subversive thought" (1976, p. 879). Thus, her call to women to "Write!" takes the approach of demanding that women author their own narratives, moving from subject to addressing subjectivity (Cixous, 1976, p. 876). For new scholars, Cixous (1976) provides some explanation for the canon's inherent sexist bias and its tradition of hegemonic masculinity. The need to conquer and control women's bodies and, by extension, their creativity, demonstrates the canon's phallocentric, white, European/American leanings. When read in conjunction with a novel such as late Nobel laureate Toni Morrison's *The Bluest Eye* (1970/2004), which copes with the burden of being a Black girl-child in a male-dominated, judgmental society, Cixous' contention that women are "the repressed of culture" seems an indictment of hegemonic masculinity and its influence on societies (1976, p. 878). Cixous (1976) brings an element of passion to the discussion of Feminism in the literary classroom that is likely to engage students in a way that, for example, Gates (1988/2001) may not. Yet, that passion may encourage many students to find their voices and articulate ideas about a text.

Black Feminism

An examination of Feminist theory would be incomplete without also addressing Black Feminism and Black Feminist critics. hooks observes that, while postmodern studies align well with critical race theory, it is often avoided by African American theorists as many believe "that there is no meaningful connection between Black experience and critical thinking about aesthetics or culture" (1994/2001,

p. 2478). Yet, Gates theorizes that Black theorists "must learn to read a Black text within a Black formal cultural matrix" (1988/2001, p. 2429). hooks' finds a connection between race and postmodernism, observing, more specifically, that "there is seldom any mention of Black experience or writings by Black people in this work, specifically Black women" (1994/2001, p. 2478). This observation of the absence of Black women from postmodern theory is not surprising but still detrimental to literature classrooms as it marginalizes an entire genre of criticism and group of critical voices. To critically analyze postmodern Black literature, or any literature representing a non-white feminine voice from this period, one must first accept that "[r]ace is a text (an array of discursive practices), not an essence. It must be read with painstaking care and suspicion, not imbibed" (Gates, 1988/ 2001, p. 2429). Critics analyzing texts addressing race should also have some firsthand knowledge of the topic rather than assuming the awkward position of externally examining this critical issue. Subjectivity and experience are two reasons why texts by critics of color should hold a more prominent place in undergraduate literature classrooms when analyzing texts by Black writers. Including critics like hooks, particularly her seminal text *Ain't I a Woman* (1981/1990), in the undergraduate literature classroom in conjunction with, for example, Octavia Butler's *Kindred* (1979), which uses the science fiction genre to provide some commentary on Black family origins in the U.S., can help students to connect the contents of the fictional text to the social, historical, cultural, gendered, and racial issues it addresses.

Classroom Discussions

Sarita Cannon describes a classroom as "a laboratory driven by experimentation and collaboration" (2017, p. 51). Experimentation is a consistent pattern when teaching and developing a collaborative relationship between instructors and students is the goal. The aim is to determine what method(s) would be most effective in encouraging student collaboration. Mollie V. Blackburn and Caroline T. Clark focus their research about group discussions on "LGBTQ-themed texts … among LGBTQ people and their allies" (2011, p. 222). While this research provides critical insight to how group discussions function and how they contribute to understanding a text, this approach does not help engage the larger community in a text that disrupts the heteronormative and, by extension, hegemonic masculinity. If marginalized groups meet and discuss texts depicting their experiences in isolation, this only furthers their isolation and deepens the hold of hegemonic masculinity on literature discussions.

Pedagogical activities that engage students in discussions must be used to help undergraduates connect to the texts in literature classrooms and to disrupt the classroom's hegemonic leanings towards allowing only the instructor (the authority) to speak. Additionally, many students may "feel that hate speech is now legitimated and normalized in ways that compromise their emotional and physical safety" (Cannon, 2017, p. 41). One might question how students can engage in a discussion when they simply do not feel safe in the space. One of the goals in today's literature classroom should be "the creation of an inclusive environment" that encourages students to express "both a visceral and an intellectual reaction to the text" (Cannon, 2017, p. 52). Such a classroom environment could help undergraduates express themselves and delegitimize hate speech while promoting discussions based on taking critical approaches to textual analysis.

Other, more direct methods, such as booktalking, can be used to engage students with a text and encourage participation during in-class discussions. Initially used by librarians to gain the attention of often-distracted middle and high school students, booktalking involves reading a book then briefly describing it and identifying key events. Linda Riesterer proposes that students can give a spontaneous "three-or-four-sentence summary of what a book is about, without giving away the ending" (2002, p. 8). Booktalks are best facilitated by students themselves, not by instructors. When students lead their own booktalks, they can take ownership of the discussion and not feel influenced or under the control of the instructor. The instructor should provide basic booktalking guidelines that reduce the possibility of expressing bias while refraining from leading the booktalks. Students selected to give booktalks can be instructed to summarize the material without additional commentary, reducing the possibility of including biases in the presentation. To accomplish this, Sonja Cole suggests limiting booktalks to between five and seven sentences: "Sentences 1 and 2 should introduce the main character and the setting. Sentences 3 to 5 should summarize the conflict. Sentences 6 and 7 should get kids thinking about what will happen next" (2007, p. 41). J. Marin Younker, taking a more technology-inclusive approach, contends that a booktalk can include "[p]odcasts, zines, videos, and blogs created by" adolescent or young adult readers (2006, p. 39). With the accessibility of information on the internet, there are now numerous sites available with videos to draw students' attention to reading material. For example, the YouTube group Wisecrack's page includes a subsection called "Thug Notes," which provides a lighter, humorous, non-biased analysis of literary texts that is also engaging and insightful. Any of these tools individually or a combination could be used to garner enough interest in a selected text to get students to complete the reading.

Classroom Discussions

Once students complete the text, instead of delving into a rather formal, structured in-class lecture, instructors might begin by asking the class one, simple question: "What did you think?". Cannon mentions beginning "class with a quick exercise in which each student shared a reaction, comment, or question about the reading" (2017, p. 51). Both approaches aim at initiating a reading discussion; either method is effective, but each may have a different student response. Sometimes, when attempting to help students negotiate the complexities of a text, one that is laden with subtext, a good place to start a discussion is with the obvious. While asking students what they think might seem straightforward, many instructors do not take this approach, opting instead for the formality, and occasional boredom, of a lecture. On the other side of this approach, many students are so acclimated to giving instructors what they believe instructors want that they forget it is perfectly acceptable to think and express their opinions without worrying about pleasing an audience. Students need not provide the correct answer, but they must respond, reflecting their understanding of the text and an effort to consider the reading material critically. Therefore, asking students what they think about a novel might create a more relaxed atmosphere, removing expectations about giving the "right" answer.

Another effective approach is connecting plot events to real-world events. If the novel is historical fiction, like Achebe's *Things Fall Apart* (1958), discussing British colonization of Nigeria is effortless as this process was repeated throughout the British empire and is often depicted in postcolonial texts. However, when the novel takes a more complicated approach to historical events that are typically misinterpreted, such as Butler's *Kindred* (1979), additional connections must be formed to clarify events for students who have often been presented with a one-dimensional or even whitewashed view of the topic of U.S. chattel slavery. In the novel, an African American woman named Dana time travels from the late twentieth to the early nineteenth century because she is summoned there to save the child version of her white ancestor, who will eventually enslave her Black foremother and force her into a sexual relationship producing children. Engaging students with material like *Kindred* could occur, following the initial question of what they think, with asking what they know about American slavery. This inquiry leads to additional questions about familial connections between masters and chattel slaves, which is relevant when discussing *Kindred*. This topic is also important in helping to dispel notions about racial superiority and its gendered outcomes—particularly on Black women in the American, antebellum South and in the almost two centuries following the Civil War.

These techniques serve the purpose of making students feel comfortable enough to express themselves in class, share their thoughts on the reading, begin a more detailed examination of the text, and engage in a discussion using theory. The instructor taking a less directive approach and yielding control of in-class discussions to students is an act of resistance to hegemony, which has dominated literature classrooms and determined who is permitted to teach and how that population teaches. Perhaps this approach might be considered Feminist or postcolonial; however, more important than identifying the theoretical mode is enacting it in the classroom so that undergraduates begin to take ownership of their education. In the process, instructors may observe students engaging more with the material, focusing less on the technological distractions, and questioning biased notions.

Conclusion

Raewyn Connell notes that the hegemonic position masculinity occupies within a given set of gendered relations is "a position always contestable" (2005, p. 76). In literature classrooms, there are ample opportunities to contravene and contest the hegemonic position the heteronormative takes over differences in gender, sexual orientation, race, class, religion, or language. Hegemonic masculinity, while a critical issue, has given rise to a series of other, rather disturbing biased notions that continue to plague contemporary societies globally. The long-term impact of colonization is still felt throughout the under-developed and developing world while neocolonial attitudes plague the developed world. The issue is not specifically hegemonic masculinity, but the biased ideas, stemming from this position, can be damaging and the possibility of perpetuating them through ignorance and avoidance of the issues remain problematic.

In academia, it is easy to convince oneself that the rarified air of privilege (educational, economic, class, gender, racial, or historical) that is breathed by so many faculty members is easily overcome. There is a notion among faculty that academe is the last great bastion of egalitarianism; however, a perusal of any given faculty population and their persistent use of only canonical (Euro-American, white, Christian, masculine) texts reveals that this is not accurate. Therefore, when English departments promote courses in the literature of the Other, specifically women of color, while staffing the faculty with examples of the Self, this obvious disparity raises questions in students' minds about representation, or perhaps they come to accept this as status quo, which does little to help them overcome their own inherent biases.

When the literature of the Other is taught, it should be accompanied by theorists who understand the lived experience of the text and with theories that contravene the norm. In addition, the 'usual suspects,' like Achebe and Kincaid, cannot be the only diverse voices heard in literature classrooms. To continue along this rather worn path of literature instruction would be foolhardy given the impact of globalization on the contemporary workforce. Literature classrooms must reflect the reality of lived experiences by including the voice of the Other in curricula; by incorporating the approaches of theorists of color to literary analysis; and by empowering students to speak so that they can think and write critically. Without the active inclusion of the Other, including women, writers and theorists of color, and student scholars in literature classrooms, the pattern of hegemonic masculinity that has become so ingrained in academia will continue to self-perpetuate globally.

References

Achebe, C. (1958). *Things fall apart*. London: William Heinemann, Ltd.

Alexander, C. (2011). Teaching against the tide: Transgressing norms in the American college composition classroom. *Akademisk Kvarter, 3*, 66–80.

Al-Suwaidi, T. (1994/2012). *The Diesel*. New York: ANTIBOOKCLUB.

Alteri, C. (1983). An idea and ideal of a literary canon. *Critical Inquiry, 10*(1), 37–60.

Angelou, M. (1969/1997). *I know why the caged bird sings*. New York: Bantam.

Baldwin, J. (1956/2013). *Giovanni's room*. New York: Vintage International.

Barthes, R. (1967/2001). The death of the author. In V. B. Leitch (Ed.), *The Norton anthology of theory and criticism* (pp. 1466–1469). New York: W. W. Norton & Company.

Belsey, C. (1982). Problems of literary theory: The problem of meaning. *New Literary History, 14*(1), 175–182.

Blackburn, M. V., & Clark, C. T. (2011). Analyzing talk in a long-term literature discussion group: Ways of operating within LGBT-inclusive and queer discourses. *Reading Research Quarterly, 46*(3), 222–248.

Brereton, B. (1998). Autobiographies, diaries and letters by women as sources for Caribbean history. *Feminist Review, 59*, 143–163.

Brontë, C. (1847). *Jane Eyre*. London: Smith, Elder & Co.

Butler, J. (1990/2006). *Gender trouble: Feminism and the subversion of identity*. New York: Routledge.

Butler, O. (1979). *Kindred*. New York: Doubleday.

Cannon, S. (2017). "Do I Remain a Revolutionary?": Intellectual and emotional risk in the literature classroom. *MELUS, 42*(4), 37–59.

Carroll, L. (2011). Teaching note: When a 'Feminist approach' is too narrow. *Feminist Teacher, 21*(2), 153–159.

Cixous, H. (1976). The laugh of Medusa (by K. Cohen & P. Cohen, Trans.). *Signs*, *1*(4), 875–893.

Cole, S. (2007). Booktalks that knock 'em dead. *Teacher Librarian*, *35*(1), 41–42.

Connell, R. W. (2005). *Masculinities* (2nd ed.). Berkeley: U of California P.

Donaldson, M. (1993). What is hegemonic masculinity? *Theory and Society*, *22*(5), 643–657.

El Saadawi, N. (1999/2009). *A daughter of Isis* (by Sherif Hetata, Trans.). London: Zed Books.

Emecheta, B. (1979). *The joys of motherhood*. New York: George Braziller.

Euripedes. (1897). *Medea*. Cambridge, UK: Cambridge University Press.

Felski, R. (2003). *Literature after feminism*. Chicago: University of Chicago Press.

Gates, H. L. (1988/2001). Talking Black: Critical signs of the times. In V. B. Leitch (Ed.), *The Norton anthology of theory and criticism* (pp. 2424–2432). New York: W. W. Norton & Company.

Gold, S. J. (2004). From Jim Crow to racial hegemony: Evolving explanations of racial hierarchy. *Ethnic and Racial Studies*, *27*(6), 951–968.

Gramsci, A. (1971/201). *Prison notebooks*. Columbia: Columbia University Press.

Griffin, B. (2018). Hegemonic masculinity as a historical problem. *Gender & History*, *30*(2), 377–400.

Hodge, M. (1970). *Crick crack monkey*. London: Andre Deutsch, Ltd.

hooks, b. (1981/1990). *Ain't I a woman*. London: Pluto Press.

hooks, b. (1997). *Bone Black*. New York: Holt Paperbacks.

hooks, b. (1994/2001). Postmodern Blackness. In V. B. Leitch (Ed.), *The Norton anthology of theory and criticism* (pp. 2478–2484). New York: W. W. Norton & Company.

Jay, M. (2003). Critical race theory, multicultural education, and the hidden curriculum of hegemony. *Multicultural Perspectives*, *5*(4), 3–9.

Jay, G., & Jones, S. E. (2005). Whiteness studies and the multicultural literature classroom. *MELUS*, *30*(2), 99–121.

Kincaid, J. (1978/1983). Girl. *At the bottom of the river*. New York: Farrar, Strauss, Giroux.

Levy, A. (2004). *Small island*. London: Headline Book Publishing.

Mahfouz, N. (1962/1988). Zaabalawi. *God's World: An anthology of short stories*. Beirut: Bibliotheca Islamica.

Marshall, P. (2009). *Triangular road: A memoir*. New York: Civitas Books.

Mootoo, S. (2014). *Moving forward sideways like a crab*. Canada: Doubleday Canada, Ltd.

Morrison, T. (1970/2004). *The bluest eye*. New York: Rosetta Books LLC.

Persaud, L. (2012). *Daughters of empire*. Leeds: Peepal Tree Press, Ltd.

Pratt, M. L. (1991). Arts of the contact zone. *Profession*, *91*, 33–40.

Redmon Fauset, J. (1928). *Plum bun*. New York: Frederick A. Stokes Company Publishers.

Rhys, J. (1930/1985). *After leaving Mr. Mackenzie*. In D. Athill (Ed.), *Jean Rhys: The complete novels* (pp. 235–344). New York: W. W. Norton & Company.

Rhys, J. (1966/1985). *Wide Sargasso Sea*. New York: W. W. Norton & Company, Inc.

Rhys, J. (1979/1981). *Smile please*. London: Penguin Ltd.

Riesterer, L. (2002). (Book)talk them into reading. *The Book Report*, *21*(3), 8–9.

Schaub, M. (2003). Beyond these shores: An argument for internationalizing composition. *Pedagogy: Critical Approaches to Teaching Literature, Language, Composition, and Culture, 3*(1), 85–98.

Trevors, G. J. (2016). Identity and epistemic emotions during knowledge revision: A potential account for the backfire effect. *Discourse Processes, 53*(5–6), 339–370.

Walker, A. (1982/1985). *The color purple.* New York: Pocket Books.

Woolf, V. (1928). *Orlando: A biography.* London: Hogarth Press.

Younker, J. M. (2006). Talking it up: Booktalking can open up a new world to middle and high school students. *School Library Journal, 54*(4), 39.

CHAPTER TEN

Queer Pedagogy and Engaging Cinema in LGBTQIA+ Discourse in Africa

STEPHEN OGHENERURO OKPADAH

Introduction

The struggle to decriminalize LGBTQIA+ individuals and practices is gaining traction throughout the world due to several counter-discourses, movements, and the adoption of oppositional cultures. Although these sexual identities and communities have received less criticism in the West (in fact, they have been given the right to life with the legalization of all identities in some Western nations), numerous countries (especially those on the African continent) have been a home for discrimination against members of the LGBTQIA+ community. Criminalization of LGBTQIA+ individuals and practices in countries such as Nigeria, Uganda, Cameroun, Liberia, Libya, Senegal, Somalia, and others are often a product of religion, morality, and a biased justice system. The belief that non-heterosexual relationships and identities are un-African is predominant in cases of LGBTQIA+ marginalization. Same-sex practices are often considered violations of the moral ethos of the African society, and in some cases, as demonic in nature. Against this backdrop, Vasu Reddy claims that "according to African stereotypes, anti-straight sexuality is a disease/sickness; a possession by evil or demonic spirits; an occult practice; or simply a despicable influence from the 'morally decadent' West" (Reddy, 2002, p. 1). Same-sex individuals and practices are seen as queer in Africa. According to Nowlan, "queers are outraged gays, lesbians, bisexuals, transgendered people, and allied misfits and outsiders who seek to move from expression of rage toward demanding satisfaction in response to what outrage them, including by seizing and appropriating what they can when this is not given them in response to their demands" (2010, p. 3). Nowlan's definition of the term "queer" implies that to be queer is to be a member of the African LGBTQIA+ community.

Presidents Sam Nujoma of Namibia and Robert Mugabe of Zimbabwe once opined that LGBTQIA+ were social misfits and not fit to live. In the words of Mugabe as cited by Chikura-Mtwazi, having a non-heterosexual sexual orientation "degrades human dignity. It is unnatural, and there is no question ever of allowing these people to behave worse than dogs and pigs. If dogs and pigs do not do it, why must human beings? If you see such people parading themselves arrest them and hand them over to the police" (2017, p. 1). In furtherance of his hate for the LGBTQIA+ culture, Mugbe also criticizes all allies of the LGBTQIA+ club. He articulates that he "find[s] it extremely outrageous and repugnant to [his] human conscience that such immoral and repulsive organizations, like those of homosexuals, who offend both against the law of nature and the cultural norms espoused by our society, should have any advocates in our midst and elsewhere in the world" (BBC, 1999, p. 1).

In light of several African cultures that openly reject anything connected to LGBTQIA+ identities and culture, there has been a dearth of critical works on LGBTQIA+, cinema pedagogy, and their intersection in Africa. In the face of the oppression that the LGBTQIA+ community goes through, cinema has brought these identities into the center of discourse to deconstruct homophobia and decriminalize queer identities in Africa. Since these films present LGBTQIA+ identities and experiences in a positive light, they hold tremendous educational promise. Thus, African queer cinema can be used as pedagogy to orientate audiences on the need to accept, embrace and celebrate sexual cultures. Presenting students films created to give voice to members of the LGBTQIA+ community and empower their ranks can help students understand several key tensions in play within many African cultures today. For instance, whether African film LGBTQIA+ narratives truly reflect an indigenous African ethos; whether queer cinema can create space(s) for LGBTQIA+ identities in Africa; and whether films about the LGBTQIA+ community are pedagogical. This chapter explores these issues along with the politics of sexuality and LGBTQIA+ identities in Africa. Furthermore, this analysis examines African queer cinema as a struggle against heteronormative and oppressive tendencies. Employing Michel Foucault's (2016) perspective on knowledge, power, and discourse as theory, this chapter uses content analysis to investigate African queer films such as Mohammed Camara's

Dakan (1997), Moses Ebere's *Men In Love* (2010) and Adaora Nwandu's *Rag-tag* (2006), among other selected African queer cinema narratives as pedagogical mediums that exemplify queer identities.

Pedagogy and the Politics of Sexuality and LGBTQIA+ Identities in Africa

It is imperative for educational institutions (especially in Africa) to adopt criti-cal methodologies and examine the current state of LGBTQIA+ discourse since the continent has failed to keep pace with their Western counterparts regarding LGBTQIA+ issues. While it is true that the hesitation on Africa's part could be attributed to hegemonic masculinity and heteronormativity, that is not an acceptable excuse. Africa must rethink its monolithic approach to addressing LGBTQIA+ issues. In fact, educators in the secondary and tertiary settings should strive to enlighten African students how to transcend heteronormativity and engage in investigative methodological approaches to LGBTQIA+ issues.

The colonial experience, globalization, and postmodernism have placed Afri-can same-sex discourse into the international discussion about implementing social justice. However, there are still lingering issues with granting LGBTQIA+ individuals in Africa the same rights and liberties as elsewhere in the world. These issues may stem from blatantly false assertions that LGBTQIA+ identities in Africa are Western constructions and the idea that the LGBTQIA+ community was not present in Africa prior to the transatlantic slave trade and colonial expe-rience. In short, some Africans believe that the LGBTQIA+ community is due to Western interference. The socio-political response to these false claims has been varied and has led to differing perspectives about inclusion and acceptance for LGBTQIA+ populations. "Politicians, religious leaders and traditional spokes-men, [have] insisted ever more strongly that the very idea of same-sex practices was foreign to Africa, and that it had been imported from the West" (Awondo et al., 2012, p. 148). However, numerous literary, descriptive, and quantitative methodological studies conducted by scholars in the social sciences and human-ities confirm that "there is evidence showing not only that same-sex intimacy was tolerated in ancient Egypt, but that at certain periods same-sex relationships were legally recognized" (Dowson, 2006, p. 96). According to Evans-Pritchard, "among the Azande, in precolonial Sudan, male same-sex marriage was legally recognized where dowry was paid to boy-wives and damages were awarded for infidelity" (1970, p. 72). The Meru people of Kenya, the Bantu of Angola, and the Zulu of South Africa also tolerated transgender men and allowed them to marry other men. Gay prostitution is also reported among the Hausa of Nigeria (Greenberg, 1988, p. 60). We must not forget that indigenous Hausas were pagans and non-Muslims. The indigenous Hausa customs created space(s) for the culture of gay prostitution. It was in the wake of the nineteenth century that the Fulani Jihad, led by Uthman Dan Fodio, displaced traditional practices, and imposed Islamic religious belief systems on the Hausa states. This dislocation and imposition included the oppression of the LGBTQIA+ community and the introduction of Islamic marriage traditions, rooted in the framework of heteronormativity. These findings suggest that at least some people of precolonial Africa expressed queer identities.

While religious "conservative voices see the queer practice as a Western imposition" (Schoonover & Galt, 2015, p. 90), one must not forget that queer sexual exploration has been part of the historical African experience. According to Aljazeera, in precolonial times, there were traces of same-sex marriage in some ethnic nationalities in Uganda (2014, p. 1). In fact, "among the Langi people of Uganda, effeminate males were allowed to marry men" (Al Jazeera, 2014, p. 1). The incursion of the West, which ushered in Christianity, brought about the change in this status quo. It also may have changed how queer was socially constructed to take on a more sinister definition. Historically, what are now considered queer practices in African societies were not considered queer. It is, therefore, wrong to "state that same-sex positioning is unAfrican" (Reddy, 2002, p. 5). Even after gaining independence from imperialist nations like Great Britain and Spain, residual control over African states remained visible. Transculturality and transnationality made possible via this lingering control helped popularize queer culture in Africa. Western ideals have been the springboard on which Africa has saddled many of its traditions. Pickett asserts that "in the 20th century sexual roles were redefined once again. With the decline of prohibitions against pre-marital sex for the sake of pleasure, even sex outside of marriage, it became more difficult to argue against gay sex. It was in this context that the gay liberation movement took off" (2015, p. 1). The debate over the decriminalization and legitimization of same-sex marriage in Africa continues to gain momentum, though many Africans still exhibit actions and express statements fueled by homophobia. To some Africans, to be queer is to be a child of the devil, and non-heterosexual identities are shown disdain. For example, in 1995, Mugabe, stood out as a reference point for African homophobia when he proclaimed that "non-heterosexuals were worse than pigs and dogs and deserved no rights whatsoever" (BBC, 1999, p. 1). In 1997, the Namibian president, Sam Nujoma, with equal measure of intolerance as his Zimbabwean counterpart, described same-sex engagement as a gruesome inhuman perversion which should be uprooted totally from society" (Lyonga, 2014, p. 97). Moreover, the support of the West sought for by the LGBTQIA+ community in Africa have yielded little to no results. Adamu Ibrahim states that, "with the role of European colonial legislation, Christianity, Islam and Western/American conservatism, and global LGBT rights activists and organizations, it appears as if the debate on LGBT rights in Africa is far from being solely African. It is a universal debate that is simultaneously taking place in other parts of the world, sometimes with the same actors involved in the West and Africa. To the extent that the homophobic discourse is transcontinental, LGBT rights activism is becoming inevitably multi-local as well" (2015, p. 266).

While the LGBTQIA+ community in Africa has begun seeking support globally, some Africans have greeted Western aid with anger. For instance, when former United States President Barrack Obama visited Kenya, the chants of "We do not want Obama and Obama, we do not want Michelle and Michelle" (Wheaton, 2015, para. 8), rang through the air. This was a warning to President Obama to desist from promoting queer activism in Kenya. The globalization of queer discourse has supplied the motivational force behind the legalization of LGBTQIA+ practices. In other words, South Africa's integration of the LGBTQIA+ community into society and the legalization of same-sex marriage stems from the assimilation of ideals of the West's paradigm of transcontinentality.

The criticism leveled upon gays, lesbians, transgenders, bisexuals, and other queer identities charted a new course in the history of LGBTQIA+ in Africa. "Perhaps the most significant recent social change involving queerity is the emergence of the gay liberation movement in the West. In philosophical circles, this movement is, in part, represented through a rather diverse group of thinkers who are grouped under the label of queer theory" (Pickett, 2015, p. 1). LGBTQIA+ liberation movements counter existing anti-LGBTQIA+ efforts. Desmond Tutu, a South African Anglican priest of international repute, fully articulates this by saying, "I cannot but be as God has made me. And so I spoke against the injustices of apartheid, about racism, where people were penalized for something about which they could do nothing, their ethnicity. I, therefore, could not keep quiet when people were hounded for something they did not choose, their sexual orientation" (Tutu, 2008, p. 1).

Tutu fought relentlessly to end apartheid in South Africa. It should be noted that Tutu's sympathy for marginalized LGBTQIA+ community members should not be construed as advocacy for the LGBTQIA+ cause. One assumes he is only concerned about the right to life and the existence of people with non-heterosexual orientations. Tutu has been instrumental to South Africa's sympathy for the LGBTQIA+ cause. "In November 2006, South Africa passed the Civil Union Act, becoming the fifth country in the world and the first in

Africa to legalize same-sex marriage" (Awondo et al., 2012, p. 157). Apart from Tutu, Imam Muhsin Hendricks has also supported the oppressed LGBTQIA+ community. He emphasizes the biological construction of sexual positioning. According to Hendricks, "when I was five years old, my mannerisms were very effeminate. When I reached puberty, my first attraction was to a boy in my class. Although I later got married to a woman, due to social pressure, we must understand that similar gender placement is not *haram*. Islam gives us leeway to think" (Qantara, 2014, p. 1). Despite the religious inclinations of Tutu and Hendricks, they are aware of the need for the inclusivity of diverse identities in society.

In Nigeria, Wole Soyinka, Charles Oputa, and Chimamanda Adichie have advocated for a sexually liberal Africa (Nigeria especially). Nigeria had been critical of the LGBTQIA+ community. President Goodluck Jonathan's administration addressed this with the formal signing of *The Same-sex Marriage Prohibition Law of 2014*. The law endorses "punishment of a sentence of up to 14 years imprisonment and also criminalizes the formation, operation, and supports for gay clubs, societies, and organizations with sentences of up to 10 years imprisonment" (Onuche, 2015, pp. 91–98). Passage of this law was met by an outcry from Nigerian pro-gay activists such as Adichie. Her manifesto against this anti-LGBTQIA+ law reads that "the new law that criminalizes homosexuality is popular among Nigerians. But it shows a failure of our democracy, because the mark of a true democracy is not in the rule of its majority but in the protection of its minority … holy books of different religions do not have equal significance for all Nigerians but also because the holy books are read differently by different people. The Bible, for example, also condemns fornication and adultery and divorce, but they are not crimes" (Adichie, 2014, p. 1).

It is pertinent to note that "Christian (and Islamic) leaders are often a driving force behind attacks on queer culture" (Awondo et al., 2012, p. 148). In the Christian and Islamic creed, fornication and adultery, just like same-sex practices, are crimes and considered sinful. In most traditional African societies, such as in the Hausa, Igbo, Zulu, Akan, and Urhobo ethnic groups, fornication and adultery are also anathema. It becomes flawed to criminalize same-sex marriage yet exclude fornication and adultery.

In Cameroon, Alice Nkom, attorney, and founder of the Cameroonian gay rights organization ADEFHO (Association for the Defense of Homosexuals in Cameroon), has been at the forefront of advocating for the decriminalization LGBTQIA+. Nkom's advocacy stems from the rise of homophobia in Cameroon (Ndjio, 2012, p. 120). Her human rights defense of gays in Cameroon has received positive appraisal from the international community.

Western governments have also criticized anti-LGBTQIA+ sentiments in Africa. According to Amnesty international, "same-sex orientation is illegal in 38 of 54 African countries" (n.d, p. 3) This contrasts most countries in the West, where same-sex marriage has been legalized. At the genesis of the criminalization of same-sex relations in Nigeria, the United States, Canada, Britain, the United Nations, and European Union called for a repeal of the decision of the Nigerian government. Nwokolo (2014, p. 1) claims that "John Kerry, the US Secretary of States called the Act a dangerous restriction on freedoms. William Hague, the UK Foreign Secretary opined that 'the Act is a disappointment.'" Ms. Linda Thomas-Greenfield, the U.S. Assistant Secretary of State for Africa hinted on the need 'to mount pressures on the President to change the law and respect human rights for all Nigerians despite sexual orientations' and lastly the UN High Commissioner for Human Rights, Navi Pillay said that the same-sex marriage prohibition law is "draconian and illegal."

The multitude of international opinions do not merely make the LGBTQIA+ debate transnational; they also broaden the horizons of LGBTQIA+ discourse. A scrutiny of the United States' perspective on the LGBTQIA+ debate suggest that the legitimization of queer identities does not necessarily promote LGBTQIA+, but instead is geared toward protecting the rights of queer individuals to live in a society where the stigmatization of the LGBTQIA+ community has reached its crescendo.

African academics have historically been critical of queer culture. Paradigmatically, Obasola Kehinde posits that "non-normative sexual positioning is unethical and unnatural. Therefore, it should be condemned in strong terms" (Kehinde, 2013, p. 77) Kehinde seems to forget that societies are subject to change when he goes further, stating that "though there has been a few dissenting voices, the general consensus in Africa is that monosexuality should not be allowed to take root. It is foreign to African culture. Its manifestation should be treated as an aberration rather than a socially acceptable behavioral pattern" (Kehinde, 2013, p. 92). Kehinde's position stems from his cultural and religious beliefs. This reveals that one cannot separate the African academia from the African cultural and religious spaces. Academics are products of cultures and religions. In fact, while scholarship influences culture, it also has been influenced by culture.

The LGBTQIA+ debate has been a subject of discourse in African cinemas that includes numerous cinematic cultures such as Nollywood in Nigeria, Senegal, Cameroon, Ghana, and South African film industries. Of the three important films that serve as case studies in this chapter, first is *Dakan* which "is commonly understood as the first gay film in sub-Saharan Africa" (Schoonover & Galt, 2015, p. 90). Additionally, Nwandu's *Ragtag* and Ebere's *Men in Love*

(2010) are also a reference point to African queer cinema. The above narratives show that African queer cinema can create inclusive spaces for LGBTQIA+ identities in Africa. These narratives can be used pedagogically to galvanize support for the oppressed LGBTQIA+ community and also show educators and students how to combat hegemonic masculinity and heteronormativity, which motivate undue harm to LGBTQIA+ individuals.

African LGBTQIA+ Cinema as Pedagogy

African queer cinema is a response to the criminalization of LGBTQIA+ practices and unfair treatment meted on community members. Epprecht observes that "African gays and lesbians have written their own memoirs, fiction, and poetry to add crucial insider insights to the discussion" (2018, p. 140). These memoirs have often been translated and adapted onscreen. Moreover, queer cinema has become a medium of perspective and advocacy for the marginalized LGBTQIA+ community. The African queer filmmaking enterprise was heavily influenced by the American New Queer Cinema (ANQC), which is "a kind of independent film-making which shares some of the main principles of Queer Theory, which is also against the idea of heteronormativity" (Maria, 2015, p. 16). ANQC's social justice and activist agenda emphasizes full integration of LGBTQIA+ communities into a world dominated by hegemonic masculinity and heteronormativity. The narration of queer lives by African cinema can be used pedagogically to teach students about queer individuals and why they should not be oppressed. Queer cinema breaks the barriers created by heteronormative cultures by centering on the lives of LGBTQIA+ culture and characters. In *Queer Images: A history of gay and lesbian film in America*, Benshoff and Griffin propose five characteristics of queer cinema. They articulate that "a movie might be considered queer if it deals with characters that are queer … Films might be considered queer when they are written, directed, or produced by queer people or perhaps when they star lesbian, gay, or otherwise queer actors … A queer film is a film that is viewed by lesbian, gay, or otherwise queer spectators … Queer films include any and all kinds of films that invite and encourage spectators to identify with characters who are considerably different from who spectators normally conceive themselves to be, and who they normally identify as. This can include films that encourage heterosexual audiences to identify with gay, lesbian, bisexual, and transgender characters, but it can also include many other kinds of identifications with 'the other' as well, including identification across lines of race and class" (2006, pp. 10–12).

One must remain critical of Benshoff and Griffin's claim that a film could be considered queer simply by the fact that it was written, directed, or produced by individuals who identify as queer. To be clear, Benshoff and Griffin erroneously claim that individuals who identify as queer who are filmmakers could write, produce, and direct a film with heteronormative themes, with no elements that challenge that heteronormativity, and the film would still be considered to land in the genre of queer cinema. The issue with their assertion is that a primary feature of queer cinema is the presentation of non-heteronormative characters and themes. Since it is possible for queer allies who do not identify as queer to also produce films that call challenge hegemonic masculinity and heteronormativity, then Benshoff and Griffin's classification of queer cinema fails to be exhaustive.

The students must understand that African queer films involve a struggle between heterosexual and LGBTQIA+ individuals. While some films some are critical of LGBTQIA+, some other films others are advocacies for the non-heteronormative sexual orientations. In Mohamad Camara's *Dakan*, the characters of Destiny, Sori, and Manga fall in love. However, they are separated by their families. While Sori gets married and has a child, Manga's mother sends Manga to an herbalist to seek a gay "cure." He eventually enters into a relationship with Oumou, a white woman. Many years later, "when the men see each other again in a bar, they immediately recognize their mutual desire. Despite their love for their families and genuine relationships with women, Manga and Sori ultimately leave everything behind to be together" (Schoonover & Galt, 2015, p. 89). In *Dakan,* world of tolerance is created. Although Manga's mother sees counter-normative identities as abnormal, she does not consider heterosexuality as a do or die affair. She sees norms as societal constructs and as such, are liable to change. The name "Dakan" means destiny, and as the title of the queer *Dakan* connotes, one could be born gay. Here, the filmmaker puts the African concept of predestination to play. Although in some traditional African societies (such as among the Yoruba people of Nigeria), there is the belief that destiny can be subjected to change, in most societies, the reverse is the case. This, therefore, becomes complex as *Dakan* defines monosexuality as a biological construction.

In Nwandu's *Ragtag*, a transnational Nigerian film, two non-heteronormative characters, Raymond and Tagbo are presented. They are separated from each other like Sori and Manga at the age of twelve. They reunite many years later, and their love for each other resurfaces as they continue their intimate and sexual exploration of each other. They continue to stick to each other despite Tagbo father's disapproval of their gay relationship. *Ragtag* and *Dakan* share the feature of displacement and reunion of the gay characters. Despite being displaced by the society, Sori and Manga finally reunite at the end of the narrative. This affirms that no matter how discriminatory members of the LGBTQIA+ community are treated, the global movement for the inclusion and acceptance of LGBTQIA+ identities will pay off. The filmmaker reassures the queer community that liberation from oppression at the hands of the larger society is a task that must be done. Sori and Manga's unity and Rag (Raymond) and Tag's (Tagbo) attitude teaches the imperative of harmony and togetherness of all queer categories to achieving acceptance.

Rag Tag is the ideal use of the film narrative to educate viewers against discriminating and criminalizing LGBTQIA+ identities. The film "challenges the tendency of closeting queerity in African films, or of representing it as evil, and abnormal. To use Naficy's words in a gendered context, *Rag Tag* destabilize[s] the traditional binarism of space" (Lyonga, 2014, p. 101).

African societies adhere to religious precepts and commandments than the West. Islam and Christianity, two dominant religions in Africa are anti-LGBTQIA+. This lends credence to the destructive appraisal of LGBTQIA+ in Africa. Unlike *Dakan,* Ebere's *Men in Love* places same-sex orientation in the domain of social construction. In this film, equivalent sex alignment is frowned at. Although he aligned with Alex sexually, Charles later becomes critical of non-heteronormative sexual orientation. Alex, his friend and gay partner is also looked at in disdain and hate by Whitney, Charles' wife on her realization that the latter engaged/engages in same-sex relationship with her husband, she frowns at it. The film even ends with a *Deus Ex Machina* whereby, prayers deliver Charles from the servitude of same-sex inclination. Films such as this would appeal to an anti-LGBTQIA+ Nigerian audience. This film advocates the transcendental approach at "unqueering" queer characters. *Men in Love*, therefore does not portray the pedagogy of LGBTQIA+, a shift in power and knowledge of sexual reorientation like *Dakan* and *Rag Tag* do. *Men in Love* is an expression of the Nigerian filmmaker's ideology, unlike Nwandu (the director of *Tag Tag*), who has been influenced by Western ideals.

Most African filmmakers that have interrogated the LGBTQIA+ condition have made the non-LGBTQ sexual inclination dominate heteronormativity. In fact, most of them align with the LGBTQIA+ minority and use their films to speak against the social injustice met on them (LGBTQIA+). *Dakan* deviates from the mainstream Nigerian film narratives that depend on the *Deus Ex Machina* for conflict resolution. This film "fits into some of the universal narratives favored by the queer" (Schoonover & Galt, 2018, p. 123). With the failure of the herbalist to cure Manga of his same-sex intimacy with Sori, the filmmaker, Camara seems to posit that same-sex is not a spiritual possession and dysfunction as popularly believed in Africa. It has nothing to do with the fetish and the transcendental.

The Anti-gay community made *Dakan* "controversial precisely for its *direct* representation of non-heterosexuality, perceived by many African critics as un-African, sinful, or an unwanted relic of European colonialism" (Epprecht, 2008, p. 132). The destructive critique of LGBTQIA+ cultures in Nollywood has led to these narratives as being secondary to the plot. *Men in Love* fully explicates that "traditionally, Nollywood films on non-heterosexuality center on heterosexual couples, with the non-straight persons assigned backseat roles as secondary characters, who attempt to ruin heterosexual relationships but fail in the end. Like films such as *Emotional Crack* (Oduwa, 2009), *Last Wedding* (Iroegbu, 2004) and *End Time* (Nnebue, 1999), *Men in Love* tows this Nollywood mainstream representation of non-heterosexuality" (Lyonga, 2014, p. 101).

Conversely, the opening scene of *Dakan* displaces the heteronormative film culture and brings the gay from the closet to the public. This scene reveals a close shot of Sori and Manga kissing passionately inside a car. While the anti-LGBTQIA+ audience is held spellbound with disgust as the sight of two kissing young men, the pro-LGBTQIA+ spectator-especially the queer categories perceives this as a "meaningful resistance to the power of the straight majority as explicated by Foucault" (Pickett, 2015, p. 5). Politics of power play is replete of the subject matter of every queer film. In films of this repertoire, there is a power tussle between the hetero and non-hetero cultures. The outcome of this scrimmage is determined by the filmmaker or the society in which the film is produced. Educators and students must understand that in the Nigerian queer cinema has been critical of the non-hetero position. Films that valorize gay rights and advocacy for social justice are frowned upon in Nigeria. This stems from the country's cultural background where the two dominant religions-Christianity and Islam perceive same-sex relations as demonic. To compound this challenge, the Nigerian Film and Video Censors Board (NFVCB) a body responsible for regulating the content of what is churned out of the Nigerian screen has always influenced the content of every film narrative. The NFVCB are well known to suppress narratives that oppose perceived moral ethos and norms of the Nigerian society.

Most Nollywood films are economically driven. The Nigerian filmmaker who is conscious of the capital which he has spent in the filmmaking process examines what he is to churn into the market to facilitate box office success in a morally conscious society. Conversely, transnational Nigerian films such as *Rag Tag* have gone beyond the frontiers of religion and African cultural beliefs to explore the question of sexual identity within the domain of the materialistic and the profane. Hence, this binarism is clear of *Men in Love* and *Rag Tag*. While the latter, a product of the Nigerian Diasporic filmmaker breaks the border of cultural beliefs, the former is subtle in its subject matter as it disapproves of same-sex desire.

Dakan, as a cinema of commitment, is a challenge to the hetero-culture "for it demands to speak and to educate in public in the traditions of African political cinema, and yet it also proposes a queer mode of publicity. The film refuses to place queer lives in opposition to postcolonial politics: it demands to be seen both as postcolonial and as gay" (Schoonover & Galt, 2015, p. 91). The queer film audience is sensitized on the creation of identities with the medium of film. While this form of pedagogy is contextualized in a particular scheme, it is also imperative to note that simply viewing a film is not enough. Observing a Film can be sometimes passive for some audiences. Hence, dialogue among the teacher and students in the African classroom setting must take place for there to be any hope that the message of acceptance and inclusion to sink into their perspectives is achieved. This is "an intentional attempt to influence how identities are created within certain social relations that do not support marginalized groups. When educators are aware of positionality, power and their own backgrounds as well as their students' backgrounds, meaningful learning can take place" (Lagomarsino, 2015, p. 9). The audience is the student who understands what it means and takes to be identified with a particular identity and the need to depoliticize the "hetero" and "homo" binary. At this point, the homo is not a distortion of sexual identity. Rather, it is a regeneration of past identities. *Dakan* aligns with this full acceptance model of LGBTQIA+ identities which supposes that "same-sex culture and heterosexuality are two aspects of sexuality, neither being the counterfeit nor the other, both being right or wrong depending on the context of their expression" (Pierson, 1990, p. 257). Advocates of the model believe that those who identify with LGBQTIA+ perspectives are born with the trait in them just like albinos, Blacks and heterosexuals are created the way they are. As such, members of the LGBTQIA+ community should neither be forced to renounce their identity, nor be marginalized by the heteronormative majority. Addressing "the question of subjugation and silencing of the oppressed and marginalized" (Binebai, 2015, p. 206) sexual minorities in homophobic Africa is therefore the thrust of *Rag Tag* and *Dakan*. *Dakan* and *Rag Tag* are produced for the purpose of "breaking discriminatory labels which have led to ill treatment and oppression of the LGBT community" (Maria, 2015, p. 18). This "cinematic visions of queerness, whether through queer characters and narratives or through representations of queer desire, have the capacity to make the global legible" (Schoonover & Galt, 2015, p. 89).

This recent proliferation of LGBTQIA+ films in Africa reveals that filmmakers have begun to utilize the medium of the queer film narrative for pedagogical activism. While the filmmakers have succeeded in this, educators must also play their role. The awareness on the persuasive power of film is not new.

Shehu posits that "film has the power to change the orientation of its viewers and influence their thought pattern" (1992, p. 78). To this end, in the classroom, educators could integrate the cinema in to their teaching process by exhibiting films that are critical of heterosexism. After exhibiting these films in the classroom, the educator could ask the students to narrate their experiences and how they intersect or differ to the situation in the films. With this, students would come out of their shell to express themselves on their perceived fears and strengths with issues related to sexuality. Educators could use the medium of film to guide the student on understanding identity construction and preservation. This is a way of protecting the student from perceived harassment and sometimes, depression.

Other African films that explore the LGBTQIA+ motif include Shamim Sarif's *The World Unseen* (2007), *Catherine Stewart's While You Weren't Looking* (2015) and John Tengrove's *The Wound* (2017). Arif's *The World Unseen* (2007), makes the student understand that same-sex disposition is apt in a homophobic continent such as Africa. In this narrative, Mariam and Amina's love and affection for one another grows and they get entangled even in the core of oppression. Stewart's *While You Weren't Looking* (2015) is a South African film with a multicultural setting which does a comparative survey of the experiences of lesbians in urban and rural settings.

Schoonover and Galt (2015, p. 92) reveal that "queer cinema could easily be considered activist films, insisting through their fictional worlds that the spectator reconfigure their assumptions about their worlds outside the cinema." Renowned African queer films such as *Dakan* and *Rag Tag* are mostly box office hits among gay communities. Paradigmatically, *Rag Tag*, the first Nigerian film about LGBTQIA+ experiences was premiered at the 2006 San Francisco International Lesbian, Gay, Bisexual, Transgender (LGBT) Film Festival.

LGBTQIA+ praxis gave rise to queer theory which aligns with Foucauldian aesthetics. Foucault's approach to power discourse and knowledge reveals that "a discourse is an institutionalized way of speaking or writing about reality that defines what can be intelligibly thought and said about the world and what cannot. For example, a new discourse of *sexuality* had fundamentally changed the way we think about desire, pleasure, and our innermost selves" (Foucault, 2016, p. 1). He goes further to submit that "discourses about sexuality did not discover some pre-existing, core truth about human identity, but rather created it through particular practices of power/knowledge" (Foucault, 2016, p. 1). Creative works within the queer genre break this power/knowledge held by the heterosexual community. *Dakan* and *Rag Tag* epitomize Foucault's aesthetics of power. Knowledge shifts from the majority (hetero) to the minority

(LGBTQIA+ community). *Dakan* and other queer films dislodge the power of heteronormativity. There is a transformation from ignorance to awareness. Sori, Rat, Tag and Manga's sexual engagements are placed before the audience without the filmmaker concealing them. Their gasp for breath when they caress with their eyes closed and mouths open, and the sound they emit in the course of caressing and kissing, makes one realize the pleasure the duo of Manga and Sori derive from it. The bond they have in the film and how the filmmaker portrays these characters is similar to James Cameron's portrayal of Jack and Rose in the classic, *Titanic* (1998). This pedagogical exercise is a struggle against heteronormative, homophobia, and oppressive tendencies. Educators could use films such as *Rag Tag* and *Dakan* that push against oppression of LGBTQIA+ to make students understand that they can stand firm in the light of oppression. Since the medium of film is a visual one, it is easier to convince students that they do not need to be intimidated by draconian laws that forbid their sexual orientation. In the same vein, educators must be selective in the type of films about sexual identity that they exhibit in classrooms. Films that balance the sexual divide-LGBTQIA+ and heterosexual orientation are what the students must experience so that they will not in turn become oppressors of heteronormative culture. Educators must then realize that queer films "would bring the self out of the closet, annexing whole new genres, revise histories in their own image, and seemingly most impressive of all, rapidly become the in thing such that you don't even have to be queer to get the picture" (Rich, 1992, p. 49).

Conclusion

Queer cinemas in Africa are a pedagogical alliance that is geared towards speaking for the LGBTQIA+ minority that has been marginalized by the non-gay community. This creative enterprise creates space(s) for the exploration of sexual identities and the deconstructing of the notion of LGBTQIA+ as unAfrican. Politics, religion, and justice have been the major drivers of the LGBTQIA+ debate which graduated into the criminalization of LGBTQIA+ identities in countries such as Nigeria, Cameroon, Uganda, Zimbabwe among others. The decriminalization agenda of African queer films led to the production of *Dakan* and *Rag Tag*. These films are a paradigm shift from the anti-queer film in which same-sex marriage had always been demonized and portrayed in a bad light. *Men in Love*, though also explore the LGBTQIA+ genre contrasts the ideology portrayed in *Dakan* and *Rag Tag*. It advocates for a LGBTQIA+ free world where heterosexuality must thrive, while other sexual identities must be oppressed. Queer films affirm that inclusivity of the LGBTQIA+ community can be a primary duty of cinema. African queer cinema resists heteronormativity and other sexually oppressive categories and this enterprise is geared towards creating praxis for the LGBTQIA+ community across the African continent.

References

Adichie, C. (2014). *Chimamanda Adichie: Why can't he just be like everyone else?* Retrieved from http://www.thescoopng.com/2014/02/18/chimamanda-adichie-why-cant-he-just-be-like-veryone-else/

Amnesty International (n.d). Making love a crime: Criminalization of same-sex conduct in sub Saharan Africa. Retrieved form http://www.amnestyusa.org/sites/default/files/making_love_a_crime_-_facts__figures.pdf

Awondo, P., Geschiere, P., & Reid, G. (2012). Homophobic Africa? Toward a more nuanced view. *African Studies Review, 55*(3), 145–168. doi:10.1017/S0002020600007241.

Benshoff, H., & Griffin, S. (2006). *Queer images: A history of gay and lesbian film in America.* Lanham: Rowan and Littlefield.

Binebai, B. (2015). Voice construction in the postcolonial text: Spivakian subaltern theory in Nigerian drama. *African Studies Review, 9*(4), 206–220.

Chikura-Mtwazi, C. (2017). Zimbabwe's LGBT community: Why civil rights and health issues go hand in hand. *The Conversation.* Retrieved from www.theconversation.com/zimbabwes-lgbt-community-why-civil-rights-and-health-issues-go-hand-in-hand-90546

Dowson, T. (2006). Archaeologists, feminists, and queers: Sexual politics in the construction of the past. In L. Geller & M. Stockett (Eds.), *Feminist anthropology: Past, present, and future* (pp. 96–98). New York: Eskridge Publishers.

Epprecht, M. (2008). *Heterosexual Africa? The history of an idea from the age of exploration to the age of AIDS.* Athens: Ohio University Press.

Epprecht, M. (2018). Hidden histories of African homosexualities. *Canadian Women Studies, 2*(3), 138–144.

Evans-Pritchard, E. (1970). Sexual inversion among the Azande. *American Anthropologist, 2*(1), 1428–1434.

Foucault, M. (2016). *Social theory-rewired.* UK: Routledge Taylor and Francis Group.

Greenberg, D. (1988). *The construction of homosexuality.* New York: Routledge.

Ibrahim, A. (2015). LGBT rights in Africa and the discursive role of international human rights law. *African Human Rights Law Journal,* (15), 263–281. Retrieved from doi:10.17159/1996-2096/2015/v15n2a2.

Kehinde, O. (2013). An ethical perspective of homosexuality among the African people. *European Journal of Business and Social Sciences, 1*(12), 77–85.

Lagomarsino, D. (2015). *Living in the contradictions: LGBTQ educators and socially just pedagogies.* New York: New York University Press.

Lyonga, F. (2014). Un-African? Representations of homosexuality in two contemporary Nigerian films. *International Journal of Humanities and Social Science*, 4(8), 97–103.

Maria, A. (2015). New queer cinema in the USA: Rejecting heteronormative categorizations in *Desert Hearts* (1985) and *Brokeback Mountain* (2005). A Master's thesis submitted to faculty of philology, University of Salamanca.

Ndjio, B. (2012). Sexuality and nationalist ideologies in Post-colonial Africa. In S. Wieringa & H. Sirori (Eds.), *The sexual history in the global south* (pp. 120–43). London: Zed Books.

Nowlan, B. (2010). Queer theory, queer cinema. In J. Juett & D. Jones (Eds.), *Coming out to the mainstream: New Queer Cinema in the 21st century* (pp. 1–16). UK: Cambridge Scholars Publishing.

Nwokolo, P. (2014). Relationship between Nigeria and the United States. Retrieved from http://rightsidewire.com/2011/06/relationship-between-nigeria-and-the-united-states/

Onuche, J. (2015). Same-sex marriage in Nigeria: A philosophical analysis. *International Journal of Humanities and Social Science*, 3(12), 91–98.

Pierson, M. (1990). *Millennial dreams and moral dilemmas.* New York: Cambridge University Press.

Pickett, B. (2015). Homosexuality. *Stanford Encyclopedia of Philosophy. Islam does give us leeway to think.* 2014. Interview with the South African Imam Mushin Hendricks. *Qantara. de.* Retrieved from www.en.qantara.de/cotent/interview-with-the-south-african-imam-mushin-hendricks-islam-does-give-us-leeway-to-think

Reddy, V. (2002). Perverts and sodomites: Homophobia as hate speech in Africa. *Southern African Linguistics and Applied Language Studies*, 20(3), 163–175.

Rich, B. (1992). A queer sensation. *Village Voice.* US: Faber and Faber.

Schoonover, K., & Galt, R. (2015). The world of queer cinema: From aesthetics to activism. *Art* Cultura, *Uberlândia*, 17(30), 87–95.

Schoonover, K., & Galt, R. (2018). *Queer cinema in the world.* Berkeley: University of California Press.

Shehu, B. (1992). The role of film/cinema in National development. In H. Ekwuazi & Y. Nasidi (Eds.), *No … Not holllywood: Essays and speeches of Brendan Shehu* (pp. 77–78). Jos: Nigerian Film Corporation.

Tutu, D. (2008). International Gay and Lesbian Human Rights Commission, Grace Cathedral, San Francisco, 8 April 2008. Retrieved from http://www.youtube.com/watch?v=ONVgf_RHrkk

Wheaton, S. (2015). *Obama faces gay rights challenge in Kenya.* POLITICO. Retrieved from https://www.politico.com/story/2015/07/your-obama-seen-as-promoting-lgbt-rights-in-anti-gay-kenya-120511

Becoming an Ally in the College Classroom: One Front in the Battle against Homophobia

OMAR SWARTZ

Homophobia, transphobia, and heteronormativity persist in society and we, as educators, can do something about it through our teaching. Using myself as an ally, I offer a discussion of best practices for creating an LGBTQIA+ inclusive classroom at the University of Colorado Denver where I engage students with issues related to diversity and the law. Before discussing these practices, I operationalize the terms "homophobia," "heteronormativity," and "ally" to help educators understand the importance of classroom inclusivity. Relying on legal scholarship, I use various court cases to demonstrate how these concepts have been used, or misused, to perpetuate harmful effects on the lives of LGBTQIA+ individuals.

Homophobia: An Irrational Hatred

The term "homophobia" first appears in George Weinberg (1973), arguing that those who harbor prejudice against homosexuals, not homosexuals themselves, are suffering from a psychological malady, an irrational state of mind (Herek, 2004). For Weinberg, homophobia is "a fear of homosexuals" associated with a "fear of contagion." He situated this fear in religious sentiments and highlighted its "great brutality" in history. Moreover, Weinberg notes that homophobia is a "morbid and irrational dread which prompts irrational behavior flight or the desire to destroy the stimulus" (Ayyar, nd). Discussing the "healthy homosexual," Weinberg declares that the "healthy homosexual is simply a healthy person who happens to be homosexual and accepts this fact" (Ayyar). Society has, Weinberg argues, invented a problem where none need exist.

Homophobia involves the belief or feeling that it is somehow "wrong" or "unnatural" to be gay or lesbian, that such a "lifestyle" is "dirty" or "disgusting." Consider, for example, the arguments of Harry V. Jaffa, that the "prohibitions upon incest and upon sodomy are not primitive superstitions: Reason and nature tell us that without these prohibitions the structure of the family, and of authority within the family, would collapse" (1984, p. 274). Under such a view, gays and lesbians are by nature destroyers of the family; consensual and loving same-sex desire is in the same immoral category as incest, which does destroy families and ruins lives. Specifically, Jaffa suggests that, in light of a thriving LGBTQIA+ community, "Moral education within the family would not be possible, and the family itself would not survive" (1984, p. 274). Jaffa's view is irrational in the sense established by Weinberg. Democratic societies that include members of the LGBTQIA+ community and bestow upon them mainstream status are thereby strengthened, as societal oppression has negative consequences for all (Bell, 2016; Freire, 2003).

Moreover, while the stability of society is undoubtedly important for many reasons, the "order" necessary to accomplish this comes at a cost. Order is always order of a specific sort, one imposed on others. What Jaffa seems to fear is not the end of the family but the end of patriarchy, the socio-political system of male privilege and authority over women, children, and property. What he calls "moral education" is education for patriarchy, the family (and by extension, societal) order under the male gaze. He is worried about the future of traditional authority under a patriarchal model, one that is rightly decaying. LGBTQIA+ communities and their allies can and should challenge patriarchy as a limiting, outmoded, and harmful institution that threatens members as well as others more generally. Less patriarchy, which means a significant shift in power relationships, means more rights for children, more freedom for women, and less toxic masculinity, a point common to writings of bell hooks, Audre Lorde, and Suzanne Pharr. Authoritarianism, whether from the state or the father, has no place in a liberal society. What conservatives such as Jaffa interpret in the LGBTQIA+ agenda is a loss of their traditional power as well as the worldview that grounds such power. Such "weakening" follows, they argue, for without a limitedly construed moral foundation, a society "cannot be a people in any proper sense. It will not fight, and it will not survive" (1984, p. 275).

Again, Jaffa is irrational in Weinberg's sense. Many people do fight for a liberal and inclusive society even if they do not believe that society rests on moral foundations in the sense that Jaffa requires. Like other natural law theorists such as Robert P. George (1993), Jaffa's arguments reduce to a rationalization of an inherited religious bias, a reading into nature of a moral worldview or theology that simply does not exist. The world does not have moral structures independent of those humans construct (Rorty, 2007). Morality, in this sense, is a human invention, a layer one reads into nature and uses for one's own ends (Nietzsche, 1997). The socio-political example of stigma is one such end. The attribution of stigma in cases of anti- LGBTQIA+ moralization is significant. According to Erving Goffman, stigma is a social phenomenon that marks a person as "different," "spoiled," or "corrupt" (1963). It is a psychological pressing, which leads to an internalization of what was, in previous centuries, a physical burning of a symbol (mark) on a person's skin, signifying social condemnation. In other words, stigma defines the "blemished" person as different from others, thus insufficiently human. Their identity becomes "spoiled" and "deserved."

Though stigma is a social fabrication, it has material consequences. Goffman's insights highlight the limitations of what he calls "normal" (i.e., a person unaffected by stigma) to move outside one's place of privilege to view the world from the perspective of the stigmatized person. Goffman explains the different attributes of stigma and then applies these variables to testimony from individuals experiencing the effects of stigmatization.

Heteronormativity and Heterosexism: Questioning Assumptions

The other side of homophobia is "heterosexism," the assumption that everyone is heterosexual or should be. A related concept is "heteronormativity," (sometimes also called heterosexism) refers to the practice of defining sexuality in terms of gender essentialism or the belief that there are two genders with prescribed and immutable characteristics tied together with corresponding social practices (Blumenfeld, 1992, p. 15). Heteronormativity is a privilege, a reified way of seeing the world in a highly exclusionary manner. It allows people to make assumptions and to act upon these to the detriment of others. For example, a Florida court in *Inman v. City of Miami* (1967) upheld a city ordinance prohibiting liquor license holders from knowingly employing gay men or even allowing them to be in the bar. The court found the law had a "rational" relation to public morality, which was to prevent congregations of people likely to "prey upon the public" or "recruit other persons for acts which have been declared illegal" (p. 52). That heterosexuals commit most sex crimes goes unnoticed or that people have the constitutional right of association denotes heteronormativity.

The heart-wrenching case of *Littleton v. Prange* provides a more detailed example of heteronormativity and heterosexism and the order they impose on the world. John Littleton visited his doctor for a minor injury and died shortly thereafter of an infection caused by the doctor's malpractice. His wife of seven years, Christie Littleton, sued the doctor for her husband's wrongful death. She had a compelling case: the doctor was negligent and was the proximate cause of her husband's death. When such tragedies occur, the law recognizes that spouses have interests in each other when an outside person tortuously interferes with their relationship. The doctor, who had no defense against the malpractice claim, successfully had the case dismissed by arguing that Ms. Littleton was ineligible to recover on her wrongful death suit because she had been born a male. Indeed, Ms. Littleton had successfully undergone a surgical reassignment program nearly 20 years earlier and had been living her life as a woman. This "technicality," which had nothing to do with the doctor's culpability, allowed him to avoid accountability for the harm he caused. As the court framed the issue, however, the case against the doctor was not about justice—compensation to a dependent for a wrongful death which is routinely socially recognized as being an important interest—but about something else entirely, something "obvious" to children. Men have a penis and women have a vagina. Thus, the court asks, "can a physician change the gender of a person with a scalpel, drugs and counseling, or is a person's gender immutably fixed by our Creator at birth?" (1999, p. 224).

The court transformed the case from the integrity of the medical system and courts righting a social wrong into an irrelevant philosophical discussion on gender and sexual binaries. As framed, the court agreed with the doctor and denied relief to Ms. Littleton, as her "marriage" was legally impossible. Important was the court's stipulation that "men" and "women" are natural kinds, "obvious" to every child, evidenced by observable sex organs. The court takes this line of argument further. It reasons that men and women cannot be reduced to their sex organs, because these can be manipulated. There is no fooling God because maleness and femaleness can be reduced to one's chromosomes, which are unalterable and determinative of humanness. As explained by the court, "male chromosomes do not change with either hormonal treatment or sex reassignment surgery" (1999, p. 230).

The *Littleton* court ruling demeaned Ms. Littleton and her deceased husband, as well as the love that binds all couples. It did not merely rule against Ms. Littleton as a matter of law but went out of the way to nullify her identity and life and, by extension, that of her deceased husband who loved and cherished her. As the court explained, "The evidence fully supports that Christie Littleton, born male, wants and believes herself to be a woman. She has made every conceivable effort to make herself a female, including a surgery that would make most males pale and perspire to contemplate" (1999, p. 213). However, she cannot be female, the court held, because her "female anatomy" is "all man-made. The body that Christie inhabits is a male body in all aspects other than what the physicians have supplied" (p. 231).

The court proclaimed that what God had created, humans cannot undo no matter how hard a person tries. The court then concluded, there are "some things we cannot will into being. They just are" (p. 231). Sex, sexuality, and family are for the court natural kinds, immutable, external, and God-given. It is wrong, indeed immoral, to maintain otherwise. Ms. Littleton had been rendered a freak for the terrible way she "mutilated" her body. Today, of course, we understand that people may be born "intersex," that is, with a sexual anatomy that does not fit the traditional gender binary as assumed by the *Littleton* court. Such people have, historically, been forced into either side of the binary, often with harmful long-long effects (Dreger, 1998), of which the law has been slow to recognize, although this may be beginning to change (Baumgartner, 2017).

Because of the court's reasoning, Ms. Littleton lost a multimillion-dollar medical malpractice suit against a physician who negligently killed her husband. There were no allegations of fraud; her husband always knew about Christie's history and loved her for the individual she was. The meaning of family and love belongs to individuals, becomes expressed in one's lived practice. Fundamentally, the court nullified Mr. Littleton's life as well—the doctor took not only his life, but also his marriage, and his agency to make decisions on how to live. With his defense, the doctor not only destroyed one family, but also undermined the integrity of millions more. For, ultimately, his defense suggests that humans have no choice, no freedom with how one defines their family. Humans have all inherited the court's limitations, all bound by its lack of imagination.

Similarly, a court in *Ulane v. Eastern Airlines* overturned a sex discrimination case against a female transgender pilot because it concluded that an individual's sex is immutable no matter how hard a person tries to change it. The court granted that the pilot was entitled to any personal belief about the sexual identity she desires. Surgery, hormone treatment, and a new birth certificate all give the "appearance" of being female. "But even if one believes that a woman can be so easily created from what remains of a man, that does not decide the case" (1984, p. 1087). Karen Ulane was a "biological male who takes female hormones, cross-dresses, and has surgically altered parts of her body to make it appear to be female" (1984, p. 1087). Such bodies are assumed to be fraudulent from the point of view of the court. In these and other cases, the court posits a nature, which is binary in form. This form, abstract and reductionist, is then elevated above substance; no facts to the contrary can exist. Categories are airtight and self-evident. Any person who acts otherwise is presumed to be in denial, mentally unhinged, engaging in fraud, or is in some fundamental way broken. Such individuals are condemned to suffer.

While there are places in the world where it is much worse human-rights wise to be a member of the LGBTQIA+ community than the United States (see below), many countries are better at protecting the civil and human rights of members of this group. Outrage at state violence meted to LGBTQIA+ individuals in Chechenia, Jamaica, Iran, Uganda, and Saudi Arabia, is not enough. Many people do not realize that places such as Belgium, Canada, Denmark, England, France, the Netherlands, Norway, and Spain, among many others, have moved to include LGBTQIA+ communities through all walks of their societies and institutions. In this regard, citizens should as a nation, look forward to the positive examples found among one's moral and cultural peers and not share similarities with societies that are intolerant, at least with regard to human rights. While the U.S. has made great strides to remove many structural and legal barriers to equality for LGBTQIA+ individuals, there is still much work to accomplish. One can always find worse societies to point to in order to feel good about the work society has already accomplished. This is easy; however, it demands no work on the part of citizens and demonstrates the lack of imagination of which some are frequently guilty. A more challenging and meaningful exercise is to set and maintain a high bar and seek to emulate the standards of those who have taken it on themselves to demand more of themselves and their communities.

Being an Ally and an Educator

An ally is someone who supports civil and human rights for LGBTQIA+ individuals, exemplified by the slogan: "Straight, But Not Narrow." This is how I position myself. I am happily married to a Chinese woman that I met in graduate school more than 20 years ago with a wonderful son and adopted daughter from China. My family is "natural" and comfortable. It works for us and we are lucky considering the divorce rates in the United States and the high rates of domestic violence and abuse that many families experience. We are aware of our privileges and society's organization along this model makes our choices seem natural. We are grateful for what we have and want others to have this experience too. I have nothing to fear from LGBTQIA+ families. As a liberal Jewish socialist-aspiring man with a bi-racial family, however, I have everything to fear from conservative and religious ideologies that seek to turn back the clock on LGBTQIA+ rights and prevent much needed social and political progress in this country.

I am aware of the fact that, until *Loving v. Virginia*, it was illegal for my wife and me to get married in the state where we wed (North Carolina). I have studied the legal history of the United States and have seen who gets hurt when the machinery of the state is used as a weapon against those perceived by the majority as "different." Cultural, political, and religious conservatives, particularly since the 2016 Presidential Election, do not hide the fact that they want to remake the United States into an intolerant society with minimal regard for civil rights, labor or environmental protections (Swartz & McGuffey, 2018). All the things that I value in a liberal and progressive society are the target of the right. Cultural and religious conservatives and the anti-intellectualism they champion are a threat to the people I love. This combined with the militarism and arrogance championed by conservatives, not the LGBTQIA+ couple next door, is what concerns me most.

A good discussion of an ally is offered by Diane J. Goodman whose work, like my own, assumes that who we are affects how we view and experience the world and that social differences should not divide people. Individuals, institutions, and society are transformable; each of us can play a constructive role. In this light, Goodman writes that allies are "people who make intentional choices to support or work for the rights of those from disadvantaged groups of which they are not part. They are committed to eliminating some form of oppression from which they benefit" (2001, p. 164). Diane Finnerty (2004) provides a real-world example of this practice when she challenges readers to consider the impact she has, as a white parent, when she challenges school district authority that her daughter is taught the legacy of racism and the opportunities available through multicultural education. She exemplifies the civic community she wants by engaging public officials about racial disparities of the criminal justice system or why, as a "monolingual English speaker," she opposes "English Only" laws (2004, p. 27).

We can all be allies. To be an ally is to be a friend (or at least a positive role model as a university professor) and, if we have but one friend, we have the capacity for friendship. Given such ability, we will be friends if we allow ourselves to be open to the humanity of others. Humans are inherently social creatures and need the comfort and closeness of others to feel welcome as part of a community. It is easy to be a friend if one does not allow a hateful ideology to get in the way. While some communities bond on the grounds of their hatred (Burke, 1969b, p. 22), it does not follow that this has to be the case. Human frailty can no longer be an excuse for our inability to construct community on positive grounds. Human history is also characterized by cooperation among members of the species rather than competition and aggression amongst each other (Kropotkin, 1989). Humans have the presumption of friendship with others.

Homophobia affects all of us, no matter one's sexual identity or moral beliefs. With an estimated 11 million LGBTQIA+ individuals living in the United States (Newport, 2018), everyone works with, lives, or loves someone who is a member of this community, whether one is aware of it or not. "Be careful whom you hate, it might just be someone you love" is an accurate slogan. Moreover, LGBTQIA+ individuals matter because people matter as people, on their own terms and in their own images of themselves.

Philosophically speaking, to be an ally involves being able to contextualize one's sense of moral order, to recognize the profoundly individualized ways in which people experience their lives. Moral principles are useful for ordering our lives only to the extent that our social practices follow certain social goals. Allies, at least intuitively, recognize this, attuned to the fact that when the goals of moral principles change, the scripts that underlie our moral languages become obsolete, even harmful. Morality should follow life, serve life, and honor life, not the other way around.

What matters are the goals posited and they are measured against our interests as humans in a particular community and of a particular historical period. The question is not how does an action comports with moral law, as such law does not exist. Rather, the proper question is how does an action help humans meet specific goals, like those of an inclusive and progressive democratic and secular society. Further, as Richard Rorty notes (while this is controversial among moral philosophers) what people refer to as "moral law" is little more than "a handy abbreviation for a concrete web of social practices" (2007, p. 47). That is to say, moral principles should not be seen as "self-evident truths but as rough summaries of past practices" (2007, p. 58). Morality stems from, and is sanctioned by, practices and changes as practices change. If morality is perceived as a tool toward a goal, and if this goal is democratically and inclusively articulated, then the ends can reflect that. Individuals must learn to think past their biases, which can be accomplished by historicizing them and subjecting them to new intellectual commitments such as solidarity (Rorty, 1989), cosmopolitanism (Nussbaum, 2002), or social justice (Swartz, 2006).

Thus, educators should encourage students to become allies of the LGBTQIA+ community by speaking up "with" them every chance they get. This will enable students' humane imaginations to feel differently and allow for including people into their moral realm that they may have shunned in the past. Such presumption of kindness is justified, in part, because the harm that LGBTQIA+ individuals suffer is consequential and the cost to the lives and experiences of cisgender, heterosexual individuals is *de minimis*. Affording members of the LGBTQIA+ community dignity and equal protection harms no one. Equity and civil rights for all does not come at the expense of heterosexuals.

Furthermore, no one's heterosexual marriage is threatened when same-sex couples are extended the right to marry; *Obergefell v. Hodges* upset nothing. If anything, *Obergefell* strengthened marriage, providing increased stability for society. Moreover, humans are all uplifted and enriched when the sphere of liberty and freedom extends to more people. As Martin Luther King, Jr., famously noted, "Injustice anywhere is a threat to justice everywhere. We are caught in an inescapable network of mutuality, tied in a single garment of destiny. Whatever affects one directly, affects all indirectly" (1992, p. 85). This is a lesson that is worth repeating with each succeeding generation, as the notion of community is expanded, and social inequities are overcome.

Best Practices for Creating a Queer-Inclusive Classroom

Question One's Privilege

As someone who writes and teaches courses on law and diversity, I wish to raise five points with regard to inclusive pedagogy. First, I enact my identity as an ally. That is, I, like Goodman, conscientiously choose to support the rights of others by publicly questioning my own privilege in the classroom. Those who have privilege should use it to empower others by challenging the institutions and practices that reify social injustice. As Michael Seal concludes his study of heteronormativity in higher education, "For those in a position of power, such as myself, it is important to come out, as it gives a message that to construct sexuality as a private thing reinscribes a public heteronormativity ..." (2019, p. 273). By "coming out" as an ally, I take seriously this politics and encourage my students to widen their thinking to allow the inclusion of more people into their sense of community.

For instance, to demonstrate how language can hinder our efforts to be effective allies, I recall an interaction I had with a woman during my first year of college in the early 1980s. As a 17-year-old, I dismissed something as unimportant by claiming it was "so gay." I will never forget how this person looked at me with shock and displeasure. With a disapproving tone in her voice she said, "I didn't expect to hear that coming from *you*." This experience served as an important consciousness-raising event for me, particularly in liberal arts setting of higher education (Holland et al., 2013). Words are not neutral; they engage in cultural work. Educators and students are responsible for what they say, even if it is not what was intended. By sharing with students my own growth, I caution them to avoid being used by language. Once there was a student who identified with "white power" without understanding its implications that caused a stir in class. Educators can use this technique to demonstrate how easily one can be misled by the vocabulary used (Swartz et al., 2009, pp. 132–133).

The reproduction of heteronormativity occurs in a million little ways by how people communicate, including micro-aggressions (Sue, 2010). Being mindful of how one dialogues makes a significant difference in the world. Robin Lakoff notes that language is more than words; rather, it is a material force that "enables us to establish [ourselves] as individuals and as members of groups; it tells us how we are connected to one another, who has power and who doesn't" (2000, p. 41). In other words, language is a blueprint for oppression. I share with students my own complicity in heteronormativity as a way to ensure transformational "safe" or "brave spaces" needed for people with privilege to not only to acknowledge them but to be able to face the discomfort of so doing. Such vulnerability, notes Amber E. George, helps "foster critical, yet real conversations likely to initiate social change …" (2019, p. 179). When students see the instructor struggle with these difficult issues, it makes it more "real" for them, encouraging them to do the same.

Modeling Compassion

Second, and following from the first, I model for students a compassionate way of interacting with others. Educators can model for LGBTQIA+ individuals that they are our peers worthy of respect and acceptance. These tend to be simple things, such as having a "safe zone/brave zone" sticker in my office, which not only communicates to LGBTQIA+ students my openness, but also to other students, letting them know that I, as a faculty member, support LGBTQIA+ students. Educators can reinforce this through their demeanor in class, how they moderate class discussions, and what readings they assign. I assign mostly legal cases which I then connect with LGBTQIA+ struggles in the news such as the struggle for marriage equality before and the fight against "religious freedom" laws now. In short, my approach to all my students, including conservative students, is to be available to them, open to the various subjectivities they embody. Just because I do not agree with them politically, does not mean that I cannot try to understand them and their concerns. I take all students on their terms and work with them from that position. I am inspired by Kenneth Burke's teaching—by expanding a person's moral imagination, "the rabid advocate of racial intolerance could become a mild one; and the mild one would not feel the need to be thus intolerant at all" (1969a, p. 305). My goal is to create a classroom environment in which the religious students can come to understand the perspectives they are gaining from listening to the narratives and input of the LGBTQIA+ students. It is not always easy and there is no "magic bullet," but the creation of a bridge in the context of class at least opens the possibility for transcending siloed thinking.

Acknowledging My Intellectual Shortcomings

Third, I acknowledge and correct for what I do not know. By recognizing the shortcomings of my academic expertise and ideological blinders, I am able to go on an educational journey with my students and embody life-long learning in which I grow from interactions with my students. There are times when I may not know an answer or make an oversight as evidenced by a recent interaction with my students regarding a book-length critique of homophobia I have been writing. I consciously decided to limit the book analysis to gays and lesbians, not as a slight to other identities, but to make my research manageable. When I shared drafts of the book with students, transgender students and their allies questioned whether transgender issues would be discussed. My heart sank. I wanted to say "yes" but I could not. I was not well enough informed to do so with integrity. I had to say no, and I gave my reasons why. I talked about how I struggled with whether or not to include transgender issues in my book and how I feared that doing so would unjustifiably conflate the needs of both groups.

My students appeared satisfied by my response; however, I was not. I felt like I had let them down. Therefore, the next week when we came back to class, I announced that I had organized an extra-curricular meeting with a transgender expert that I recruited, and I invited any student in my program to attend. Quite a few students did, and we had a useful discussion on issues important to transgender people in which I learned a great deal by listening to my students talk about their experiences, and I began to integrate Trans* issues into my scholarship while being respectful of the differences. This example demonstrates how educators can support students who have their own expectations of what is important by embracing the limitations of one's knowledge and avoid taking the easy way out.

Valuing All Student Perspectives

Fourth, the biggest issue I face in teaching my diversity courses is how to be respectful of religious people who oppose LGBTQIA+ rights. The legal position, the position determinative of our rights, has, in our society, no room for religious bias. However, as an educator when discussing these issues, I realize that my positions make some students upset. When I can identify these students, I try to reach out to them, and I am generally successful. Yet I had one sobering case a few years ago in a graduate class in which I was guest lecturing on the Marriage Equality movement where I failed to perceive a student who became upset. She never said anything in class, but later complained to her instructor that she felt offended by my discussion of religious objections to LGBTQIA+ relationships. This got me thinking: Clearly, I cannot remove the religious critique from my presentation on Marriage Equality. It is not reasonable to discuss same-sex marriage and not talk about arguments that oppose it. The question becomes, how do I present the material in a way that does not make conservative or religious students feel uncomfortable? Otherwise stated, how far do I have to go to make the oppressive group more comfortable while critiquing their oppression?

What I have learned is this: When holding accountable what I consider a socially undesirable ideology or practice, I do two things. First, in my presentation style, I make sure to not mock the other side or imply that my class agrees with me. I realize how frustrating it can be for a religious or conservative person when I, a liberal teacher, engage in a way that presumes that all of my students are also liberal. Teaching in Greensboro, NC, from 1995 to 1998 made it clear that my students did not find extreme religiosity offensive or harmful (to the contrary). So, I learned to differentiate between different types of moral reasoning. I do this by explaining, repeatedly throughout the semester, that "ethics" is not one thing nor religion monolithic; rather, ethics is an argument made in the context of a particular community. For example, one way to argue ethically is from the "religious perspective," defined as adherence to religious doctrine, interpretation, or tradition grounded in a particular sacred text, such as the Bible, Koran, or Torah. These traditions are often important for my students. I found that I can honor them while grounding my pedagogy and practice in the "humanistic perspective." Here I ground my argument that practices that dehumanize persons/groups for, among other things, race, gender, age, or ethnicity, are wrong (Johannesen et al., 2007; Rorty, 1989). That is as far as I can go in terms of justifying my moral principles beyond saying that I value all positions that work to increase the conversation and solidarity among people rather than to shut it down.

This is a delicate issue and my experience with the student I upset with my marriage equality lecture has had a big impression on me. I bring it up before any lecture when I discuss LGBTQIA+ issues. I want my students to know that I value all of them, regardless of their stance on this issue. I reach out and work with any student who approaches me regardless of their beliefs. I help them to construct better arguments for their positions, so they understand them better. At the same time, I feel obligated to do the work of teaching for social justice, which means asking questions and presenting histories that may make some people feel uncomfortable. To be effective in this task requires getting the people who disagree with me to feel like I have listened to them. Happily, in the nearly twenty years I have been teaching diversity courses on both the undergraduate and graduate levels, I have managed to do fairly well, gaining the respect even of students who are profoundly different them me in their religious/political views.

That being said, how do I deal with students who do, in fact, cross the line? That is, how do I differentiate between different viewpoints and something else: "hate speech," aggression, or personal attacks? Sometimes it is easy, as in the case of aggression and personal attacks. University policies allow me to ask disruptive students to leave the room (my male privilege allows me to do so easily). So-called "hate speech" is something different. Three times, when teaching in North Carolina at three different universities, I had students stand up and passionately defend the Ku Klux Klan. Another student proudly told my class that her parents belonged to a segregated country club. Did these students cross the line or engage in "hate speech" or did they present a "real world" check-in and a teaching moment? Like the student who clung to the phrase "white power" without understanding how it positioned her, I engaged these students. That is all I can do—offer students an opportunity to expand their moral imaginations. I cannot change them nor is it my job to do so, although outside the classroom I do everything I can to construct the inclusive world I believe in (see points one and two above).

Practice Mindfulness

This suggests my fifth and final point: mindfulness. I am engaged in teaching a vast array of students with dissimilar needs and experiences in a metropolitan university. Thus, it is essential to be mindful that each student is an individual and deserves to express their perspective in the classroom. This involves a student-centeredness that replaces the traditional teacher authority and is grounded in dialogical practice/learning (Freire, 2003), in which knowledge about self and others is co-created through communicative interaction grounded in lived experience. The class is about them: their lives, their perspectives, and their growth. Even the students I profoundly disagree with, I wish well, as I believe in the ameliorating power of education. Censorship, in any form, is unlikely to change people's minds. Free speech is imperative to destructing these attitudinal and presumptive negative attitudes toward LGBTQIA issues and people.

Conclusion

A person's sexual identity or sexual relationships have nothing to do with that person's moral stature or with their status as a citizen in our diversely rich multicultural democracy. What people take to be "common-sense" morality is little more than allegiance to past practices and beliefs and such phenomena may or may not be relevant for our society today. Assumptions about the undesirability or wrongness of same-sex desire belong in this category. It is irrelevant to public policy and how rights are allocated in society.

Values are wonderful things; however, they are not static: they need questioning and growth in order to be healthy. This means also that we must be on the guard against those who pander to people's intolerance to achieve political or social power. We must concern ourselves with the political power that comes to extremists who pander to people's homophobia, among other things. For example, in his well-known polemic against gay people, Cardinal and future Pope Joseph Ratzinger (1988) expressed concern with what he called the "overly benign interpretation" that liberals have of gays and lesbians. While he allowed for what he calls "homosexual inclination," the expression of same-sex desire is "an intrinsic moral evil; and thus, the inclination itself must be seen as an objective disorder." Intrinsic moral evil? When I think of moral evil, I think of genocide or chattel slavery. I do not think of the loving caresses of people's bodies touching or other forms of consensual adult sexual intimacy. Such a view is, no matter how we look at it, clearly disproportionate.

Moreover, to the extent that homophobia and other extremist views advantage the political agenda of the radical right, my family is threatened by attacks on reproductive rights, cuts in education spending, and a devaluation of science and scientific research. Simply stated, support for LGBTQIA+ rights require supporting people qua people, to stand against those who want to impose their rigid morality on others, and to not allow them to punish individuals for being different. To support—to be an ally in the struggle for LGBTQIA+ rights—is to support liberalism or progressivism that represents the best that is the United States.

References

Ayyar, R. (n.d). George Weinberg: Love is conspiratorial, deviant & magical [Interview]. *Gay Today.Com*. Retrieved from http://www.gaytoday.com/interview/110102in.asp.

Baumgartner, N. (2017). Intersex parenting: Ethical and legal implications of the treatment of intersex infants and the ramifications for their families. *Women Leading Change: Case Studies on Women, Gender, and Feminism*, *1*(3), 45–55.

Bell, L. (2016). Theoretical foundations for social justice education. In M. Adams & L. A. Bell (Eds.), *Teaching for diversity and social justice* (3rd ed., pp. 3–26). New York: Routledge.

Blumenfeld, W. J. (1992). Introduction. In W. J. Blumenfeld (Ed.), *Homophobia: How we all pay the price* (pp. 1–22). Boston: Beacon Press.

Burke, K. (1969a). *A grammar of motives*. Berkeley, CA: University of California Press.

Burke, K. (1969b). *A rhetoric of motives*. Berkeley, CA: University of California Press.

Dreger, A. D. (1998). Ambiguous sex or ambivalent medicine? *The Hastings Center Report, 28*(3), 24–35.

Freire, P. (2003). *Pedagogy of the oppressed*. New York: Continuum.

Finnerty, D. (2004). An open letter to my white lesbian, gay, bisexual, transgender sisters and brothers. Retrieved from https://www.academia.edu/3322291/An_Open_Letter_to_my_White_LGBT_Sisters_and_Brothers?auto=d

George, A. E. (2019). Building alliances for nonhuman animals using critical social justice dialogue. In A. J. Nocella II, C. Drew, A. E. George, S. Ketenci, J. Lupinacci, I. Purdy, & J. Leeson-Schatz (Eds.), *Education for total liberation: Critical animal pedagogy and teaching against speciesism* (pp. 171–184). New York: Peter Lang.

George, R. P. (1993). *Making men moral: Civil liberties and public morality*. New York: Oxford University Press.

Goffman, E. (1963). *Stigma: Notes on the management of spoiled identity*. New York: Simon & Schuster.

Goodman, D. J. (2001). *Promoting diversity and social justice: Educating people from privileged groups*. Thousand Oaks, CA: Sage.

Herek, G. (2004). "Beyond homophobia": Thinking about sexual prejudice and stigma in the twentieth-first century. *Sexuality Research and Social Policy, 1*(2), 6–24.

Holland, L., Matthews, T., & Schott, M. (2013). "That's so gay!" Exploring college students' attitudes toward the LGBT population. *Journal of Homosexuality, 60*, 575–95.

Inman v. City of Miami, 197 So.2d 50 (1967).

Jaffa, H. V. (1984). *American conservatism and the American founding*. Durham, NC: Carolina Academic Press.

Johannesen, R. L., Valde, K. S., & Whedbee, K. E. (2007). Ethics in human communication (6th ed.). Long Grove, IL: Waveland Press.

King, M. L. (1992). Letter from a Birmingham jail. In J. W. Washington (Ed.), *I have a dream: Writings and speeches that changed the world* (pp. 83–100). Glenview, IL: ScottForesman.

Kropotkin, P. (1989). *Mutual aid: A factor of evolution*. New York: Black Rose Books.

Lakoff, R. (2000). *The language war*. Berkeley, CA: University of California Press.

Littleton v. Prange, 9 S.W.3d 223 (1999).

Loving v. Virginia, 388 U.S. 1 (1967).

Nietzsche, F. (1997). *Daybreak: Thoughts on the prejudices of morality*. New York: Cambridge University Press.

Newport, F. (2018, May 22). In U.S., estimate of LGBT population rises to 4.5%. Retrieved from https://news.gallup.com/poll/234863/estimate-lgbt-population-rises.aspx

Nussbaum, M. C. (2002). Patriotism and cosmopolitanism. In J. Cohen (Ed.), *For love of country?* (pp. 3–17). Boston: Beacon Press.

Obergefell v. Hodges, 2015 U.S. LEXIS 4250 (2015).

Pew Research Center for the People & the Press. (2011, May 13). Retrieved from http://people-press.org/2011/05/13/most-say-homosexuality-should-be-accepted-by-society/.

Ratzinger, J. (1988). Letter to the bishops of the Catholic Church on the pastoral care of homosexual persons. In J. Gramick & R. Nugent (Eds.), *The Vatican and homosexuality: Reactions to the "Letter to the Bishops of the Catholic Church on the Pastoral Care of Homosexual Persons"* (pp. 1–10). New York: Crossroad Publishing Co.

Rorty, R. (1989). *Contingency, irony, and solidarity*. New York: Cambridge University Press.

Rorty, R. (2007). *Philosophy as cultural politics*. New York: Cambridge University Press.

Seal, M. (2019). *The interruption of heteronormativity in higher education: Queer Studies and Education*. Cham, Switzerland: Palgrave Macmillan.

Sue, D. W. (2010). *Microaggressions in everyday life: Race, gender, and sexual orientation*. Hoboken, NJ: John Wiley & Sons.

Swartz, O. (2006). Reflections of a social justice scholar. In O. Swartz (Ed.), *Social justice and communication scholarship* (pp. 1–19). Mahwah, NJ: Lawrence Erlbaum Associates.

Swartz, O., & McGuffey, L.W. (2018). Migrating pedagogy in American universities: Cultivating moral imagination and social justice. *Communication Education, 67*(1), 102–109.

Swartz, O., Campbell, K., & Pestana, C. (2009). *Neo-pragmatism, communication, and the culture of creative democracy*. New York: Peter Lang.

Ulane v. Eastern Airlines, 742 F.2d 1081 (1984).

Weinberg, G. (1973). *Society and the healthy homosexual*. Garden City, NY: Anchor.

Editors' Biographies

Amber E. George, Ph.D., is an Assistant Professor of philosophy, social justice, and sociology at Galen College. She has co-edited several books including *Education for Total Liberation: Critical Animal Pedagogy and Teaching Against Speciesism* (2019); *The Image of Disability: Essays on Media Representations* (2018); *The Intersectionality of Critical Animal, Disability, and Environmental Studies* (2017); *and Screening the Non/Human: Representations of Animal Others in the Media* (2016). She is the current editor-in-chief of the *Journal for Critical Animal Studies (JCAS).*

Russell W. Waltz, Ph.D., Ed.D., serves as Associate Professor of Philosophy at Galen College where he teaches courses in philosophy, sociology, critical thinking, and diversity, equity, and inclusion. Additionally, he has published in the areas of social and political philosophy, applied ethics, political communication, social epistemology, and media studies. He is the former editor-in-chief of *Auslegung: A Journal of Philosophy*. Lastly, he has recently finished a second doctoral degree researching the effects of implicit bias on critical thinking development in undergraduate student populations.

Contributor Biographies

Camille S. Alexander, Ph.D., is an assistant professor in the English Literature department. She completed her Ph.D. in English at the University of Kent and has an MA in literature with concentrations in composition and rhetoric, Caribbean literature and feminism, and gender studies from the University of Houston, Clear Lake. She is currently researching the impact of feminism on African American film, manifestations of Indian culture in Indo-Trinidadian literature, and symbols of the divine feminine in Trinidadian culture.

Jessica Ruth Austin, Ph.D., is an associate lecturer in the English and Media department at Anglia Ruskin University, Cambridge: UK. Her Ph.D. thesis is concerning fan identity construction in the Furry Fandom. She has written peer-reviewed articles about online research ethics, reception of the *Star Wars* movies by female fans, an evaluation of pornography in the Furry Fandom and the effect of necropolitics in South Korean horror movies. Her research interests are in the fan studies discipline and posthuman theory.

Crystal Benedicks, Ph.D., is Associate Professor of English at Wabash College. Benedicks is the coordinator for Writing Across the Curriculum, member of the Teaching and Learning Committee and Gender Studies Steering Committee. Her research interests include gender studies, queer theory, and disability studies.

Mária I. Cipriani, Ph.D., is an adjunct Assistant Professor of English, American Studies, and Media Studies who teaches at the City University of New York, the State University of New York, and Hofstra University. Dr. Cipriani earned a Ph.D. from Stony Brook University in Comparative Literature and Cultural Studies in 2014, and since 1996, has worked as a psychotherapist specializing in trauma, LGBTQPIA+ stressors, and gender identity.

Emily Donovan is a graduate student in creative writing at Florida Atlantic University and a scholar of queer exclusion. She teaches first-year English composition.

Jenn M. Jackson is a Ph.D. candidate in the Department of Political Science at the University of Chicago. Her research is in Black politics with a focus on group threat, gender and sexuality, and political psychology. She is also a writer whose work has appeared in Washington Post, Teen Vogue, and EBONY.

Zuzanna A. Jusińska is enrolled in an M.A. program in the College of Interdepartmental Studies in the Humanities at the University of Warsaw where they study philosophy and gender studies. Jusińska's baccalaureate thesis was 'Semantic and Pragmatic Analysis of Expressions with Grammatical Gender.' Their long-term goal is to contribute to the development of feminist philosophy of language and analytic feminist philosophy.

Stephen Ogheneruro Okpadah is a Ph.D. Candidate at the Department of the Performing Arts, University of Ilorin, Ilorin, Nigeria. He holds a B.A. (Hons) degree in Theatre Arts from Delta State University Abraka, Nigeria, and a Master's degree in Performing Arts from University of Ilorin, Kwara State, Nigeria. His areas of research include performance aesthetics, ecology, geo-politics and film studies.

Purnur Ozbirinci, Ph.D., completed her Ph.D. in the Doctorate Program in English Literature at Middle East Technical University in 2007. Her dissertation entitled "Mythmaking in Progress: Plays by Women on Female Writers and Literary Characters" was published in the United States in 2009. Further, her book *Dunya Kadina Karsi* (*The World Against Women*), which is about the historical strategies working to suppress women, was published at the beginning of 2012 in Turkey. Her recent research and publications have aspired to answer the questions underlying rewriting, adaptation, and gender. She has taught courses in writing, literature, drama, and gender studies.

Omar Swartz, Ph.D., J.D., is Associate Professor and Director of the Master of Social Science program in the College of Liberal Arts and Sciences at the University of Colorado Denver, where he has also coordinated the law studies minor for the past 16 years. His primary areas of research and teaching are law and diversity, First Amendment, cultural criticism, and philosophical problems in the social sciences. He is the author or editor of 13 books and more than 100 essays, book chapters, and reviews.

Hilary N. Tackie is a Ph.D. student in the Comparative Human Development Department at the University of Chicago. Her research focuses on youth identity development, the experiences of youth of color in schools, and trauma.

Adriel M. Trott, Ph.D., is Associate Professor of Philosophy at Wabash College. Trott is the chair of the Teaching and Learning Committee, the entity through which discussions about teaching occur on campus. Trott is also the chair of the Gender Studies Steering Committee. She specializes in ancient Greek philosophy and contemporary social and political philosophy including feminist theory.

.

Index

RADICAL ANIMAL STUDIES AND TOTAL LIBERATION

Anthony J. Nocella II, SERIES EDITOR

The **Radical Animal Studies and Total Liberation** book series branches out of Critical Animal Studies (a field co-founded by Anthony J. Nocella II) with the argument that criticism is not enough. Action must follow theory. This series demands that scholars are engaged with their subjects both theoretically and actively via radical, revolutionary, intersectional action for total liberation. Founded in anarchism, the series provides space for scholar-activists who challenge authoritarianism and oppression in their many daily forms. **Radical Animal Studies and Total Liberation** promotes accessible and inclusive scholarship that is based on personal narrative as well as traditional research, and is especially interested in the advancement of interwoven voices and perspectives from multiple radical, revolutionary social justice groups and movements such as Black Lives Matter, Idle No More, Earth First!, the Zapatistas, ADAPT, prison abolition, LGBTTQQIA rights, disability liberation, Earth Liberation Front, Animal Liberation Front, political prisoners, radical transnational feminism, environmental justice, food justice, youth justice, and Hip Hop activism.

To order other books in this series please contact our Customer Service Department:

PETERLANG@PRESSWAREHOUSE.COM (WITHIN THE U.S.)

ORDERS@PETERLANG.COM (OUTSIDE THE U.S.)

To find out more about the series or browse a full list of titles, please visit our website:

WWW.PETERLANG.COM